# What do I have to do to sell a book!

*The essential guide to book marketing in the UK for the independent author*

First published in Great Britain by
Pen Press Publishers Ltd
The Old School
39 Chesham Road
Brighton BN2 1NB

ISBN 1-905203-58-6
ISBN13: 978-1-905203-59-8

Printed and bound in the UK

A catalogue record of this book is available from
the British Library

www.indepublishing.com
www.penpress.co.uk

Self-publishing is changing the way the book industry works as more authors turn to self-publication in order to overcome the barriers that existed in the past and use their book as a sales tool to prove they have a market. Authors who truly seek publishing success can find their route through the many avenues offered to them – the supply chain, the retailers, the media, the internet and direct selling opportunities – in order to reach their end customer.

It's merit-based success functions harmoniously with mainstream publishing as serious self-publishing authors work to raise awareness of their title and allow the customer to decide its value.

# CONTENTS

# INTRODUCTION

This book is for authors seeking to sell books. It doesn't matter whether you are a mainstream published author or a self-publishing author; you can still play your part in increasing the sales of your book.

"What do I have to do to sell a book!" is aimed primarily at the serious author, the one who really wants to make it. There are, however, plenty of tips and guidelines that will also help the hobbyist author who is keen to promote his book.

The big question everyone is asking is how to sell a book? And why is it so difficult to actually sell a book? You are proud of the product you have created, yet nobody is buying it. Your friends and colleagues have all said that it is very good and very impressive. The local paper gave you a small write-up and the local bookshop bought ten copies. In fact, you even have a letter from a large and recognised publishing house saying that it is well-written (although not for them) and it deserves publication (although not *by* them). So why isn't it selling?

Let's take a step backwards. Publishing is the process by which a book is produced to an established standard and reflects the story within. If the cover attracts attention and clearly communicates to its target audience, the book should sell. If the title is intriguing and full of promise, and the back text confirms the reason to believe, the book should sell. If the overall package is right then the *browsing* customer can readily be converted into a *buying* customer.

The issue for many self-publishing authors is usually because the overall package isn't right. Most authors rush into self-publishing as though publication is the end-goal; in reality, publishing is the meat in the sandwich. Before you start to publish, you should understand whether your book has a market that you can actually talk to, reach out to and sell to. Don't think it, but know it. Once you know your market, *then* you publish. Your initial research will tell you what you are producing and how you announce your book to that audience. "What do I have to do to sell a book!" sets out to help you assess your market.

### *Marketing is not a bolt-on.*

By my launching "What do I have to do to get a book published!" first, one would assume that is the order you should work in. NOT. The reality is that marketing should come *before* the creation of any product. A manufacturer does not set up a factory to create a widget without doing his research to confirm that there is a large enough sector of the community who want to buy that widget. He wouldn't get the financial backing for starters, and would be wasting his time when he could be earning more money elsewhere.

Most self-publishing authors pay for publication on a gut-feeling that the book will sell. They write in isolation, publish in a vacuum then back-fit the marketing activity, trying to push a square peg into a round hole... it nearly fits, if only you could smooth down the corners. The truth is that, if the author researched *prior* to writing, he will have understood the market need and would have shaved the corners off during the course of creation and publication.

Marketing is a skill that authors historically never needed. Traditional publishing is where writers write then hand over large royalty percentages to publishers do all the publishing, distribution and 'salesy' stuff.

In a mainstream publishing house, the crux of a decision as to whether to take a new author on is a joint decision between Commissioning Editor and Marketing Director. Increasingly, it is a marketing decision. As the publisher, the self-publishing author would be well advised to take note of this important fact before embarking on many months of writing (which is time investment) and several thousand pounds of financial investment to publish and promote their book.

In fact, any author wanting to secure a publishing contract would be well-advised to know their market before approaching a publisher. Demonstrating well-researched knowledge of the target audience and big market potential will go a long way to securing that contract. And, in the new order of publishing, authors need to become increasingly more involved as promotional budgets become more polarised to fewer authors. Authors are constantly urged by their publishers to become more pro-active at marketing their books, building and using their contacts, doing road-shows and events, talks and signings. Remember, that publishers do not earn their money by taking on new contracts and authors; they earn money by selling books. All hands to the mill. Unfortunately for authors under contract, their efforts rarely earn them a larger part of the pie.

The wise new author will rise to the challenge of self-promotion in order to give his writing career every chance, yet it is a rare author that takes to self-promotion without nerves and apprehension. There are best practice sheets throughout this book to help authors grow in confidence with their self-promotional activities.

### The product (your book) has to be good.

Some people have asked me why I published "What do I have to do to get a book published!" before this title, despite the fact that marketing must come first. The reason is obvious – because if you don't have a great product to sell, then it won't sell. Endorsement is the bedrock of success in the book-selling world.

What publishing and marketing cannot do is sell something that people don't want or aren't ready for. Your first book launch is the most expensive, in terms of time and financial investment. Most fiction and non-fiction titles are a one-off purchase (unlike educational titles). Whereas consumer brands like Coca-Cola get repeat purchase, the sale of each book represents a sizeable piece of marketing.

If you are hoping to launch several books, then you can begin to amortise the costs of the first launch, but the first book must be good in order to get people the second time round.

### *Marketing is a thorough process in itself*

Many authors self-publish their book and use it as a sales tool. After all, it is easier to sell the value of a product than an idea or concept. But marketing is a thorough process, designed to maximise the opportunity within any conversation. Say the right things to the right person, and you will be heard.

**Marketing is communicating…
the RIGHT information
to the RIGHT people
in the RIGHT place
at the RIGHT time
…repeatedly**

That's the answer in a nutshell. Do your homework. Plan it out. Answer the above questions then keep recycling the communicating, building and developing each time, tweaking the message to widen your audience and keep issuing new news.

### *Magic and logic…*

Creative writing is MAGIC; publishing is LOGIC. Marketing books is a bit of both… the best marketing follows a process, a set of steps to a destination point, a continual recycling of communication to audiences, building and growing – combined with sometimes just saying the right thing to the right person. Suddenly a lost cause can become a fantastic sale. A little bit of magic through the use of words.

> *"The author is the most powerful and potent tool in marketing."*
> *Julian Rivers, Publishing News, 11/7/05*

Never a truer statement has been made. The author is the most powerful tool in marketing and the author is the person who can convert an opportunity into a sale. "What do I have to do to sell a book!" will show you how.

*Jo Anthony*

# PART I

# HOW TO SELL

**Overview of the publishing process**
*Publishing process timeline*

**How to use this book**
*Do people want to read what you write?*

**The basics of marketing**

**Understanding the purchase decision**

# OVERVIEW OF THE PUBLISHING PROCESS

In "What do I have to do to get a book published!" we concluded with a timeline to publication. This book starts where its partner title left off, and now we are expanding this publication timeline to include all marketing activity.

In order to successfully take a book from manuscript to market, you should follow a pre-planned series of activities. By skipping over the preparation and groundwork will only result in a lot of bother and problems further down the line, and undoubtedly mean that much time investment is wasted because the book's message was poorly communicated or it wasn't being communicated to the right people.

## (i) PLAN
- o Research the potential success of your books; create a Marketing Plan
- o Read "What do I have to do to get a book published!" and "What do I have to do to sell a book!"

## (ii) PREPARE
Most people arrive at this point having missed the critical planning and preparation as follows:
- o researching the book: talk to the intended audience, develop your own perspectives and meet the audience's needs;
- o researching the options – how to publish the book
- o initial immersion, find out what contacts you might have easy access to
- o research all self-help guides out there; talk to people; start to immerse yourself in the world of books.

## (iii) PUBLISH
Create a high quality published title (see *"What do I have to do to get a book published!"*) and plan out the pre-marketing schedule ie. collecting endorsers and supporters.

## (iv) PRE-MARKET
Another area that most authors miss this out, not realising the critical importance of it. Instead, they go from having the first printed copies of it to selling it. However, it takes time for your book data to filter out to the shops' databases, so start promoting the book to the trade and media whilst preparing your promotion to the audience. It is wise to print only a small run of review copies, collate endorsements and add to the cover before a final, longer run.

## (v) PROMOTE:
Implement your planned Promotions campaign, recycling success and exploiting new opportunities. This phase includes managing sales & customers, maintaining the database and noting down relevant updates. Remember to keep your website live.

This is an endless round of promotion until you have saturated your market or promotional avenues, and ideally you have established a regular sales channel and cost-effective route to market.

*(In this book, I am generally referring to fiction, non-fiction, gift books and humour. Whilst many of the same rules apply for text books, academic and reference books etc. there are some marked differences as these have different selling opportunities and channels.)*

**For a comprehensive Timeline to Publication and Launch, go to Indepublishing.com and download it as a PDF in the Downloads section.**

# HOW TO USE THIS BOOK

The purpose of this summary is to advise you how this book works, as the advice contained within is multi-layered and frequently cross-referenced.

Unlike publishing where the self-publishing author must follow clear steps to publishing success, selling cannot so easily be done by numbers. Plan and implement one activity, assess and recycle any success, feed it into the plan, follow another lead, assess and recycle... it's continual. You don't see results immediately and sometimes good luck seems to come out of the blue. Although the chances are that it was your hard work that created that luck.

I recommend you read the book once through, then start back at the beginning, working your way through to create a marketing plan and the order in which you are going to implement it.

**This book is going to look at the four distinct parts of the selling process:**
- Know what you are selling – covered in *"Creating the Marketing Plan"*
- how to make the book available – covered in *"Selling through the Supply Chain"*
- how to raise awareness of the book – covered in two sections *"Promoting through Media"* and *"Direct Marketing"*
- how to sell the book – covered in three sections *"Promotion and Publicity"*, *"Selling Online"* and *"Selling Direct"*, which goes to show how many opportunities there are out there for the independent author!

**We then conclude the main parameters of Marketing Planning with the money aspect:**
- how much to spend and what on – see *"Marketing Budget"*
- other potential income-earning opportunities – see *"Generating other income"*

Your marketing plan will vary as each book will cut its own course through the jungle of bookselling, but it demonstrates how to break the whole plan down into achievable bite-size chunks, then build and recycle success in order to achieve the end-goal.

Marketing and selling books can be overwhelming as the market is so large and disparate. Many authors fire off their marketing effort in a random fashion and waste much time, effort and budget in the process. A focussed plan will help you sift and prioritise to ensure your effort is best placed to convert into a sale, then you convert that sale into an opportunity, the opportunity becomes the next sale along which in turn becomes another opportunity... and so the wheel turns.

Before we start the planning, let's just do a quick review on the product... why do we read books? What do customers want from them?

# Do people want to read what you write?

*"It's a fine line between writing what we want to write
and writing what people want to read"*
Mary Sandys

People have been sharing stories since time began; stories invariably based on fact but woven with exaggeration of incredible heroism or success as it is told and retold until eventually the story has no connection to its original version. Stories that may have started as factual accounts end up as fictional flights of fantasy and imagination that stun and amaze their audience. There is pleasure in allowing the imagination free rein to dream up fantastical ideas, just as there is pleasure in hearing of the impossible. We like to hear about heroes who can single-handedly save the world, about women so beautiful that they eclipse all known beauty; we like to feel that the 'goodies' always win and 'baddies' always get their come-uppance. Harry Potter can wave his wand and Anakin Skywalker his lightsabre. So what if it's impossible? It's fun to dream, fantasise and escape.

We love to be delighted by fiction and gain insight from non-fiction. We read for two overriding reasons – purpose or pleasure.

## We read for a purpose

We read in order to learn and understand. Other people's life experiences can provide important insight for our own life journey. We can understand life better through other people's experiences, and can better perspectives when judging others.

Reading can provide information that wholly endorses or clarifies your opinion. You may read something you disagree with, which helps you understand you own justification better; or it teaches you a new viewpoint previously unconsidered. It may change your opinion or re-affirm what you already believed in?

Reading can provide the 'if' factor. Maybe the story parallels with your own experiences; maybe the hero of the piece took a different route. Reading can teach you a new way of dealing with issues in your life.

## We read for pleasure

We read for pure entertainment – passing the time on a journey or sunlounger, to experience other people's lives, to relax, to pre-occupy, to amuse. Reading is a pleasant, stimulating and intriguing way to pass the time. A good book can be like a long conversation with friends, debating various points of view and you contemplate whether you are prepared to change any of your own views. It is like embarking on a journey together. Reading is like meeting a new range of friends as you live their experience with them, laughing or crying with them, getting involved in their decisions and experiencing outcomes with them. A good book does it well and stays with you for days afterwards. A badly written book leaves you indifferent.

## We read for social reasons

A You Gov survey discovered recently that many people's reading material is comprised of books chosen for 'social reasons', which is a modern-day phenomenon. A high number of people admitted that they buy a book in order to look intelligent and/or to be seen with the right book when commuting to work, sometimes keeping two books on the go – the intelligent one for the train, and the escapist one for bedtime reading. They admitted they will scour the prize-winner lists and literary review pages, and buy the 'right' books yet sometimes never finishing them. Oh, and furthermore, they will never be seen with a book that has a price-promotion sticker on the front of it!

This is as a sad indictment on the evident social pressures people feel – not only do their clothes, shoes and accessories have to have the right labels, but also their reading material and other social pastimes. Even books have become a part of the complex process of self-branding.

Fortunately a very high two in five people still rely on recommendations by friends and family for their reading, which means that the majority of people seek to read for the sheer pleasure and genuine purpose of reading.

The reason why an author *wrote* the book is often a very motivating reason for somebody to read that book. When you read an article in a newspaper about an author's new book, the first two questions answered are invariably what's the book about and why did you write it? In order to convince potential buyers that your words are worth reading, you need to answer these questions quickly and clearly.

The answers may be very simple i.e. for pure enjoyment; the emotional experience that the lead character went through; to understand a different perspective… Therefore, an essential part of the planning a book must include the author questioning himself: *"Why am I writing this book?"* and *"Why should anyone read this book?"*

## So why do we write?

Having a greater understanding about why we <u>read</u> should inform us about why we <u>write</u>. Are you looking to show a new perspective? Are you looking to provide pure enjoyment? Are you writing to help yourself or to help others? There is merit in every reason for writing the book; the critical task is to communicate that reason.

Most writers feel compelled to write. Writers of fiction have an urge to bring their creative thinking into a tangible form so they can share it with others, they can mould it and shape it to make it live and last. Some people desire to have their life story in book form, as everyone's life story is different. We all tread a different path and learn about the secrets of life in our own way. There is merit in wishing to write this down, maybe to share with family and future descendents; maybe for a sense of immortality. This is as meaningful a reason as any.

Writers of non-fiction seek to share knowledge and insight into a specific subject. Maybe your specialist subject-matter has suddenly become a hot topic, and you have a distinctive point of view that you wish to be heard. A high percentage of new titles commissioned by the large publishing houses each year are in response to mass-market trends. As soon as a Hot Topic is identified, everyone jumps on the bandwagon and floods the market with their version. This gives us a wide range of information which is a positive, but the end-reader is overwhelmed with choice.

Maybe you have written a self-help guide to help and inform other people, to give them the benefit of your own learning in life. By sharing your knowledge, you can help others and avoid them reinventing the wheel. Probably, they will develop and build on your knowledge and in turn, will share their experience thus effecting positive change in society.

Maybe you are looking to cause change but are simply not being heard. One way to get your theory, philosophy or call for change out into the public consciousness is to write it down – in a book or on a website, anywhere that people can see it and hear it. For some authors, it is so important to get their message out there that they decide to give it away for free. As the author of a piece of text, it is your right to do this.

Maybe you are writing with a view to making money? This is a risky strategy but some people who are honest with themselves may realise that this is their motivation. They hope to be able to create a book with an idea so strong and so desired that it will catapult them to the top of the bestsellers. This is as brave as it is a gamble, and certainly contra to any advice successful authors such as Ali Smith (author of *The Accidental*) would give:

*"A secret shared by all the better writers is that the only way to write a book of real worth is to ignore the sales reps and promotions,*

*to refuse to think about whether you will get on the right shelves or be nominated for the right awards. Authors who can do that have a chance of producing good books, not bad ones written from ambition rather than talent."* The Independent Online 4/12/2005

## What does this mean to the self-publishing author?

Whatever reason you are writing for, you must understand that reason and ensure it is clearly stated in all communication about your book. The planning remains paramount and is the basis of your marketing planning; understand why you are writing the book and know why people will want to read the book, then ensure you communicate this clearly on the jacket of the book and all associated publicity. Without this, your book will not be understood in a world full of choice.

Most self-publishing authors do not approach book writing and publishing with a commercial eye, and there is an honesty within this. But in order to sell your book, the self-publishing author should understand what a large enough percentage of the market will buy, or where there are gaps in the book market, and understand how to package it correctly then make it visible!

If you are seeking to show a new perspective, make sure that the succinct little summary line from your marketing planning is clearly visible on the cover of your book – front or back. If it is pure, escapist enjoyment then make sure that is clearly communicated. If the book is seeking to help others, again, make it clear in one sentence HOW and WHO. Know whether you are too early to market and no-one understands what you are trying to say; or too late to market and too many other better-known people are already writing on that subject.

Work like crazy to shout about it and get it heard. If someone else creates their version of it, then remember you got their first – then your story will be how you were the catalyst to a whole new genre. That is publicity in itself.

For what it is worth, there is one observation I have made about self-published titles. They tend to be written more from the heart. Never have I read so widely than since coming to self-publishing. I find myself reading well outside my usual genre and comfort zone, and am enjoying my reading so much more as a result. True, some of it is not brilliantly written and invariably the self-publishing author leaves in too much superfluous detail, allowing their story to side-track and deviate. But the fact remains, the stories are gritty and more genuine that some of the commercially-produced material out there. Many self-publishing authors feel the urge to write and self-finance the publication of their book because they are desperate to share a message about their own experience, life-learning or perspective, and this is where the real value is.

# THE BASICS OF MARKETING

The purpose of this chapter is to provide readers with a crash course in marketing in the real sense of the word; what marketing is and what it *isn't*, then explore what you could be doing about it.

Firstly, I want to dispel a huge myth in the market that *discounting* is *marketing*. IT ISN'T. Discounting is not marketing and marketing is not discounting. Discounting is just a price promotion. Marketing is far more than simply a price war between competitors.

**What is marketing?**

> **Marketing is communicating...**
> **the RIGHT information**
> **to the RIGHT people**
> **in the RIGHT place**
> **at the RIGHT time**
> **...repeatedly**

Marketing is communication. Once you have a consistent message to impart, you need to have a focussed strategy to impart it – this strategy is called the Marketing Plan. It is the blueprint of your communication and is the springboard for all promotional and publicity activities

*Focus and target for maximum return*

A marketing plan helps an author to focus efforts on the areas that present the biggest and best opportunities. Some people have an unerring and instinctive ability to market; most people have to work at it. Rather than adopting the risky strategy of *"let's just throw enough mud at the wall and see what sticks"* self-publishing authors should create a plan to keep them focused, motivated and clear about the daily priority. It is easy to feel overwhelmed, and take a random approach to selling books.

Random book-selling results largely in unanswered phone calls, emails and correspondence containing expensive review copies. All your efforts vanish into the ether, as do many of the review copies that you despatched with so much hope and enthusiasm. Twenty copies issued as review copies can represent £160 of possible income and £80 of certain costs – money that will never be seen again.

We saw in the partner title to this book that an average investment to producing a self-published title is around £3000, and this is based on costs alone. The personal time investment is never calculated for the one good reason that it is a rare person that receives a real return on his time investment – although when they do, it usually more than compensates. Everyone knows that is a gamble from the off, and that the real benefit to self-publishing can be many things other than financial reward.

But in order to maximise the financial return, or minimise the investment, the self-publishing author MUST ensure that efforts are focussed. You must minimise the amount of time you spend on reinventing the wheel or chasing after lost causes. You must maximise the time you spend on following up leads and potential that could convert into real sales.

### The complexity of marketing books today
Gone are the days of writers simply writing, publishers simply publishing and bookshops simply selling a book when a customer walks in through the door.

There are millions of books out there fighting for reader attention. Books are competing on a different level today, competing with other leisure time activities such as watching DVDs, listening to CDs, playing computer games and surfing the internet. It's a tough market in a saturated consumerist age; none of us need any more stuff, but if the price is right we buy it anyway.

Perpetual discounting is standard across the book industry nowadays and the selling channels are extremely disparate. The middle-men are many and they cut into what little profit is left between the unit cost of product and the discount selling price.

Books are following the music industry practice where discounting happens at launch, rather than at the tail end of interest. Click onto Amazon and most books carry a discount of sorts. There are many who decry this practice but statistics demonstrate that the shopper is all in favour of this, and the book business is booming as the book prices hit rock-bottom.

Budgets dictate what is heavily promoted in the bookshops, rather than shop-window and front-of-store displays being merit-based. The cost of such a siting can be £10,000 upwards, which means that many authors simply don't get promoted. In any town around the UK in any category, we are experiencing the gradual homogenisation of the high street, offering bland and narrow ranges of products.

High street bookshops are under tougher competition than ever before with online bookselling giants and supermarkets taking so much trade away from them. They will only give a book a chance if there is evidential marketing activity driving the sales. This means we increasingly see only the big name authors and famous celebrity titles.

The high street chains are difficult to penetrate with the major chains increasingly having centralised buying, or at least centralised promotions planning, and recent ordering strategies have reduced stock-holding to only one copy of most titles except blockbusters. Small publishers turn desperately to the independents, only to find them fast disappearing.

The supermarkets, high street booksellers and behemoth websites, like Amazon, cream off the profits in blockbuster titles, leaving the independent booksellers unable to compete. Their smaller buying power means they don't get the discounts that the high street chains and supermarkets get. Some claim that the independents offer a wider range, although their space restriction can make this not the case. But what is fair to say is that the independent bookseller better supports niche titles by hosting events and creating book displays of unusual titles. They rarely sell their shop window or primary display, instead preferrig to choose their own displays.

There have sadly been some notable closures amongst the independents due to the price-competitive market, but before it all sounds too bleak, there have equally been some quality new arrivals, and Guardian Unlimited has an online listing of interesting independent bookshops.

On the publishing side of the business, publishers are over-producing volumes in order to get economies of scale which enable them to offer better discounts; the aim is to gain on volume of sales. This perpetuates the problem of dominant mass-market titles and books selling for too cheap a price. The range of books in the spotlight glare becomes increasingly narrower as supermarkets, book retailers and big book websites seem to be promoting only a handful of titles.

The quality and extent of marketing of books by mainstream publishers is restricted as the marketing budget gets spent where it is likely to receive a return on investment i.e. on big names, celebrities, blockbuster authors etc. The rest of the authors will be entered into all catalogues that the publisher uses, some reviews sought and for some, there might be a book tour, but very few get any tangible marketing budget spent on them. Billboard announcements only really work for established authors. It is an efficient way to announce, "Nick Hornby's next book is out…"

The window of launch is getting smaller, with many now citing a three-month display in bookshops before books get returned to them, yet the most expensive launch is the first book. The best opportunity for publishers to find a book's market is at launch, yet increasingly books get one shot, one season. Books that turned over a low but steady number during the launch phase will get moved from front of shop to the alphabetical shelf-siting at the back of shop.

The internet provides a fantastic route to the world, but it relies on people knowing you are out there or finding you amidst the billions of web pages that exist. Amazon, and similar sites like Abebooks, enable all registered books to be found but the browsing customer will never find you on page twenty as they rarely move off page one. As everyone scrambles for market share, publishers become online retailers and retailers are becoming publishers – Amazon's purchase of Booksurge now offering self-publishing.

This sounds like a catalogue of bad news for self-publishing authors, and this tirade of issues will no doubt have many authors shutting the book at this point – but DON'T. Because, bizarrely, this chaos leaves many opportunities for the independent author and small publisher. All you need is to be a bit clued-up, work your way around the problems and cut your own route through the jungle.

**So where's the opportunity?**
There are two major opportunities open to the self-publishing author. One is, of course, the internet and the other is the aspect of self-promotion and hand-selling. Mainstream publishers and booksellers simply cannot compete with the amount of dedicated time and knowledge that the self-publisher can offer his book/s. These are both looked at indepth in later sections – Direct Selling, Promotion and Publicity and Online Selling. For the moment, let's just glance at the benefits that the internet brings.

Whilst high street bookselling has a very short selling window before books are de-listed, the internet is picking up book sales in what is called "the long tail of the sale". This means that years after a book is released, it can still be listed in catalogues and pick up the ad hoc sales. The long tail of the sale is allegedly worth 2 billion dollars to the book industry!! That is a phenomenal change to the business of bookselling.

The internet has, in short, extended the life of a book. Where, historically, a book no longer in demand would have been remaindered, pulped or not reprinted, books can now live forever in catalogues and databases, you can order it as print-on-demand long after the last hard copy of the print run has been sold.

The internet also cuts through the traditional supply chain, enabling an author to put up a website at minimum and a shop-site at best. This means you do your own fulfilment. If the demand is so high that you are struggling to keep up with fulfilment, then you have an immensely successful book on your hands and you will easily be able to sell to a publisher.

Equally, if you only sell a few books, then you still stand to gain. By cutting down the quantity of middle-men in the selling chain, you can afford to sell fewer books and make more profit per unit. This is beneficial when you might only be able to reach a small audience or saturate demand quickly. The internet offers a win-win situation for the self-publishing author.

Another recognised phenomenon that the internet has produced is in the creation of "communities". Suddenly, groups of people who share a common interest in a specific subject-matter can come today on a worldwide scale. However obscure the topic of your book, the chance is that on the internet you will be able to find the hundred or so people who happen to want a book on that subject.

But it is not only the independent author who increasingly turns to the internet to reach his audience. Increasingly booksellers are using the internet to search for the books that they do not stock. As the volume of published titles increases year-on-year and more self-published titles come on line, booksellers are relying on the internet to help them hunt and find. Many of the independents are becoming information specialists, crossing the divide from high street bookseller to librarian in order to pick up every sale they can by servicing every customer that walks in their door. If, as an independent author, you are not on the internet, then you reduce your chances considerably.

The obvious importance of the internet in the mix means that the data-based information on your book needs to be very good, inspiring and accurate. Plan it and take the time to get it right. You do this by creating a marketing plan – a blueprint for all communication.

**Back to basics**

Mention marketing plan or marketing campaign and most people look either wary or dazzled. Marketing is a kind of mystery to those with no experience. Most authors say *"I can't do the marketing bit,"* or *"I'm useless at selling anything"*. But it really is not that difficult, and this book is going to take you through the steps to show you how easy it is. Just plan what you are going to say and say it whenever you get the opportunity to. The most important thing to remember is that the first time you talk to someone about your book is probably the first time they have heard about your book. What do you want them to know about it? But more of that shortly. First, let's go back to basics.

**Manufacturing is the creation of a product**
*(ie. publishing is the creation of a book)*

**Branding is the activity that defines that product towards specific target audiences**
*(conveying product benefits and appealing to consumer needs)*

**Marketing is the communication plan**

**Promotion is the activity the pushes the brand forward**

**Publicity is the noise around a brand.**

**A purchase is when the customer has understood!**

It is important to understand that your book performs in a similar way as Pantene shampoo or Persil washing powder. As with grocery products, there is such a plethora of books out there that potential buyers need to be able to read the codes and messages on a book cover or piece of promotion in order to disseminate whether it is for them or not. The buying market is at crisis point trying to find the material that they want to read, and as both publisher and bookseller, it is up to you to help them. You can do this in a multitude of ways – by jacket design and text, by what you say about the book, how you promote it and by the channels you use to promote and sell it – it all goes to present an image in the customer's mind, and that by definition is a brand.

### So what's a brand?

A brand is a product with a set of values that differentiate it from other similar products – its characteristics, benefits and reason to believe.

In today's society, consumers have a fantastic range of products for every need and occasion, to the point that we struggle to find the one thing we are looking for. There is such a plethora of choice and sea of noise that it feels purely by luck when we finally find a product that is exactly what we needed. The fact is we find our product of choice because of a complex array of branding, marketing, promotion and publicity activities.

We like to surround ourselves with products that define who we as individuals are. The man that chooses to drive a BMW is making a different statement about himself from the man that chooses to drive a Jaguar. Western affluence enables us to make these statements. We are, in effect, branding ourselves. What clothes labels we wear; what brand of watch / car / technology we buy; what music we listen to and films we see; what art is on display on our walls *and* (accordingly to the You Gov survey) what books we read. All of these items build up a story about each individual, and we use it to find, attract and mingle with like-minded people.

Branding has become very sophisticated as sellers exploit our desire to express ourselves through the products we surround ourselves with. In order to make a sale, sellers ensure they are 'speaking clearly' to the consumer. A packet of coffee is simply a packet of coffee – but visit the supermarket to see the array of different brands, each one appealing to different tastes, moments, occasions, lifestyles, hopes and dreams. Lavazza is selling Italian authenticity, Harrogate & Taylor sells the magic of weekends in New York, whilst Café Direct appeals to the conscientious, socially-aware individual wishing to buy Fair Trade. The fact is – most of them taste the same. All they are selling is a concept, a mindset, a set of values that we wish to buy into as it makes us feel good about ourselves and who we are. The packaging is designed to talk to a very specific target audience and emotional need.

Successful branding is when you believe that the product you are buying will deliver something over and above simply being a product, and you feel good about using it. Your book needs to deliver that promise; the jacket needs to evoke that message.

The jacket cover on the front of a book needs to act in the same way as a branded coffee does. The cover must offer the promise whilst accurately reflecting the book's story and purpose.

Look at the book jackets in the stores at the moment – it is easy to gain an impression of what is fashionable and desirable at the moment. The colours, the font, the choice of cover text all contribute to building the brand message.

One self-published author, K D Lather who wrote *The Changeling*, was picked out from the crowd by store manager at Ottakar's in Witney simply because he thought the cover image was striking and intriguing.

## What is a brand message?

The brand message is the story behind the product in order to differentiate from other similar products. Let's look at cars as an example: Audi's "Vorsprung der Technik" versus Land Rover's "It's how the rough take the smooth" versus Jaguar's "Don't dream it. Drive it." Each strapline makes a distinctive comment about the product quality and benefits. The fact is, cars have the added advantage of looking distinctly different from each other. Now you see how difficult it is for books...

A good strapline ensures you remember the one critical and defining point about the product. It is delivered consistently, every time you see the product, advertising or promotional material. I observed on the spine of SHE magazine their strapline:

### *"For a life less ordinary"*

Fantastic. From this, the reader understands that underpinning every single article is the angle that the reader is seeking to make her life less ordinary. Ergo, SHE magazine endeavours to delivery hundreds of ways to make your daily life experience exciting and unique. Imagine if you had a strapline like that on a book you had written for 30-something stay-at-home mums?

Can you succinctly define what your book is about in a way that conveys the "what and the why"? Do you know what image, feeling and benefit you are trying to conjure up? If yes, then count yourself amongst one of the very few self-publishing authors who is naturally good at marketing. If no, then count yourself amongst the other 99% of self-publishing authors who need guidance with their marketing. Chapter 2 will begin to show you how to understand your book's brand and how to create your brand message. Once this is done, then you can move on to communicating it.

## Marketing is communication

Marketing is a term used very loosely in the publishing world. Some people seem to think that marketing consists of telling the media the book exists then discounting it until it sells.

But this is such a small and over-simplified viewpoint, and it won't work for a self-publishing author. It barely works for the majority of mainstream published titles! The good news is that there are many activities that a self-publishing author can do to market his book as long as you are prepared to work at it. Understand your book's brand in order to maximise all the opportunities you create to talk about your book.

> *Talk clearly and people will hear you;*
> *Mutter and you will be ignored*

Marketing is the communication plan. Once you have a consistent message to impart, you need to have a focussed strategy to impart it – to the right people, in the right place at the right time and your marketing plan helps you to identify these different elements.

> *The marketing plan is the springboard*
> *for all promotional and publicity activities*

The bookselling marketing is very disparate – high street bookstores, online bookstores, book reviewers in magazines and newspapers, catalogues and membership clubs, co-retailers, auction sites... whatever, wherever, however. How does one person possibly cover off all the avenues? The answer is you don't because you can't.

In fact, not even large organisations can actually afford to throw more money at full advertising and distribution of each title they produce, so independent authors should not experience a sense of futility. Quite the opposite. If you are prepared to invest personal time and some small budget into promoting your book, then you may well be putting in more individual and focussed effort than goes into a mainstream published title.

There are hundreds of opportunities, and they are all time-consuming to implement which is why it remains of paramount importance to create a marketing "blueprint" so you can simply cut and paste information as you open up each new communication or sales channel. The marketing plan ensures you stay focused and consistent when promoting and publicising, achieving as many economies of scale as are possible to the self-publishing author.

## What this means to authors

The quality and extent of marketing of books by mainstream publishers is generally broad-brush, and any author (under mainstream contract OR self-published) can exploit the opportunities that self-promotion brings.

Most authors can sell around 300–500 copies of their book simply through personal contacts, work colleagues, links with communities and local activity. As the person earning the bulk of the percentage, this can prove to be sizeable. If you have access to a small, specialist-interest market this would be a beneficial route to take at the outset.

If you are simply trying to get 'found' then self-publishing is increasingly becoming a route to success, with regular stories emerging in the press about 'yet another self-publishing success story'. It provides the potential to use a book as a sales tool and build your own personal value.

One major drawback for mainstream-published authors is the one-shot, one-season aspect. Too many authors fall by the wayside as the window of opportunity shrinks from what used to be years of promotion, display and backlist cataloguing to nowadays being a few months of promotion and display, with low-selling titles quickly getting remaindered or pulped. Backlists are resevered for titles with a steady sales track record. If you don't make it big within two or three books then you are dropped from a publisher's list.

Self-publishing authors can market their book (and all ongoing books) on the slow-burn for far longer periods. Self-publishing authors can better exploit the early opportunities ie. the 'low-hanging fruit' and get a far higher return per book. It is worth taking the time to create a marketing plan, to earn income from the low-hanging fruit and build a value.

### *Don't rush it, but take the time to do it properly*

The fact is that mainstream publishers increasingly need authors to actively participate in the selling process. I have heard from a couple of sources that self-published authors often have a better relationship with their publisher than many other midlist authors because they have a better understanding of the pressures facing the publisher.

### *A marketing plan may help you secure a mainstream deal*

Additionally, demonstrating good marketing potential in your pitch to them will be the difference between securing a contract and not. As the publishing industry becomes increasingly market driven to compete with other industries, so too does the way a publisher must choose his titles. They look for titles with a big, ready market (as they need to sell in volume), markets with needs (ie. gaps in the market) and titles that match new needs.

### *"The marketing potential of a book is the difference between being published and not"*

Unsolicited manuscripts are assessed by a Commissioning Editor and the marketing department. If the market potential is not easily identifiable, the manuscript is rejected. A manuscript has to be good enough to get past the Commissioning Editor, but ultimately it is a marketing decision. This obviously impacts heavily on the kind of titles that are commissioned. Show your market and how you believe you can reach them, and you improve your chances immensely.

Irrespective of whether you are intending to approach a mainstream publisher or self-publish, authors must understand why anyone will BUY their book. Authors cannot rely on someone taking the time to read the book in order to discover its merits. This underlines the importance of authors understanding how to draw up a proper, targeted and real marketing plan at the outset.

> **Authors must promote the book's merits**
> **in order to get someone to read the book**

Yes, the chances of making it big are slim, and only a few authors do but this is commonplace in any trade, profession or art. Only a handful of people experience phenomenal success – actors, musicians, businessmen, whatever. They happen to be in the right place at the right, maybe they knew the right people, maybe they tapped into a trend that suddenly exploded in popularity. Ultimately, the person who tries is the person who at least gives himself a chance. Therefore, any "vanity" jibe shouldn't stop you from participating, and enjoying the process of publishing and selling for the life experience that it is.

With such a volume of books out there, it is comforting to hear one philosophy currently making the rounds to reassure publishers and booksellers, "The more there is to read, the more we will read." Phew! To a certain extent this is true. Apparently more people are reading more books than ever before, in all age groups.

# UNDERSTANDING THE PURCHASE DECISION

*"The creation of any product always starts with understanding the reason why people will buy it"*

The curious fact about marketing planning is that you need to start at the end by understanding the purchase decision.

Anyone producing a product needs to understand how the customer will find it and buy it; therefore you need to shape your marketing plan to fit with how you will bring it to their attention and make it available for sale. This is your marketing plan. Marketing has to be undertaken at the outset whilst understanding the end-selling point.

**So how do people choose what books to buy?**
The current routes to the book reading audience are:

1. via distribution to the sales outlets
2. via display in retail outlets
3. via media presence – reviews, features, advertising
4. via direct selling
5. via the internet.

The self-publishing author will struggle to get visibility with many of the traditional bookselling routes, and he has to work hard to earn their respect and this means "fitting to category". Remember – *if it looks like a duck, walks like a duck and quacks like a duck, then it is a duck.* Rightfully or wrongfully, self-publishing authors are advised to follow industry-standards and category codes in order to be taken seriously by the traditional channels.

From a piece of research undertaken by Book Marketing Ltd, the single biggest influence to the purchase decision is the jacket of a book – a staggering 74% per cent of books are bought on the strength of the jacket. The cover must be arresting and appeal to the type of reader it is written for so the likely purchaser of the book picks it up. It must set up positive customer expectation, instantly conveying the genre of the book and what mood it sets.

### Book covers make a promise to the reader.

It is up to the author to deliver against the expectations raised by the cover. Self-publishing authors must work hard on the cover, and get the communication right. Know what you are selling and what readers want to buy.

Don't forget the You Gov survey: many readers also seek to be seen with the right book ie. a prize-winning or short-listed author, a much-reviewed or much-debated author or an intellectual book. This doesn't help the self-publishing author who may not fall into one or all of these reasons, but he can help himself by *looking* like a credible book. Study your category, emulate (without copying or plagiarising) the books that you love. Make your book looks like a book that people are happy to be seen with.

This self-same piece of research also revealed that there are several ways in which people become aware of books, the first three of which are fairly evenly balanced.

*Familiarity with the author's work* is highest but only by a small majority. On the flipside, many people say that they don't like to read ALL of an author's work as they can tire of the style, or it doesn't deliver as well as the first book they read by that author. This means that new authors do have a good chance of being bought and read; consumers do not edit out a new author as a choice.

### Seek opportunities where unknown authors or niche titles are promoted

*Recommendations by friends and family* remains high, as does *browsing in a bookshop*. The former is good news for self-publishing authors as it demonstrates that using local activity, talking directly to communities and roping friends and family in to help will stand you in good stead – and most of this comes fairly cheaply.

Obviously the latter point, *browsing in a bookshop*, is a limiting factor for self-publishing authors. Bookshops increasingly are the domain of best-seller, mass-market, big-promo-spend books, and therefore getting into the bookshop remains the task and objective for authors, rather than the expectation.

### Make a big noise in a small area to get visibility

*The media* will certainly bring the book to the awareness of the reading public but scores relatively low in terms of this converting to a sale – which is fortunate for self-publishing authors as the chances of securing national media coverage is also pretty low. So celebrate and exploit it when you do get it.

*Advertising* reputedly scores zero per cent in terms of helping authors choose their books. Personally, I am a bit suspicious of this figure, even though I don't believe in advertising your book as a money-making venture. I think people subconsciously take in advertisements although in research, respondents deny this as nobody likes to feel 'sold to', particularly the reading market which prefers to be seen as more discerning.

Two of the most important learnings from the above knowledge is (i) the importance of the book cover and (ii) the importance of endorsement. Never under-estimate how powerfully these can work for you.

The fiction and biography categories have a lot of volume, dominating the market with 40% share; which is just as well given the sheer quantity of manuscripts and new launches that are created each year. But it's an elusive audience. It's hard to find them and even harder to tell them that they really do want to read your book… just as it is very difficult for the potential reader to know exactly which book is meant for them.

Knowing your audience is critical, and this is explained in the next section, but in the meantime, remember that most authors are also readers. You too buy books and this makes you perfectly poised to understand the problems of selecting a book. How do you select your reading material? Why would you choose your book? Understand the purchase decision in order to help yourself understand the selling decisions.

## SUMMARY

To understand the purchase decision, you will need to answer the following questions. But don't just take your first answer as the only answer. The next section endeavours to help you interrogate yourself properly, by asking around the question and answering it from the point view of a very distinct and definable target audience.

### *What does the market need from this product?*

- o BOOK: What is the book about? What is the benefit or message?
- o GENRE: What genre is it? Where will they look for or find this book?
- o AUDIENCE: Why do they want this book? What need does it fulfil?
- o COMPETITION: What gaps does it fill in the market? Why do they need filling? What topical issue has arisen that demonstrates the need? Why is your book better or different from the competitors?
- o AUTHOR: How is the author relevant to the book? What is
- o the story behind the story ie. the inspiration for the book?

# PART II

# CREATING THE COMMUNICATION

**Creating a marketing plan**

    a.  **The right information**

    b.  **The right people**

    c.  **The right place**

    d.  **The right time**

    e.  **The competitive context**

    f.  **Selling the author behind the book**

*Issue: The importance of research*

# CREATING A MARKETING PLAN

The purpose of this chapter is to demonstrate how to create a marketing plan. Success is in the preparation – all the business books tell you this and a marketing plan focuses where your effort and priorities should lie.

## WHAT IS A MARKETING PLAN?

A marketing plan is a list of planned activity; it is the "blueprint" of what you are going to tell people and when, in order to make them aware of the book and inspire them to buy it. In short, a marketing plan is a summary of:

**WHAT you are going to communicate**
**WHO you are going to communicate it to**
**HOW you will communicate it**

**and the order in which you will IMPLEMENT it ie.**
*how you will build-on and recycle that communication*
*to the trade, the media and the end-customer*

You will be talking about your book to many people and in many different forms over the life of the book. Firstly you need to understand precisely what you are trying to say about your book however differently the same question may be phrased. How many times have people asked you about your book and you have struggled to articulate a succinct but very interesting answer that will have them hopping around begging to buy a copy of it – or at the very least understanding that they would actually reap benefits or enjoyment by having a copy of it.

Non-fictional books are easier to define in succinct terms whereas fiction has a more indefinable 'reason-to-read'. I hear too many authors rambling on about their book without ever inspiring me to pick up and read it. One author recently did articulate her book summary well, and as a result I couldn't wait to read her book. I longed to be transported on the journey that she had clearly once experienced and had written about in her book (*The Crab Man*). She captured the central and defining moment within the book which inspired me to want to read the book – and that is what all authors need to do. Planning out your communication and understanding what people want to hear is critical.

Therefore, you will need to interrogate yourself about your book's merits and what you want to say. How have you written yours to make it unique, fascinating, page-turning, intriguing and un-put-downable? Is the real strength of the story in the plot? Is there a surprise or twist that will stun or amaze readers? Or is it in the lead characters? Are they so strong, identifiable or likeable that you wish to know them better, and live their story with them? Is it in the writing style that is so beautiful and lyrical that it reads like a song?

## MARKETING IS COMMUNICATION

1. The right information
2. To the right person
3. In the right place
4. At the right time

*Underpinned with research:*

5. Knowing the competition
6. Understanding connection between author and book

### *Publishers talk to many audiences*

The reason you need to have a clear and consistent communication plan is because you are talking to many different groups of people, and they all need to hear what is relevant to them. Everyone will have a slightly different reason to believe that your book will have a benefit to them.

As a self-publishing author, you are talking to the trade, the media, the public and often to agents/publishers as well if you are trying to secure a mainstream deal. Each conversation about your book is a potential opportunity.

One sad insight is that you are often talking to yourself. You pump out the information to book reviewers and book shops, but rarely get a response. You are left wondering if they got the email / flyer / review copy etc.

It is for this reason that you have to keep the information focussed and tight – and sent out as cost-effectively as possible. Strike the balance between telling as many people as you can whilst communicating on a one-to-one level. Minimise the amount of time you will waste telling people about your product who will never be interested in it, as it is not 'for them'.

**Remember...**
- o Make each pitch relevant to the person to whom you are talking
- o Don't reinvent the wheel each time you talk about your book
- o Understand your book well enough that you can angle your pitch to suit a need
- o Think about the market you are selling to rather than the product you are selling
- o It's not what it is but what it means to your customer. How will it impact on his life?

**How to approach the creation of a marketing plan:**
1. Set aside a whole day in a quiet room to work through the questions, interrogate yourself, write out descriptors and rewrite them.
2. For every question you ask yourself, put it through its paces – ask yourself Who, Why, What, When, Where

and How. Some of these may not be relevant, so just cross them out and move onto the next one.

3. Answer the questions quickly. Just write down the first answers that pop into your head and keep up a good pace.

4. Create a Good Words List: keep a list of words or phrases on a separate sheet of paper; feel free to add to it as new thoughts occur to you; cross words off as their relevance diminishes; put the list in an order of priority.

5. Then go back to the beginning and ask Why? What does that answer mean, and more importantly, what does it mean to my readers? How does it pertain to my book and my book alone? How can I use this piece of information?

6. Then put it aside for a few days whilst you continue working on your manuscript, bearing in mind the questions and answers you had arrived at so far.

7. Then revisit the plan and start crafting it.

8. Make sure the lead words or phrase from your Good Words List appears somewhere in your final statement on "What the book is about".

9. It is difficult to be too formulaic about what questions to ask, as I would pose a different set of questions for a fictional title to a non-fictional title.

## 1. THE RIGHT INFORMATION

A marketing plan communicates the right information on what the book is about in an inspirational, succinct, motivating and relevant fashion.

To define "the right information" you have to ask yourself the right questions, and this section seeks to help you ask yourself the right questions.

I cannot be prescriptive here, as no two books will have exactly the same set of questions. You have to start with the generic questions listed here, but these are only to act as a guide. Each time you answer a question, re-interrogate it and ask yourself why? Keep digging deeper until you have run out of different answers, and find that you are repeating yourself or simply going round in circles.

*An example:*
*I recently interrogated an author about the purpose of her book, "Brown Jade". We derived some positive angles and answers but the real hook was missing. She went away to think further about it, and emailed me two days later saying "the book is really about hope." She was right, and suddenly the whole marketing plan came together.*

My experience is that authors always know the answers to the many questions I pose to them, and in fact they thoroughly enjoy the interrogation and the wide range of thoughts that it prompts. The answers all lie within, and a good marketing plan will focus on the best and richest veins of thought.

### What's the book about?
The book description has to live in a variety of ways – both as a snappy one-liner to booksellers and the trade, on promotional material, as a headline or sub-title on the jacket cover; and as a paragraph in a catalogue or online bookshop, on press releases, promotional material. It also has to live

verbally ie. when friends, potential buyers, book reviewers and journalists ask you what your book is about.

It is for this reason that you do not want to be working with some hastily written descriptor that was not properly "worked through" or researched. The first descriptor you write out is only the beginning.

Sometimes you may alter the emphasis on one element than another, but the essential meaning doesn't change. The one-liner summary is usually a very heavily distilled version of what you would write on the back cover of the book, and what you might use in a catalogue or online shop listing.

**It has to be succinct**
**It has to interest and attract**
**It has to secure the sale**

Good one-liners focus on the book's strengths. This gets the customer interested. Once you have identified the core strength, it is easy to adapt it for different audiences and flesh it out for different uses.

### What are the book's strengths?

Most authors can rattle off a number of answers at this point which are a combination of features (ie. elements within the book), benefits (ie. what it gives to the reader) and advantages (ie. how it is different). But this is only the *top* half of the purchaser's reason to buy. Underneath it lies the world of self-agenda - shoppers buy in response to a need or want. The core of your communication needs to clearly and distinctly hit that nerve.

### (i)  Human interest revolves around self-need

The strength of a book needs to lead with a claim that is invariably more 'self-ish' than any of these (ie. about the self, not as in being greedy!). Does your book satisfy a human need? People buy in response to a personal need or want, and the main strength of the book revolves around this reason-to-buy. Will it provide people with any of the following:

- o Help you make money
- o Help a loved one
- o Improve your future
- o Impress others and/or improve yourself
- o Help to prevent something bad happening
- o Further your career
- o To share personal learning on a subject / help others
- o Experience new/different; go on a journey
- o Gain pleasure
- o Gain deeper understanding and insight

## (ii) Shoppers need a reason to believe

Once you have identified what basic human need (or self-need) your book provides, you should tack onto it the feature or benefits that make it specific to your book. This feature or benefit will revolve around the *reason* for the potential buyer to believe, or buy into what you are claiming.

Fiction

- o Most fiction titles will revolve around the basic human wish to gain pleasure or gain a deeper understanding and insight or to experience something new by going on a journey that another person has experienced. To hammer home the reason-to-buy, your strength will need to explain why or how ie.
    - o *A moving story about…*
    - o *an uplifting story of…*
- o Many fictional titles revolve around some form of social comment or observation about today, and this will be the main strength you should seek to communicate ie.
    - o *a fascinating insight into…*
    - o *an extraordinary observation…*

o  The strength of fiction can often lie in the quality of writing – the strength of the plot, character, main event, writing style.
>    o  *Led by one extraordinary woman, this is the story of…*
>    o  *A beautifully written account of…*

## Biographies

These predominantly revolve around the human interest or need of 'sharing personal learning' whilst also overlapping with the above strengths for fiction. The benefit to biographies is their stretchiness – by that I mean that fact is stranger than fiction and oftentimes more extraordinary events take place:

o  *A curious set of coincidences…*
o  *A strange childhood that led to…*

and the writing style within the book often reflects the bizarreness of reality:

o  *The funniest biography I have read…*
o  *A crazy, mad-cap journey through…*

## Non-fiction or information texts

Non-fiction books such as historic studies, business, self-help etc tend to have a very clear human need and their strength will focus more around how successfully it provides new information or insight, answers a question or solves a problem.

o  *Free up your life by…*
o  *Secure your future by…*
o  *History reveals that…*

## (iii) Relevance to different audiences

Every book has many audiences – the trade & bookseller, the primary target audience, the purchaser which is sometimes different from the reader ie. children's books are bought by adults, people buying as a gift, a school librarian etc.

Therefore, the main strength of a book will depend on to whom you are talking, and you will need to angle it accordingly.

> *Focus on the person you are selling to,*
> *not the product you are selling.*

### How to determine what is the right information

Sometimes authors struggle with being able to pin down 'one great strength', feeling that they are ignoring other important messages about their book, and often a third-party is required to help them with this (which is how Indepublishing.com seeks to help authors).

> *"What authors need more of is critical assessment and*
> *independent perspective"*

### Summary

However, to help you further at this point to work this out independently, try the following exercises:

o   Write out a description of what the book is about in your own words, allowing it to be as long or short as you wish but ensuring you capture all the things you want to say. Underline the critical words and re-write them on a fresh piece of paper (see Good Words List on page 42, point 4).

o   If you have already written the book and commissioned an independent critique or edit, then browse through their report. A different pair of eyes or a different perspective can really help you to define what it is you are creating. Underline the critical words and add them to your paper.

o   Ask a couple of close friends to read the manuscript and give their views about what they liked about it, where the strengths were, what was the best 'bit' of the story or the most interesting piece of information. Note down the critical words – the adjectives they use, the strengths they comment on. Add these words to your paper.

o   Distil the words down: cross out the ones that repeat, cross out the ones that are synonomous with each other; choose words that capture best what you want to say. Try to be left with 5 good, strong, descriptive words that you can always grab when talking about your book. See if you can construct them into a sentence.

o   Ask yourself why should someone read it?

o   Ask yourself why you wrote it. What are you trying to change? What do you want the reader to feel as a result of reading it?

o   What does your book mean to people TODAY? Are you telling them something new, or putting a new spin on something old? Is it part of a fad? If so, what cycle is the fad in? Are you early to market (therefore undertaking an educational role); or you peaking or in the tail-end? Is it new news? Are you out there first or have more credibility than the others?

***Books that do most well are books that touch on a nerve,***
***or are in tune with a hot topic in society.***

If you are still having difficulty, or feel that you are only scratching the surface, then try doing the same exercise with another book, be it a fictional John Grisham or a factual John Harvey-Jones. Sometimes this will help you to stand back from your own book and see it with clearer eyes. The problem for many authors is that they are simply too close to their book.

## 2. THE RIGHT PEOPLE

The most important *reason* to know WHO is going to buy your book is to help you to understand HOW you are going to talk to them. How are you going to make them understand that this book is aimed at them and written for them? You need to understand what language and tone to take with them, what visuals and graphics will appeal to them.

### *It's not what it is, but what it means to your customer*

Good, cost-effective marketing always targets the "low-hanging fruit" first. Who did you write this book for? Why will they enjoy it? What will they gain from it?

These are all questions you asked yourself in THE RIGHT INFORMATION. Now you are taking these and thinking about the person who is sitting down and reading the book.

### *Target the "low-hanging fruit" first*

Who is going to buy your book, therefore who are you selling to? Don't write 20–64 year old adults as your target audience as this is not a target group but a general demographic description who you can only reach by doing mass advertising on television, radio and in bookshops – which you can't afford nor should you be spending as you will not make your money back. Instead you should be asking yourself who will enjoy this book the most.

### *Broad-brush descriptions are worthless*

But how do you get beyond the 'general demographic' description? Most people think of an age range of people – this book is for young children, for teenagers, for 20-something, 30-something etc, OAPS etc. But you have to dig deeper than this. If you are targeting 20-somethings, then start to define which

20-somethings. Some are party-animals, others are career-minded, or community-oriented. Chicklit has distinctive codes – over-bright colours, zany lettering, cartoony or charicatured illustrations. Is it any coincidence that magazines, DVD's and CD's, computer games and consumer brands targeted at this age range all have similar graphic codes? Of course not.

Chicklit appeals to a certain type of 20-something girl. If your book, however, has more classic tones, a gentle romance or social observation then the language, graphic codes and colours will need altering in order to address them. Compare how you may modify your language to address two different audiences:

*"Suky was always a little bit crazy, but this time she'd gone too far. Even her best mate couldn't defend her this time…"*

Versus:

*"Susannah had always been remote and dreamy, but reality was about to hit. Her closest friends could do little but watch…"*

Start adding the layers to these two books – zany illustrations and fonts for the former, classic fonts and a fine art print for the latter; gaudy colours as opposed to traditional earthy shades or cool greens. Endorsements by young trendy magazines will resonate with the chick-lit crowd for the first book, whereas the latter needs respected authors and establishment voices to endorse it. Plastic, over-gloss finish, maybe with some gilt or embossing works a treat with the first book; a matt finish with subtle varnishing appeals to the more intellectual audience. Potential book-buyers subconsciously understand all these codes.

All this, and we're still in production. Now you have demonstrated you understand WHO they are, you need to find them. Match your promotional material to the visual codes and production values of the book, to reinforce your message.

Now think where your chick-lit-lover hangs out, what she reads, how she receives information; compare that to her shyer or more career-oriented counterpart. One may get referred to the book by way postcards in a wine-bar whereas the other will hear about a new book at her reading group. One may hear about a book whilst booking a package holiday to Ibiza whilst the other will read the review in the BA Inflite magazine.

Understand your audience, then position your book so they see it.

## How will they find me?

This is a real worry for most self-publishing authors, as they invariably lack distribution and in-store presence. Assuming that most people will go to a bookshop to look for a book, self-publishers fear that they won't ever be found.

To overcome this, the self-publishing author should do some research – a little bit like locking yourself out of your own house to see how easy it is to break in. The only difference being that you will be pleased if you find your route to your book quickly and easily.

Go and research how you would find this book. Research how you would find other books like it. Did you ask the shop assistant for his advice? Where did he point you to in the shop? What advice did the library give? Did they point you to an aisle or online? What magazines did you refer to? What search terms did you put into the internet? What online book sites and book-finder sites did you get referred to? What books did your friends recommend to you? Why?

Once you found it, what was it about the book that drew you in? That hit the right nerve and convinced you that this was the right book? Was it the summary description? Was it the cover of the book? Was it the endorsements? Was it intriguingly different yet clearly of a genre you recognised?

*Research how to find your book,*
*and other books just like it*

### How will I find them?

This is where your marketing plan begins to take real shape as you can start listing out the media and locations that you need to target your communication through and to. Once you have begun to define and profile your target audience, it is easier to start locating where they are and how you will help them to find you, by listing out the places they would automatically go to in order to find a book such as yours.

> *Reaching your audience is a two-way street:*
> *you reach out to them and you help them to find you.*

*TIP:* Staying with the "low-hanging fruit" analogy - define the primary audiences who you know have a definite requirement for your book and focus all your energy on talking to them. Don't worry about whether you are closing the door on other audiences because you aren't. Once you have started the ball rolling and got the 'easy pickings' then you can devote time and energy on the next defined audience along.

### How do I get them to demand my book?

You make a person demand your book by selling it to them; not in the financial sense of the word, but by convincing them that they must have it as it will be beneficial or pleasurable to them. You cannot always be standing in front of them singing the book's praises, therefore the book itself has to do this. Make the cover beautiful or engaging or full of promise. Get the language right.

> *A book must talk directly to its audience*
> *and sing its own praises*

Sometimes an author is lucky and writes a book on a certain subject that suddenly becomes a hot topic for the media. The wise author will be watching for media attention on his topic and will seize any opportunities as they arise, and this is explored further in "Raising and Driving Awareness". Sometimes this may result in the author becoming an 'expert' or 'spokesperson' for a certain social issue, and this we look at more closely in "Selling the Author" (page 59).

In order to talk directly to these people in a meaningful way, you need to think about how they are receiving the information. You need to aim your message directly at them so they cannot miss it. This will influence the design of the book in order to arrest their attention and make them pick the book up. This will dictate what language, words and tone you need to adopt to make them understand it is for them.

> *Reaching your audience means aiming the*
> *book design and tone of language at them*

Whilst writing the book, you may wish to include a very specific group, place or voice; include other businesses or quote potential endorsers as they are more likely to take an interest if they are positively mentioned. Remember the low-hanging fruit? You've just added a whole new branch, or two.

### What promotional material will best attract them?

In understanding your audience, you will also come to understand what promotional material and activities will draw their attention. It needs to tie in with the book and be relevant to the content. Great publicity is unusual and eye-catching; it brings a concept to life. Whilst your book may have to fit category standards, the publicity material can be different and challenging. This is explored in "Promotion and Publicity" (page 213).

### Summary

Identifying the right person will provide you with the necessary information on how to talk to them. This will inform

all design elements from book cover to promotional material
as well as how you address your audience in terms of
language, tone, font and content across all communication.
Understanding your target audience will also play a large part
in what sort of promotional activities and type of promotional
material you choose to implement.

If you get these elements consistently working in harmony
your target audience cannot fail to see you. It is then up to you
to put your book into the right places and the right time…

## 3. THE RIGHT PLACE

By now you will have a good understanding of your primary
target audience which will help you to identify the 'right'
places' to go to so your audience can find you. At this stage of
the marketing planning, you are hazarding some guesses and
making some assumptions. Ultimately you want to get your
book in as many places as possible.

I want to pause for a moment to reassure anyone who I am
losing at this point… if you have got this far, then be
comforted by the fact that you have done the bulk of the hard
thinking and from here on in we are just building and sifting.
Once we get to the implementation, the real fun begins.

### Where will people look for this title?
Firstly, do your research and create a list of all the many,
many places you would go to in order to find and buy your
book. Building on the lists created in RIGHT PERSON,
research and list out the following:

◊     What shops? High street bookshops, specialist shops, co-
retailers (see "Channels to market" page 108)
◊     Where in the bookshop will people find it? Have you
categorised the book correctly so that
(i) the store puts it on the right shelf and
(ii) potential buyers are directed to the right place in the

store to find it.
*(as per the BIC Classification Guide on Nielsen, or using Amazon as a guide to categories)*

◊ Where online? What categories might they browse in to find you? What search terms would they put into a search engine? Have you registered the right keywords and metatags (see "Selling online" page 262)

◊ Libraries? Is it the type of book that may have high appeal to libraries (see "The Library Market" on page 100).

◊ Abroad – maybe in export markets ((UK language markets) or foreign markets (all other languages). This is explored further in "Selling Rights" on pp 341, and you may wish to also refer to indepublishing.com for further information.

## Golden rules

Self-publishing authors are not in control of the supply chain and end-selling point, and this makes them vulnerable. Some retail outlets will readily accept your title and others will prove impassable. It is seemingly a random decision based on the mood of the moment. To minimise the risks of not being available and not being found, you should follow the below golden rules:

o Implement the mandatory – database collators such as Nielsen and Bowker.

o Follow the easiest and shortest line to the buying public – the path of least resistance – to make sure the book is available to buy.

o Take control – ensure you have at least one avenue where you know for certain that your book is available; that it can always be found and can easily be bought ie. online bookshops such as Amazon.co.uk (can be tricky initially) and Indebookshop.com.

---

    o   Ensure you clearly communicate WHERE your book can be found on ALL forms of media and promotional communication.

## 4. THE RIGHT TIME

In order to strike the right moment, self-publishers can only be PRO-ACTIVE or REACTIVE. You can either pre-plan to tie in with a nationally recognised event or date that pertains to your subject matter ie. Valentine's Day for romance etc, or you can simply set a date and work towards that, looking for any opportunities in the media that you can swiftly react to.

In the first instance, the main question you have to ask yourself is *"when do people most need this book?"*

### (i) Critical calendar dates (pro-active)
Itemise any and all critical dates in your subject matter's calendar. Do your research properly and find out if there are any events, festivals, celebrations, talks, roadshows, dedicated days etc that you can be involved in.

### (ii) Search for more information (pro-active)
Don't fight shy. If you want information, sometimes you just have to get on the phone and ask for it. If you have written a crime thriller, then contact the Crime Writer's Association. Become a member. Get a copy of their annual calendar of events. Ask how you can participate. If you have written a Romance, contact the Romantic Novelists Association. If you have written a sci-fi fantasy, contact The British Fantasy Society. Hunt online. Ask in bookshops. People are generally very helpful and friendly.

**(iii) Ask yourself when people need it? (pro-active)**
When you decided to write your book, it was possibly prompted by a certain need at a certain time. When was this, and what can you now do to ensure other people can find it?

**(iv) The media need spokespeople (pro-active)**
Remember, the media are often aware of certain social issues or hot topics but simply lack the necessary resources to put somebody onto researching the topic and finding the spokespeople – particularly for local newspapers. And just because you live in Kent doesn't mean you cannot be a spokesperson in Northumberland ie. on issues of underage drinking? Make yourself known to them. They may well be grateful for the information. (see "Selling the Author" pp 59).

**(v) What's news? (re-active)**
Keep a tab on the news; don't live in a vacuum. Be prepared to pounce on any news story that can remotely link back to your book. Get your friends involved and tell them to look out for any news stories on your topic. Think out of the box (creatively) in order to make connections between the news story and your book.

**(vi) Make news (pro-active)**
There are several ways to make news. Some, like Dave Chick, are fighting for a cause. Hair-raising publicity stunts like risking life and limb on cranes by Tower Bridge or on the London Eye will certainly make news – although he still needed to write his book to get the truth out there which had too often been inaccurately reported. Another way to make news is to research some data yourself, then report on it. Think of an issue associated with your book then do some research. Write up an article and try to get it into your local paper or specialist interest magazine – or even a national paper.

## 5. KNOW THE COMPETITIVE CONTEXT

Every element within the marketing plan must be considered in the context of what the competition is doing. You cannot market in a vacuum, and this is where the basic principles of marketing do not come naturally to an author. Authors write in isolation. It tends to be a more solitary, inside-your-own-head pastime.

Author publishers must assess their book in the context of the competition because this is how people will judge it. If your book is the only one to meet a certain need then it stands on its own merit; but if there are plenty of me-too's and same-subject-different-angle, then your book will be judged differently.

◊   BOOK: who is the competition? What is same/different? Who's doing what better? What claims do they make on the cover?

◊   AUDIENCE: is your audience the same or different? What's the difference? Why?

◊   PLACE: how/why different? What other channels do they sell in?

◊   TIME: how/ why different? What times of year do they seem to be most active?

◊   PROMO & PR: what promotional activity are they doing? What publicity are they securing? Who's reviewing them or writing about them? Who isn't, and is there any interest to be had from them?

◊   AUTHOR* – what gives you/them the edge? Why are you more relevant to speak on the subject? *(We look at this next).*

It may be appropriate (or indeed it may not, and you are the best judge of this) to talk to authors of competitive titles. Maybe you are building on a theory that they first proposed and it would be a positive action to garner their opinion and credit them with their positive reaction. If you are offering an alternative opinion it may be better to not involve them – although if you are trashing their theories, you should expect a reaction at some point. And being an author, they may have access to some very public channels and media routes to launch a derisory attack on you. You might decide to hear their objections in private first?

Remember, when assessing the competitive context, it isn't in the last few minutes before launch but many months before if not years before. Watch the market to see what books follow your lead, or totally contradict you. You can use any of this for publicity purposes.

# 6. SELLING THE AUTHOR BEHIND THE BOOK

The book is the product that people are buying, but invariably the story behind the book is as interesting as the book itself. Who is the author, and what prompted him to write the book? What is the connection of the book to its author? What event happened in his life that prompted this story, and what are they hoping to achieve by writing about it?

> ### *The author is the bridge-link between the book and the audience*

In summary, this can be labelled the 'author brand' with the caveat that this label has a variable definition. For the purposes of this book, when I refer to the 'author brand' I am referring to the "who/what/why" of the author. Some people use 'author brand' to label the author who has invented and writes solely on a whole new genre.

Ask yourself what human interest or human need does your book provide? What insight, perspective, observation, social issue or problem does it address?

How are you the bridge-link between that problem and your book? What is your point of view and what are you seeking to change? What is your voice? What are you a spokesperson of? What are you representing? How do you help people experiencing the same problem?

> **An author brand is the "who/what/why"**
> **definition of the author behind the book**

### Establish your reason

Ask yourself what prompted you to write that story:

- o Is it a topical social issue that you have experience of?
- o Is it a human interest issue?
- o An observation on human behaviour?
- o Provide a different perspective?
- o Is it a bizarre story?
- o Does it change something?
- o Are you trying to right a wrong?

Assuming you have written a romance, the reader wants you to express your individual thoughts, feelings, experience. Maybe you have experienced something that you haven't previously seen written about and you wish to bring it to the world, to share and help others to learn from your own mistakes.

If the heroine's an alcoholic, then readers will want the author to demonstrate personal understanding of alcoholism. This may not be as the alcoholic himself, but from a third party perspective – being the partner, son/daughter, parent of an alcoholic; being a medical person or therapist treating alcoholics etc. Readers will want you to provide them with a new, deeper and/or different understanding of the problem.

> **Great fiction often provides**
> **new perspectives and other-person insight**

**Establish a voice or style.**

You might choose to write about modern-day issues ie. career women, house husbands, wild children, single-parenthood etc. You might choose to write about this topic in many different ways, from many angles and experiences, across a number of books. This puts you in the ideal situation to promote yourself as the voice of that issue, and the media may happily run with it whilst using you as the spokesperson.

- o Are you writing many stories on same theme? ie. build up a voice that the media can play on
- o Do you have a very compelling style?
- o What experience gives you authority to write on it? What is relevant to your issue and builds a distinctive image *(this forms the basis of your biography).*
- o What expertise? This is critical for non-fiction.

***Authors have nearly a one-third greater chance of selling a book if readers have heard of you***

This is fantastic for already existing authors – but the difficulty is becoming known. In order to give the media a reason to write about you, you will need to establish a clear voice or style. To achieve it, you need to <u>make</u> yourself known by working at establishing yourself as a spokesperson on the subject you are writing about. Contact the relevant media with a range of different angles over a period of time, and at some point there will be a connection. You will happen upon the person who has need of your 'voice' at that time, and they will gratefully pounce on you to help them with their own article or research.

**Establish why you have the authority to write on that subject.**

Once you have understood the brand of your book, you must then list out the reasons why you have the authority to write on that subject. Who writes the best books on a subject? It is obviously the person who has the experience or the knowledge of that subject. We can all pontificate on a subject matter, but unless we actually have experience or knowledge we run the risk of trotting out the same old, same old.

Non-fiction is obviously more identifiable. The important element is what you are saying that is different or unique? Are you challenging anyone? Are you communicating a new development?

Fiction has an indefinable and elusive audience. Famous authors have worked hard to establish their brand and what they represent, and subsequently have the advantage that there is a lot of branding information locked up in their name and reputation. Marion Keyes is one such author whose books are an unusual blend of comedy and darkness, covering topics such as depression, addiction and illness. This is largely down to Marion's own experiences with a drinking problem by the time she was thirty. The daytime chat shows invited Marion onto the show to talk about drinking issues, a fact which publicised her book. Marion's ultimate success is down to the quality of her writing and the characters she creates. Whilst it was unsought publicity, this demonstrates the point I am making. Erin Pizzey is another author who put her name to an issue, writing about battered women and being the Founder of the Modern Women's Shelter Movement.

New authors are relying more heavily on other clues as to what they are writing about ie. most motivating element, benefit, reading need or type of book, in order to start the connection.

*Authors must weave their own story:*
*the connection between them and their book*

### Creating your biography

Every author needs to have a "Biog" about themselves – maybe even a couple that address slightly different aspects of the book. The moment you speak to the press, they ask for your biography. This is because newspapers generally write about human interest issues, and focus on the human behind the story and not just the story itself.

Ask yourself the following questions in order to start trying to formulate your 'author brand' and what will become your stock-in-trade response. The more people you talk to, the more this will morph and develop. Allow that to happen, and keep updating your marketing plan as your communication hones itself to perfection:

- o   Who are you?
- o   What do you write about?
- o   What experience do you have on that subject?
- o   What uniqueness do you bring?
- o   What tone/style?
- o   What message do you have?
- o   What voice do you want to be?

Don't feel the need to answer all these questions in one biog but, as you did when writing out the RIGHT INFORMATION, underline the most salient points and create a short, snappy biography that best encapsulates your link to the book.

It is also important to remember that when you write your biography, that this is not just a curriculum vitae or domestic description. People *will* want to know the basic parameters – married, with kids, living in windmill in Yorkshire etc – but if your current lifestyle or background did not play a large part in why you wrote the book, then don't burden the biography with excessive detail. Keep it all relevant, and focus on the connection between you and your book.

**"Keep the link between you and your book clear."**

What experience gives you authority to write on it? What is relevant to your issue and builds a distinctive image. If you have written a story about a single-mother struggling to keep her teenage son from a certain journey to jail, and you are a single-mother, then include this. What expertise do you have? When writing non-fiction, people will want to see your credibility either in terms of formal education (degrees), informal education (experience) and other people's endorsement of what you are saying.

> *"Your biography should build your credibility."*

The press are notorious for working at speed and not double-checking their facts. Sometimes they read only one-third of a sentence and therefore report inaccurately. In order to manage what is said about you and reported in the media, keep it brief. Say only what is relevant and don't feel inclined to tell everybody everything about your life.

> *"Manage other people's perception and comment about you."*

It is wise at this point to get a range of professional photographs done – in colour and black & white, close-up head shot as well as possible in a relevant environment with your book. It is worth investing in professional photographs and ask him to get the character right – not too serious and not too casual. You want to look friendly, approachable and obviously your best without looking posed and starchy.

## THE GOLDEN RULES OF COMMUNICATION

### (i) Communication is an ongoing process
◊ Keep recycling and tweaking the communication, pushing as many reasons for people to read your book as possible. At some point, your book sales will either settle into a small but regular pattern, or may reach saturation point. Usually, however, most self-published titles saturate their ability to reach their market before they saturate their market.

◊ Give people different reasons to sell you or promote you by using new endorsements or reviews.

◊ Exploit successes – show great media to bookshops and great sales to the media.

◊ Redefine your audience as you progress, broadening it or finding new audience groups

◊ Listen to and use your feedback

**(ii) Avoid wasted opportunities; make sure the book is available**
There is often a temptation for self-publishing authors to have a book launch within a week of receiving the first print run of the book. However, depending on when you registered your book information with Nielsen, the shops may not have updated their databases and all your marketing efforts will be wasted. It is critical that the unknown or self-publishing author ensures his book is available to order via all major bookstores and online etc before approaching the media.

From the media perspective, the most motivating news about the launch of any book is the fact that it is new to the market; the second most motivating or interesting news is the need or desire that it fulfils. And they are not going to run the same story twice just because you didn't have your distribution properly sorted out the first time, so don't be tempted to rush it. Make sure your book is available before you market it.

**(iii) Make it easy for people to find your book**
All marketing and promotional activity must also point people clearly towards where they can buy your book from. As an unknown author, you must make it easy for people to find your book and therefore buy it. The best way is to have a website – even if this is just a one-page site that tells people how they can contact you or how they can buy your book.

How they will hear about it, how you will direct them to it and how you motivate people to talk about it and refer each other is all discussed in "Raising and Driving Awareness"

## TIP: *Don't rely on the bookshops*

Any unknown, self-publishing author can take it as read that it is as good as impossible to get your book nationally distributed by any chain bookseller in the country at launch. Many booksellers may stock your book at relevant localities against evidence of your own marketing activity ie. events, media promotion etc. If it seems to do very well, then Head Office may decide to extend the book into other key locations and may invite you to do an event, or provide materials for a display. If it still sells well, they may roll it out nationally. But this is a good 3–6 months down the line, if not a year after launch.

### (iv) Maximise your routes to the audience

There are many routes to the audience as itemised throughout this book. Whilst it is critical to cover off the-most-obvious-yet-least-likely (distribution in the high street bookstores), the independent author must cover off a wide range of other routes (see "Selling into the Trade" and "Selling Online").

### (vi) Exploit any specialist-interest avenues

For non-fiction titles, there are often many 'specialist-interest' avenues you can follow such as book clubs, trade fairs, targeted media and doing talks with groups. Again, you will need to know how easily and cheaply you can use these routes, and this is all explored in later chapters.

### (vii) Understand the selling context

Any product must be evaluated and planned in the context of how it will sell. In the partner title to this, authors were urged to do their in-store and online research to see exactly how their book would be sold in order to help them design and categorise their book. This self-same visit will help you to plan your marketing campaign ideas and promotional material requirements, all of which is analysed in later chapters.

## (viii) How else might your book live?

When people write a book, they tend to stop seeing it exist in any other form except as a book. But ultimately what you are creating is CONTENT, and according to the DTI, the future of books lies in how many times you can resell the same content. So having created that content, what else can it become?

o   Fiction = films, serial, audio, extract
o   Non-fiction = documentary, radio debate,
    reference, expert spokesperson

We look at a range of different rights that you can sell in "Selling Rights" on pp 341.

This concludes the creation of your communication strategy. The next two chapters are going to explain the process of implementing it to the best possible advantage.

# Issue: *The importance of research*

## *"You can't market in a vacuum"*

Marketing is communication; communication is a two-way affair at minimum. If you attempt to talk to people without considering how they will receive the information, the chances are you won't be heard.

People remember about 3% of what you tell them, and you need to make sure it is the right 3% that will inspire them to go and buy your book. Therefore you need to understand what they want to hear, and how that connects with your book.

### Research before you start

Most authors are the same. By this I mean that they have a great idea for a book and set about writing it. But just because it is a great idea, doesn't mean that it has a market. Clive Sinclair had a great idea when he invented the electric Sinclair C5 but it didn't make a success. He was too early to market and the aesthetics were wrong: people didn't want to be seen in it nor travel in a vehicle that did 15mph at top speed. He would have researched before investing his millions, but obviously missed some of the finer points of detail and thus missed his mark.

Ask yourself – are you early to market? Is your cover design wrong? Does your book fill a need? In order to clarify this better, I will use the example of Elizabeth Singer Hunt, successfully self-published author of the Secret Agent Jack Stalwart series:

*"Secret Agent Jack Stalwart was born many years ago when I was travelling. I learned so much from the experience of travelling, yet it occurred to me that we do not share these experiences adequately with school children. The idea was to bring the world to school children; Jack Stalwart is sent on missions around the world, and each book is set in a different country - China, Cambodia, England etc.*

"*However, before sitting down to craft my story I decided to connect my idea to its audience and find out exactly what children wanted to read, what parents and teachers needed to encourage children to read and learn, and basically what gap in the market needed filling. The 'need' was apparent immediately. Many school boys struggle to transition from picture books to text-solid books, so Jack Stalwart was presented in a way to encourage these 'reluctant readers'. The paragraphs are short, the spacing is wide and the overall impression of the page does not look onerous. To visually appeal to the target group, I then researched illustration styles and we found one that really appealed to the target group.*

"*Having got the package right, I then set about selling it. Because I knew that the demand was there, I was confident about going out and really promoting it. I had a ready audience, and this was really down to the fact that I researched my idea and tailored it to the potential buyer and reader.*"

This approach evidently paid off, as she now has an 8-book deal with Random House.

### Feedback – getting it and using it

Criticism can offend, particularly when aimed at creative artists and within this term I mean authors, illustrators, actors and musicians. Therefore most people prefer to decline comment if they don't like it rather than risking offence or embarrassment by saying why they didn't like it, or what they would have like to see changed. Authors often feel compelled to justify or defend what they have written, and end up challenging the person offering the criticism.

The fact is, you don't get the opportunity to challenge the man-in-the-street who has bought your book. Your book must therefore live or die on how people receive it without a verbal justification to go hand in hand.

> *If people don't understand your meaning or intention*
> *then you haven't articulated it*

Many authors I have spoken to say that it is not easy to get research. Certainly, Elizabeth Singer-Hunt's approach comes from previous work experience. But authors need to find a balance between organising official focus group research and simply writing a book and waiting for it to be discovered.

The important thing is to *talk* about your book or idea – with friends, a reading group, by paying a reader etc. Maybe do it anonymously ie. as a marketer or researcher, rather than the author. Approach a school (for children's books) and ask if they would like to participate in some research. Draw up a list of questions, photocopy a page/chapter from your manuscript and invite children to say what they would like to see happen next. If none of them are inspired, you are on the wrong track. If none of them seem to understand what you're talking about, you've got the wrong audience.

Maybe approach an old people's home if you have written a biography. Give them 25 free copies of your book and ask them to read it. Go back 2 weeks later to do your research, under the guise that you are reprinting soon and wondered if anyone had noticed any typos or inconsistencies. Once you have got them talking, you may discover interesting truths, benefits or errors that you hadn't seen previously. People may tell you why they found your book of interest, what was missing from your book, whether the characters were plausible. Note down the good, descriptive words that they use.

People will often give you information that may not have even occurred to you, but proves to be very useful indeed.

However, if you are either very sensitive to criticism or grimly determined to see your text remain unchanged, then don't research.

## Six Golden Rules of Research

o   Inform yourself and be aware of what is happening in the outside world. Tailor your message to ensure it penetrates people's busy lives.

o   Think of people as types rather than ages in order to better focus your communication towards them.

o   "Six degrees of separation" is a very true phenomenon. The more you talk to the people around you, the closer you get to the spokespeople who can help you.

o   Feedback can help shape and improve your book. Listen to it, and question it.

o   We only see light because we can contrast it with dark. We only understand good because we also know bad. You need to understand what your book is by seeing what it isn't – and this means comparing it to similar books and understanding how it differs.

o   Not everyone sees the world as you do. You may think you have discovered some incredible truth, or solved a world problem. Before you go riding out with guns ablazing, talk to others about your 'discovery' or announcement. Maybe it is not as unique or as wondrous as you thought. Equally, maybe you have truly discovered something incredible. By talking to people, you will find your way through to journalists and spokespeople who will catapult your message to the world.

# PART III

# SELLING THROUGH THE TRADE

**1. Database collators and promoters**
*Best Practic & Examplee: AI Sheets*

**2. Wholesalers and Distributors**
**Evaluating the different services**
*Best Practice: Selecting a wholesaler/distributor*

**3. Libraries**

**4. Book Retailers:**
    **High street chains**
    **Independents**
    **Supermarkets**
    **Co-retailers**

*Best Practice: Approaching booksellers*
*Best Practice: Managing booksellers*
*The Issue of Bookselling Today*

# SELLING THROUGH THE TRADE

## Making books available

The purpose of this chapter is to look at the myriad ways that an author/publisher can make his book available for sale. It is critical before approaching the end-purchaser that availability and methods of purchase are sound and easily accessible.

One of the major complexities about bookselling for the independent author is the disparate nature of the bookselling channels – the channels that make your book available for sale, the media you promote through and the ultimate purchaser.

Given enough time and budget, it would be possible to cover off all the options, but most small publishers do not have the luxury of time or an abundance of money. Large publishers pay for displays in shop windows or front tables. They pay for dump-bins and shelf-talkers, posters and on-counter leaflets. They pay to participate in summer and Christmas promotions. Independent authors cannot compete.

Many self-publishing authors cling to the notion that their book MUST be in the bookshops. And "yes", books will sell if they are (i) visible and (ii) heavily promoted, but small publishers do not have that kind of budget. Given enough exposure, it is true that someone may well buy the book on the off-chance and, yes, in-store presence may result in sales. But it is expensive to get that exposure, and independent authors must see self-publishing as the route to trying to *achieve* that presence, rather than anticipating that it will be forthcoming at the outset.

The resistance many authors get from the Trade is very frustrating, and it begs the question whether books should be in bookshops purely on the strength of budget rather than the book's merit, but this is the status quo. Given time, new bookselling routes will emerge whereby books are promoted by reader merit and endorsement rather than the marketing budget behind it. In the meantime, authors need to work hard at getting exposure of their book and focussing on the many other communication channels to talk to their audience – online shops and communities, direct mail to a specific target group.

Fortunately, there are many alternative routes to the end-reader today and with a good understanding of the choices and with careful planning, you can achieve reliable routes to your book-buying market.

## What is "The Trade"?

The Trade is, in effect, the supply chain between you and your customer. People buy books wherever they are made available for sale, primarily in high street bookshops, supermarkets and online. They are there because of a complex supply chain comprising many middle-men between the author and his reader – agents, publishers, wholesalers/distributors, sales agencies, book database companies, cataloguers and all forms of book retailers.

Most self-publishing services companies have a distribution arrangement already set up which offers hard-copy distribution as well as online distribution, but it is a good idea to understand the process so you can chat to them about their arrangements. Most good self-publishing companies are open to any suggestions that may improve distribution, as distribution is generally difficult for independent authors and self-publishing services companies.

If you are "going it alone", without the support of a self-publishing services company, the advice is to read closely and implement the following guidelines item for item. It is very tough to get any form of visibility in the market, and very time consuming to attempt to cover off all the options. Think carefully about your target audience, how and where they want to buy this book, and go with the channel that appears to service that area best.

As you start approaching what appears to be a wide range of options, the alternatives quickly narrow down. Some specialise in an area not suitable for you, or their terms and conditions aren't suitable to your needs, or the cost of carriage between the two of you eradicates any profit in selling books.

For the self-publishing author, the supply chain is not only a whole new learning curve, but increasingly a real road-block. Many wholesalers are reluctant to service the individual author because of the incremental time investment in servicing low-income earning accounts. Each account needs setting up and managing, statements and payments issued, stock management and returns control etc. It is simply not cost-effective, and therefore many self-publishers find themselves at a closed door before they have even started.

Low-selling titles occupy valuable income-earning potential in shops. Retail space in the bookshops is at a premium. Whilst on one hand, there has never been more space dedicated to bookselling as bookshops become vast arenas displaying thousands upon thousands of books. On the other hand, many bookshops are now diversifying and giving over space to complementary products and services such as stationery, gifts, toys and coffee shops. The vast bookshops do not necessarily mean a far broader and richer range of books, but invariably result in the large displays of blockbusters, 3 for 2 promotional tables and luring people in via other products and services.

The traditional channels (wholesalers, bookshops, media presence) are slowly squeezing the independent author as competition hots up. It is a buyer's market as there are so many books published each year, only a fraction of which will gain any form of high street and/or promotional coverage.

Another issue area for self-publishers using the traditional routes is that they sacrifice a far higher percentage via the supply chain and payment periods are ridiculously long.

## Who are "The Trade"?

1. Database collators:
   - o   Nielsen
   - o   Bowker
   - o   Google / Yahoo
2. Middlemen:
   - o   distributors
   - o   wholesalers
3. Libraries
4. Retailers*:
   - o   High street bookshops
   - o   Online booksellers
   - o   Supermarkets
   - o   Co-retailers

*Book clubs could technically fit into this category, although I have listed them under Direct Selling as they invariably buy firm in volume, rather than buying incrementally on a sale/return basis ie. acting as a middleman. Book clubs, in terms of income to the author/publisher, behave more like an end-purchaser. The fact that they then on-sell does not affect subsequent profit/loss to the author. No books get returned to them.

## 1. DATABASE COLLATORS

There is a comprehensive section about the UK-based book database companies in *"What do I have to do to get a book published!"* and therefore it is not necessary to repeat the same facts here. Should you wish to obtain this information without buying the first book, contact me and I will email you the section of text (Joanna@indepublishing.com). In the meantime, here is the list of companies:

- o Nielsen: www.nielsenbookdata.com
- o Bowker: www.bowkerlink.com
- o PubEasy®: www.pubeasy.com
- o Googleprint.com

This is the point where book publishing and book selling truly overlap. You cannot publish without completing this task, nor can you sell. This demonstrates how critical it is to complete, and complete accurately.

The database collators also set the standard in terms of the basic information required to promote your book to the trade. The information they require comprises the following, and this should in turn form the basis of your Advanced Information Sheet (AI Sheet) which is the one-pager you need to issue to any part of the book trade when approaching them about your book.

## BEST PRACTICE : AI SHEETS

The Advanced Information sheet is the basic sheet of information about the book that the book trade will base their decisions on. Everyone will ask for it when you contact them. In order to get cut-through, it is critical to ensure you have all critical information as well as GOOD information.

You should prepare this six months ahead of launch for wholesalers/distributors, libraries and bookshop head offices. Smaller bookshops can be approached a bit closer to the time although contacting them early won't hurt.

An AI sheet is an A4, one-sided page, containing:
- o Pithy description or announcement (5-10 words max)
- o Title and Author
- o ISBN and price
- o Publication date
- o Sales of author's last book *(if…)*
- o Location of story and/or author *(as relevant)*
- o Book image, sample illustration

## AI SHEET: Example

# Written a book? Want to publish it? Here's how...

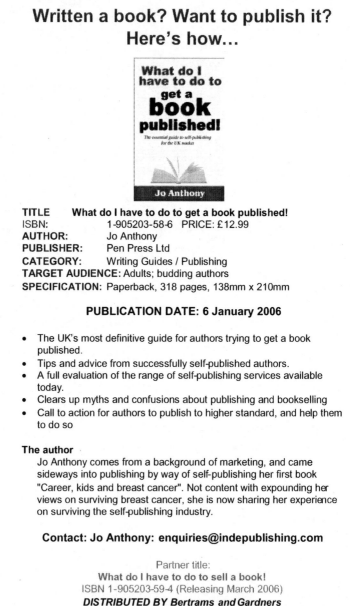

**TITLE**     **What do I have to do to get a book published!**
**ISBN:**     1-905203-58-6    PRICE: £12.99
**AUTHOR:**     Jo Anthony
**PUBLISHER:**     Pen Press Ltd
**CATEGORY:**     Writing Guides / Publishing
**TARGET AUDIENCE:** Adults; budding authors
**SPECIFICATION:** Paperback, 318 pages, 138mm x 210mm

### PUBLICATION DATE: 6 January 2006

- The UK's most definitive guide for authors trying to get a book published.
- Tips and advice from successfully self-published authors.
- A full evaluation of the range of self-publishing services available today.
- Clears up myths and confusions about publishing and bookselling
- Call to action for authors to publish to higher standard, and help them to do so

**The author**

Jo Anthony comes from a background of marketing, and came sideways into publishing by way of self-publishing her first book "Career, kids and breast cancer". Not content with expounding her views on surviving breast cancer, she is now sharing her experience on surviving the self-publishing industry.

### Contact: Jo Anthony: enquiries@indepublishing.com

Partner title:
What do I have to do to sell a book!
ISBN 1-905203-59-4 (Releasing March 2006)
***DISTRIBUTED BY Bertrams and Gardners***
***AVAILABLE FROM Borders, Waterstone's, Indebookshop.com and Amazon.co.uk***

## Book description

Headline this section with your one liner summary then add a few bullet points to flesh out the key benefits or features about the book or storyline that will inspire someone's interest.

## Key selling points

Ask yourself the following questions and come up with one powerful, overriding key selling point:

*What's new? What need it meets? Why publish it (ie. what is adequately different about it from any competition)? Why should they stock it? Why will it sell?*

## Who's buying it and why

Ask yourself the following questions and come up with one powerful, overriding consumer 'reason to purchase'. Remember that with children's books, you are sometimes talking to the mother (aka the purse-holder). Whilst bright colours and pester-power works, if the product doesn't look value for money or doesn't justify its own purchase, then the purse-holder has the casting vote and may not buy.

*What main features support the benefits of the book? ie. pictures to help children transition from all-picture books to all-text books.*

*Are the any promotional highlights so far in media, famous endorsers, potential rights purchases etc?*

## Promotional activity and material

Provide details of promotional activity and material to help distributors/sales reps/booksellers understand it and therefore how <u>easy it will be to sell</u>. If you demonstrate to them that you have thought this through and that you are making it easy for them, you have just increased your chances of being stocked and displayed a hundred-fold.

## 2. WHOLESALERS AND DISTRIBUTORS

### The definition of services

Most self-publishing authors will undertake 'self-distribution' which means they hold the stock and fulfil it upon placement of orders, either from a bookseller or direct from the public. Whilst this puts you in control of the cash-flow and the speed of fulfilment, it is also extremely time-consuming and expensive.

Ideally I would like to define exactly who does what, but the precise definitions for wholesaling and distribution are a bit blurry and variable. So I will describe it by activity:

3rd party pick, pack, despatch: this is one step on from what the self-publishing author would be doing himself only he shares some royalty percentage by getting a company to fulfil. The books are taken on consignment (ie. not bought outright) and they charge a small royalty percentage (ie. around 5%) before returning monies to you; you pay for any carriage costs and warehousing, which is nominal. Any cost-savings you achieve by their economies of scale will undoubtedly be lost in these costs, but for the self-publishing author this really has to be a Holy Grail solution. Fulfilment is time consuming and soul destroying, and you have shifted that responsibility which is great! (see example – Bertrams on pp 90). This form of activity should never be exclusive.

Full service on consignment: this is when the company stocks the title and undertakes the whole process of fulfilment, invoicing, credit control, handling returns and holding accounts with all booksellers. Cost-savings are undoubtedly to be found in freeing up the self-publishing author's time from fulfilment AND invoicing, but for the small self-publisher you may have difficulty (i) obtaining an agreement and (ii) speed of fulfilment as one-off titles may show up as out of stock, or stock doesn't get re-ordered. This is usually non-exclusive.

**Full service, bought outright**: this is when the company purchases a stock of the book and undertakes the whole process of sales force presentations, fulfilment, invoicing, credit control, handling returns and holding accounts with all booksellers. Not all books are accepted; they have to be convinced that their sales force can sell them. Cost-savings are undoubtedly to be found in freeing up the self-publishing author's time, but very few self-publishers are likely to secure this deal unless they have (i) contacts within the business or (ii) have written something truly superb with evidential proof of market demand. This is often on an exclusive basis because they are investing time in selling on your behalf.

**Specialist wholesalers/distributors** trade in certain niche areas such as educational texts (including language, teaching, research, scholarly studies), faith-based, special needs, self-help guides, business, cultural guides, transport books, maps, environmental, medical, regional-interest; special interest (archaeology, natural history); specific formats ie. comics, sheet music. Some companies offer sales/marketing services, or have strategic links with other distribution channels ie. export markets, foreign-language markets.

**Exclusivity**
Some distributor/wholesalers request exclusivity, and this is invariably when they are investing both in the stock of books and the sales force to go out and sell those books. Consignment-based arrangements (where they simply hold stock without buying it first) are invariably on a non-exclusive basis.

There is no negative to exclusivity if you have an exclusive arrangement with a distributor who has excellent reach ie. accounts with all booksellers and offers a top quality, fast and efficient fulfilment service. To answer this, you may need to phone random bookshops, both independent and chain, around the country to satisfy yourself that you will benefit from such an arrangement. If the company cannot reach every part of the trade, then you should not sign up to an exclusive arrangement.

Equally, one caveat I heard about having too many wholesaler / distributors agreements is that it can increase the number of returns. This is because booksellers may place an order with both or all listed companies, see which one comes in first with the best 'deal' then return the others. Personally, I have difficulty in believing this because it is a rare bookseller that has the time to over-order then return the unwanted orders. It certainly has never been my experience at a self-publishing level, at any rate.

The advice ultimately is to ensure you have at least one wholesaler/distributor agreement that provides a guaranteed fulfilment service with your book always being in stock until such time as you no longer supply them with books. If you can get a complementary service from someone else, then you are more than covered.

**What a good wholesaler / distributor can do for you**
Primarily, publishers require a fast, efficient fulfilment service upon placement of orders and good stock management. Beyond that, publishers may desire a host of additional services for which they pay a higher, agreed percentage. It is up to the publisher to know exactly what he needs when deciding between alternative services.

*For example:*
- Do you need to warehouse your products? Wholesalers can provide a cost-effective solution to this, with the benefits that it brings. Whilst a wholesaler holds stock of your book, Amazon shows a 24–48 hour delivery, book-sellers see fast delivery of orders placed etc; publishers also benefit from bulk-purchase of fulfilment.

- Are you actively promoting online? Therefore you need a company with a simple and efficient online ordering system and a high-speed link.
- Do you wish to off-load all customer invoicing, royalty calculations, managing sale & return etc? Some publishers are keen to stay close to their customers and see invoicing as an avenue to this. A good distributor will manage the whole supply chain function which often includes a digital tracking system that you can log onto to track book orders.
- Do you seek to target a very specialist market? Why spend days researching where your audience are when a specialist distributor has their names and addresses at their fingertips?

Independent authors need to weigh up the cost of their time against the loss of percentage royalties and decide where they would rather 'spend' the money.

## EVALUATION OF SERVICES

### General distributors / wholesalers

◊ Bertrams: the UK's leading book wholesaler with increasing international customers
◊ BR&D Book representation & distribution
◊ CBS: Combined Book Services – a leading independent UK book distributor, including calendars & art stationery, journals and series publications
◊ Central Books: independent distributor of books & magazines
◊ Gardners: the UK's leading book wholesaler for any British or American book in print.
◊ Gazelle: book distribution across Europe spanning 200+ subject areas

◊ GBS Ltd (Grantham Books) – individual book distribution for independent publishers; only services publishers who guarantee in excess of £1m booksales per annum

◊ Macmillan Distribution – distribute to UK and Worldwide for 30 publishers including the Macmillan Group

◊ NBN International – distributors for 80 publishers across UK, Europe and North America

◊ Signature Book Services: representing around 20 well-known independent publishers in the UK

◊ TBS The Book Service Ltd: Britain's largest distributor in the UK

◊ The Manning Partnership: total sales, marketing and distribution services for publishers in the UK and English language Export markets.

◊ THE: Total Home Entertainment - the UK's largest wholesaler and distributor of books, audio, video, multimedia and computer games.

◊ Thomson Publishing Services

**Specialist distributors / wholesalers**

◊ Countryside Books: Publish and distribute books of regional interest

◊ Cordee: specialises in travel guides, books, DVDs and maps covering all aspects of adventure sports. www.cordee.co.uk.

◊ Worldly goods and eco-logic books: have been distributing and selling books that promote practical solutions to environmental problems for 15 years and now started also publishing it own range of titles.

◊ Vine House: non-fiction titles only

*Further information:*
A up-to-date, comprehensive list of distributors, wholesalers and book services companies can be purchased at The Bookseller.

All of the following descriptions of each company are taken, with permission, from their own literature and/or websites, with the exclusion of the interviews which are written in my words and approved by them.

## GARDNERS BOOKS

*"Gardners Books are the UK's leading book wholesaler offering the largest range of titles in stock and easy ordering facilities for any British or American book in print. We pride ourselves on delivering the books and services required in today's demanding retail environment. From the local bookshop to the multinational company, we specialise in meeting the needs of the bookseller, whether in the UK or internationally. Our comprehensive stockholding, high fulfilment rate, next day delivery and a full range of customer services combine to offer an unparalleled source of supply for today's bookseller."*

**Services**
- Over 50 dedicated personnel await your call
- A simple 2 step sourcing and ordering service for over 2,000,000 British & American Books in print; an electronic ordering system Gardlink, designed exclusively for booksellers by booksellers. Gardcall Fast Track enquiry line 01323 521444 and using your telephone keypad you can gain access to availability 24 hours a day 7 days a week, all at the touch of a button.
- A fulfilment service provided by Gardners Books allowing you to send items direct to your consumers door.
- A loyalty card scheme for booksellers to run for their customers.

- A unique interactive website which is free to all Gardners Account Holders; it offers our customers the ability to order in real time including placing drop-ship orders, check availability, view invoices, backorders, promotions, bestsellers and much, much more.

## Catalogues and promotions

- Seasonal and topical catalogues are regularly produced to reflect customers' requirements; run throughout the year. From exclusive deals, subject based offers and publisher specials we always have extra discount to take advantage of.
- An illustrated 'buying guide' of books and display material, available from all publishers, is published monthly. Independently compiled by our experienced buying department, it offers an objective view of all new titles and their sales potential. This is supplemented by our "Select" magazine for independent booksellers.

## Sales team

- Regional Account Managers are based throughout the UK providing regular shop visits. A personal touch, which helps keep booksellers fully informed of all the latest new titles, promotions and current sales trends.
- Booksellers throughout Europe and around the world can also benefit from the kind of service we offer UK customers. Gardners Books was one of the first wholesalers to establish a separate export department to service our overseas customers
- The department is managed and staffed by professionals with a wealth of export experience, and is geared to the special requirements and services demanded for the international market.

**Contact**

Gardners Books have developed an unparalleled range of services for our publisher suppliers aimed at helping them to significantly grow their overall business, whilst at the same time considerably reducing their costs. For more details or to discuss any of Gardners Publisher Services, please contact Gardners' Publisher Services Manager , Bob Kelly on 01323 521555, email on bob.kelly@gardners.com or fax on 01323 525507.

**Interview with Bob Kelly**

"A wholesaler/publisher relationship needs to be cost-effective and equitable to both parties. The books that come to us must be both marketable and marketed, which means that both parties stand to mutually benefit as a result of the efforts they put in.

"We are a large organisation servicing publishers from one man band's to the biggest global corporate. We receive around 200 pallets a day of books and 3,500 new titles to be entered into the system per month. Whilst we will differentiate our service according to size, the small independent publisher is not penalised by being small. We have installed sophisticated system to ensure our services work for every size publisher; equally we are a business and we must focus our energies on where the income is.

"However, ALL publishers must approach us with knowledge of the supply chain and bookselling business. We do not have the time to educate people about the supply chain, and for this reason we direct new publishers & authors to our Publisher Services on the website:

(www.gardners.com/pubmenu/pubindex.htm).

This should help newcomers to the industry, but ultimately we prefer authors to come via an intermediary such as a self-publishing services company like Pen Press or Book Guild because they invariably do most of the supply chain stuff themselves, as well as educating their authors about the distribution process. The new self-publishing booksite, Indebookshop.com, should also be a real help to authors as this is underpinned by a co-operative wholesaling/distribution agreement which is ideal. It is a genuine and unique solution to the issue that both parties (wholesaler & self-publisher) must mutually benefit."

### *Have you any advice or perspective to share with first time authors?*

"Historically self-publishing was seen as the books that couldn't get published, but more frequent successes begin to change opinion, and if a book has a market saturation point of 1000 copies then it makes sense to get 70% gross sale return rather than 7%. Authors just have to work harder to earn their money.

"My real advice for authors is to not compete on price and never spend money on advertising as, in the book world, it doesn't return the investment on unknown authors. The internet is key to selling self-published books. Focus on your content and invest as much time as possible to infiltrating the online communities. As long as you can easily point people to a purchase-point and you are backed up by good fulfilment, you should maximise your sales."

### BERTRAMS

*"Bertram Books is the UK's leading book wholesaler, with a growing number of international customers. Founded in a chicken shed 40 years ago, Bertrams has developed and expanded to become on of the premier forces in the book trade. The book distribution & wholesaling facility is now in a purpose-built distribution centre in Norfolk, and Bertrams Library Services is based in Leeds."*

### Bertrams Wholesaler Services

Bertram Books is a trade wholesaler. Our stock consists of around 190,000 titles in paperback, hardback, audio and print-on-demand formats from over 1,800 publishers and their imprints across all bookseller categories. Our range is also adapted to suit seasonal trends with supporting promotions such as Back to School, Summer Reading and Books for Christmas.

We can also supply ANY British or American book in print and are developing a range of European-language titles through other international databases.

Our database is updated daily with electronic title information from major publishers, bibliographic data providers, international wholesale partners and many others to ensure that our data is as accurate and up-to-date as possible.

Bertrams offers two comprehensive book management systems – Bertline 301 for National book orders and Bertline 150 for International book orders. Both systems enable complete ordering and stock control management, leaving you in control.

- Fast & efficient system
- Electronic acknowledgments & invoices
- Accurate stock management
- Goods receiving & stock-take facilities
- Sales reporting
- Links to BookData & Whitakers bibliographic databases
- Online stock enquiry
- Integrated stock catalogue & Bertrams Buyers Notes
- An open system which allows users to select the supplier of their choice
- Dedicated customer support

## Bertrams Distribution Services

This is a new and logical extension to our wholesaler services. It provides publishers with the opportunity to reduce their costs of distribution, simplify the supply chain to their customers and ensure maximum visibility to a much wider customer base.

Our sales & marketing skills enable us to offer tailored or packaged services to publishers. We are active members of BIC and the IPG. Our services are designed to meet your bespoke needs.

### Service

- Secure warehouse storage
- Pick & pack operation which scales from a single home address delivery to several pallets of books to your largest customer
- Managed IT systems and networks which are secure, recoverable and protect with 24/7/365 technical support
- Internal warehouse location alternatives to best serve the profile of your stock
- Real-time stockholding that constantly reflects every stock adjustment and allows perpetual inventory
- Despatch notes laid out and branded to your requirements
- Flyers, leaflets and other promotional materials in your packaging
- Daily electronic confirmation of orders, backorders and inventory reports
- Daily despatch file to help you control your own invoicing
- Online access to our system to analyse stock levels and progress of orders

*Routes to market* which includes marketing to:
- the major bookshop chains
- raditional independent stores
- supermarkets and mass market retailer
- numerous web-based book vendors covering both mass-market and specialist niches
- media accounts including newspapers, magazines and TV/radio fulfilment
- sites at major tourist attractions and entertainment venues
- garden centres and a range of non-traditional outlets such as sports shops
- public libraries.

*Key marketing tools*
- Buyer's Notes is a monthly book & CD which announces 3,500 new titles to our range; this goes to all leading independent bookshops and through the Library Services website.
- Bertnews is a monthly magazine reviewing instore promotions and previews of next books, with promotional offers and packaged deals for key dates such as Mother's Day.
- Seasonal & Thematic Catalogues such as summer holidays, back to school and Christmas. We assemble tailor-made ranges to help bookshops select a winning range.

*Additional marketing services*
- Bertrams can also offer production facilities to help independent publishers create trade & consumer catalogues, promotional collateral (posters, leaflets, bookmarkers, postcards and shelf talkers).

- We can create web-based advertising to promote books and promotions on national newspaper and magazine publishing houses
- we offer a Direct Marketing Service which is supported by one to one fulfilment to enable bounce-back promotions. Bertrams Library Services runs a library specific website and a school supply website.
- Bertmail: a daily email and promotions update service with information on new books and promotions, Bertram's services and news from the book trade.

### Interview with Graham Wallace

"The real problem for the self-publishing author exists in their 'Single title' status. The supply chain is very complex and not an area easily understood overnight by an author wishing to publish one, or even five, books. Wholesaler & distributors need scale of individual title sale and/or volume of range to make the relationship mutually worthwhile, which is virtually impossible for the self-publishing author unless he signs up to some form of co-operative – much like what Indebookshop.com is setting out to do.

"New titles are getting an increasingly shorter and shorter window of opportunity; the most exciting thing about a new book is that fact that it is new. If it doesn't find a regular selling channel or volume within six months, it is invariably returned by bookshops and enters a different phase of its life. Bookshops and supermarkets seek only 'assured volumes' but this is where the internet comes into its own.

"The proportion of DVDs sold in the 'longtail' on the internet far outweighs the volume sold in the frontlist. The longtail is, as it sounds, the incremental sales over the longer period.

"What does this mean to authors? It means, get online. Ensure you have a facility to sell online in the longterm. Ensure you have good fulfilment. Ensure your title is completely searchable by getting your keywords right and relevant."

## GAZELLE BOOK SERVICES

*"Gazelle Book Services is one of the most experienced book distribution companies in Europe, offering a flexible, fast and effective distribution service stretching across Great Britain, Ireland, Western and Eastern Europe. We represent a range of international publishers with diverse lists covering more than 150 subject areas."*

### Services
- Supply of bibliographic data to all relevant book listing agencies
- Review copy service to journals, magazines and other media
- Liaison of advertising opportunities in magazines and other media
- Promotion and direct marketing through flyers, catalogues and advertising
- High quality mailing lists of booksellers, specialist libraries and institutions
- Sales representation to booksellers and libraries
- Presence at major book fairs and relevant exhibitions and conferences
- Selective academic calling
- Consignment stock insured at Gazelle's own expense
- Regular and prompt reporting on sales and stock levels
- For US-based publishers, payment in dollar cheques

### How we work
- We operate on an exclusive basis supplying books to the trade.
- Publishers supply stock on consignment and pay the costs of transportation to Gazelle's warehouse.

- They take books on consignment and hold, initially, a small working stock.
- Each book has its own code, based on the BIC coding system, and is catalogued by genre.
- One copy of each title is sent to Promotions to create an Information Sheet. A small sales force will present it into the trade, issue AI sheets and mail out catalogues regularly.
- A report is generated each month
- Payments are made after 120 days
- Gazelle take their commission against sales, and their percentage is 33% royalty on monies returned, or 67.5% of RRP.
- We trade electronically via EDI orders; non-EDI orders are processed by customer services staff who maintain good contract with many key book-buying customers ie. wholesalers, library suppliers and specialist booksellers.
- We deliver books promptly and reliably via tried and tested courier services.

### Marketing and promotion

- Information sheets are the main tools for our sales force. They are mailed out to booksellers who stock that genre.
- We issue monthly promotional mailings about Forthcoming and New Titles.
- We produce annual catalogues in over 50 subject areas.
- The Promotional Copy of the book is sent to selected magazines for review or to a specialist bookseller as a sample to encourage stocking.
- Our publicity and promotional activity is based on promotion by subject area, publisher or title.

- Our targeted mailing system is also used for individual promotions of topical books, using email marketing wherever possible due to its efficiency.
- We have a Sales Force which cover general trade outlets, specialist booksellers, university bookshops, high street retail chains and other retail outlets such as airports and museums.
- Our European market is served by freelance reps in each country.
- We have specialist representation to the educational markets through the Paul Roberts Educational Services.

### Listings

We supply full bibliographic information and a colour image of the front cover to the below list of trade listings. We even send reviews as and when they are generated in magazines and newspapers. All our books are listed on:

- Nielsen BookData
- Amazon.co.uk – under the auspices of Amazon Advantage system
- BookFind – a monthly CD which is used by booksellers and libraries to source new titles and locate distributors. Also available online at www.bookfind-online.com
- TES BookFind – produced each academic term in conjunction with The Times Literary Supplement, this cross-references BookData records with TES reviews and 20 other leading journals
- The Book Pl@ce – BookData's trading internet site where buyers can browse the entire database, link to publisher's homepages and place secure orders with trade suppliers
- Gazelle website – which has a Trade Books section and offers a secure ordering system.

## BEST PRACTICE CHECKLIST: SELECTING A WHOLESALER/DISTRIBUTOR

Make a list of services offered overall then analyse in detail:

**Systems**
- What systems are in place for communicating orders, sales & stocks?
- Can I log on from anywhere?
- What is the process to getting a book listed?
- Warehousing books – what stock held / for how long?
- What stock inventory & management systems?
- How quickly do you issue stock out? Even the one-off orders?

**Sales process**
- Sales reps
  - How many sales reps
  - What region do they cover
  - Can I present to them and do they feedback to me
  - Can we attend sales conference?
- Catalogue
  - How many and how often produced?
  - Any seasonal specials?
  - What is lead-time to get info in?

**Financials**
- What discounts are requested?
- What are the costs of carriage?
- What are bookseller terms and conditions of payment?
- Any additional fees, legal indemnities, insurance?
- What are the return rates?

**Terms**
- How often do they pay? ie. 90 days or on payment from bookseller.
- What titles / areas / audiences are they strong in?
- How many publishers do they represent?
- Are other publishers compatible?
- Are books insured in warehouse and on consignment?

**Contract**
- What is the duration? What are the termination terms? Can we see a copy?
- BEWARE any contract with a low percentage sales fee and high catalogue charges for storage, shipping, collection, catalogue listings and marketing fees.

**Background history**
- Gain some background history so you can be sure of their financial security. When a distributor goes bankrupt, your stock is counted as part of their inventory. Most of the main names in the UK industry can readily prove their standing.

**Can you get references?**
- Ask Booksellers: find out how well they do service the stores?
- Ask other small publishers: how many did they sell? Do they pay on time?

## 3. LIBRARIES

The library network is an area that many self-publishing authors overlook. The percentage returns appear to be too low for what is a complex network, a steep learning curve and high time investment to organise. The information is difficult to access, most of the library distributors target certain regional areas or specialist audiences.

In the UK market today there are around 208 public library authorities which service nearly 4,500 local libraries. Each public library authority follows its own procurement and management systems.

This is not taking into account the 2,500 special libraries such as academic libraries (across all educational establishments), government, medical & hospital libraries, church and religious libraries and libraries held by museums, art galleries, photographic & other arts bodies.

There are a handful of library suppliers who promote books to various different library systems, but they (like most distributors) look for economies of scale, and it is difficult for the lone author to establish accounts with these middle-men. And for what return? The percentage return is allegedly very low.

### Public Lending Right

Under the United Kingdom's PLR Scheme authors receive payments from government funds for the free borrowing of their books from public libraries in the United Kingdom. To qualify for payment, authors must apply to register their books with us. Payments are made annually on the basis of loans data collected from a sample of public libraries in the UK.

To register and/or learn more about the PLR Scheme, and the statistical data generated by it on trends in public borrowing visit the website (www.plr.uk.com), but have a good read through the Frequently Asked Questions first.

The PLR year runs from 1 July – 30 June each year. If you register your book(s) at any time during the PLR year, you will be credited with loans of your books for the whole PLR year. They are unable to make retrospective payments for earlier years since the whole PLR fund is distributed each year amongst registered authors.

**Libraries today**

Libraries have gone through a very difficult time in recent years. Book borrowing from libraries is in steady, year-on-year decline. Increased footfall in libraries must not be confused with an increase in book borrowing, as this increase is attributed to the presence of computers and internet access. The cost of running a library is excessive, as reported by consultant Tim Coates in *The Bookseller* (3/06/2005) when he investigated the Library Authority in Richmond upon Thames:

*"When allocated to the various processes, the costs of selecting and preparing a book for the shelves are more than the cost of the book itself... Of the £5.2m only £3.2 is spent on the library and the services the public uses. If the £.52m was spent on libraries and the procurement was efficient, the service would be excellent."*

Libraries have increasingly turned to offering reader development services, in particular for children, which is great but doesn't address the fundamental issues such as book range is severely limited, the opening hours are too restrictive for working people and the buildings are often unwelcoming, run down and shabby.

Procurement has long been a major issue for libraries although this is now set to change. By 2008 there will be a new national model for library book buying with a national purchasing agency for libraries being set up. This joint ordering and shared procurement system is estimated to save libraries anything from £7m to £20m which could be reinvested in books. Library suppliers will only need to tender once for business, enabling libraries to obtain higher discounts. What this means to the independent author remains to be seen, but one thing is evident. The more centralised a system becomes, the more it squeezes out the small independent.

The other limiting factor for libraries, which the internet never suffers from, is opening hours. Libraries tend to be open only five days out of every seven from 10am to 5pm at best with many, smaller libraries open for fewer days and at very restricted times.

This issue is now being addressed with a new service managed by the Museums, Libraries and Archives Council (MLA). The "Enquire, Discover and Read" web-based service provides public libraries with 24 hour a day access to library staff to help answer any question, guide you through the web and explore books and reading online. Simply type in your question and you will be answered either via a live chat link or by email – you choose. Simply go to:

www.peoplenetwork.gov.uk

or link in via your local library.

### What is the value of the library to authors?
Any platform or environment that gives authors the opportunity to be visible is always of benefit to the self-publishing author. Local libraries will support local authors, they will host events, put up posters and display flyers. None of which can be ignored.

Unfortunately, given the sheer volume of new and backlist titles, the chances of your title being (i) in the right library and (ii) being found when someone is searching for your book is fairly slim.

It is difficult for authors to achieve much presence in the library network as most local libraries will stock largely the big sellers and big names. If you have been into a library recently, you will have experienced what most people experience – the book you are specifically looking for is invariably not there, at least not in that branch although another library under the same authority may have it. The chance of finding the book you want is a sorry 57% chance. This means ordering the book in and returning again another time to collect it.

If you have written on a specialist subject matter with easily identifiable search terms, you increase your chances of being accurately logged into their systems and promoted directly into the heart of specialist audiences.

Sometimes people may use libraries to check out a range of non-fiction titles on a certain subject before committing to buying it. Or they may realise the non-fiction title is more useful than simply borrowing it for three weeks, and will then go to buy it. However, very few fiction books will convert into a sale once read. Even if referring the book to a friend, it will usually remain within the library network.

## What this means to the self-publishing author

The traditional library network may offer limitations to the self-publishing author. It requires too high a time-investment with very little return. As the price of books comes down through fierce competition, dominance of discounting and growth of the second-hand book market means that books can be bought for as cheaply as one pound. People are happy to spend the odd pound here and there on the off-chance the book turns out to be pretty good. But this prohibits the self-publishing author from participating.

However, as libraries become increasingly online-driven, with services such as The People's Network, the opportunities start to increase.

The real opportunity for self-publishers in the modern day, if you are computer and web literate, lies in the internet. As services such as People's Network launch, self-publishing authors have a far greater capacity for finding audiences. Using search engines such as Google will enables shoppers to locate a far wider range of books in response to specific search terms.

Authors need to focus on activities that cost the least and provide the highest potential for return and this is investigated more fully in Section VII, Selling & Promoting online.

## Promoting books to libraries

There are a number of wholesalers/distributors that promote directly to libraries. A good startpoint is Bibliographic Data Services (www.bibdsl.co.uk) which provides a bibliographic record to meet library requirements for cataloguing. By submitting a review copy of the book to them, they can supply an enhanced catalogue record.

*"We are the premier source of industry-standard information on book publications and home entertainment releases. BDS offers libraries, publishers and booksellers the data solution they need to remain efficient, cost-effective and up-to-date.*

*BDS specialises in the promotion of publishers' information in the MARC format, a data standard used by libraries to store and exchange information. It allows the information to be downloaded direct to the library system. The rich content included in the record is designed to aid selection, either pre-publication or on publication. Both home and export customers use BDS services."*

### *Other library suppliers are:*

Listed below, most of them require initial approach by post. They need to receive information four months ahead of launch, and they largely work in regions as opposed to nationally.

Askews: www.askews.co.uk
Bertrams Library Services: www.bertrams.com
Holt Jackson: www.holtjackson.co.uk
Madeline Lindley Ltd: www.madeleinelindley.com
(children's titles only)
J S Peters & Son: www.peters-books.co.uk
G A Turner & Co: www.turnerbooks.co.uk (education titles only)

## Library Directory

You will find this information in the *Libraries and Information Services in the UK and Republic of Ireland* directory (published annually by Facet Publishing) which should be available in the reference section of your local library. This lists the library headquarters address for every library authority in the UK and Republic of Ireland.

## ADDITIONAL LIBRARY SERVICES & BODIES

### The Reading Agency

"TRA was founded on the principle that reading has infinite potential for making life richer and that libraries are the most democratic medium for bringing reading to people. As a charity we work to improve the reading experience by inspiring, challenging and supporting libraries. We work closely with the main library bodies. Our mission is to inspire a reading nation by working in new ways with readers, writers, libraries and their partners."

www.readingagency.org.uk

### The People's Network and Library system

This is a brilliant new development, seemingly bringing libraries into the 21st century with a great online service.

*"This site helps everyone to make the most of the online world: to enquire, discover and read online for free 24/7 from anywhere with access to the web. It's just like going to your local public library to ask for help or find information, but doing it online from anywhere at any time instead. Libraries across England are working together to bring you these valued and trusted services from one website so you can get the information you need when you need it most."*

www.peoplesnetwork.gov.uk

Visit the site, and click on the following to be linked through to different services:

- o   ENQUIRE answers your questions in real-time by real people.
- o   DISCOVER offers you a personal guide through the web's hidden treasures, and
- o   READ enables you to explore books and reading, and share them with others.

It is a thoroughly enjoyable website, managed by the Museums, Libraries and Archives Council (MLA). I contacted them, praising the fairly radical service for libraries and trying to find out how an author might get their book included for review within the linked sites:

*"Thank you for your kind words regarding the People's Network. The main reader development site is Reader2Reader. www.reader2reader.net and people are able to suggest titles for reviewing, or share other reading experiences.*

*"The People's Network is not directly responsible for purchasing books on behalf of public libraries. This happens at a local level. However, I know that public libraries have a pretty good track record of stocking titles from authors backed by many different types of publishers."*

### *What this means to self-publishing authors...*
Make sure your book is available through the library network and therefore given a chance to be reviewed on this site, and contact the other linked sites independently. Most of the linked sites are local library or government agency such as The National Literacy Trust, or educational ie. The Open University.

As the role of libraries begins to change, self-publishing authors would be wise to devote a day or two to gaining presence on the library database and systems.

# 4. BOOK RETAILERS

Book retailing is in a state of change and has been since the abolition of the Net Book Agreement in 1997 and the emergence of online book retailing and supermarkets as serious competitive threats to traditional bookselling avenues. The real question is 'where is it going'? What is the future of bookselling? More and more independent booksellers are being forced to shut up shop, unable to compete with such intensive price discounting; whilst writing this book, HMV is endeavouring to buy out Ottakars, making the Waterstone's/Ottakar's bookselling chain a force to the reckoned with in the high street scenario. The high street will in future be Waterstones/Ottakars, Borders and WHSmiths, with a handful of independent booksellers who, likely as not, will seek to specialise in order to retain a market share as they are unable to compete with the mainstream titles.

As with most industries, we just need to look across the water to our American & Canadian cousins to see a possible future scenario. America has a handful of large distributors (Ingrams, Bertrams, Baker & Taylor) and large bookselling chains (B&N, Borders), which are supported by many, much smaller state-based distributors and booksellers. This is more like the UK is today. Canada, on the other hand, has one major bookseller, Indigo Books & Music, with some very small independent town-based bookshops, usually with very specialist or unique selling point. This is arguably where the UK is heading to.

Is this a good thing? One person I spoke to tried to convince me that having fewer chains will reduce the disparate nature of the distribution process and that this is a good thing. However, the overwhelming reaction from the publishing, distribution and bookselling trade is that one dominant bookseller is a bad thing:

*"Rejection by such a large high street store could destroy an author."*

*"Taylor lamented the 'potatoes only diet' of the big chains, saying that there are the same three-for-twos in every shop. They are a denial of choice as opposed to being an expression of it."* The Bookseller, 16/9/05

The majority of the industry craves the democratisation of book industry rather than a world where discount pricing dictates stock in shop – but are the readers going to bite? Will they support the endeavours of the book-loving world or do they really just want cheap?

*"The Power Shopper is informed, demanding and disloyal… Power Shoppers do not just want cheaper prices, but they believe them to be their right. Nurtured by myriad Rip-Off Britain campaigns and promotional pricing in the high street, Power Shoppers are those who know the price of everything and the value of nothing."*
Danuta Kean, various articles from The Author, 2004

## The major bookselling channels

70% of annual book sales are sold through bookshop chains, supermarkets, bookclubs and Amazon. The following figures reveal the market share in terms of demonstrable through-the-till sales, but do not include direct sales:

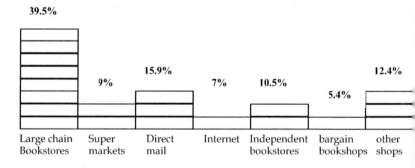

*Market share by volume (Source: Book Marketing Ltd)*

The big chains, supermarkets and behemoth online booksellers are demanding ever-higher discounts whilst also asking publishers to pay for marketing. Seemingly they are strangling the very industry that they rely on.

## How retail outlets work

- Booksellers take their information from a variety of sources – their own knowledge of what's selling, advice from trusted publishers and sales reps, book trade media, the distributor/wholesaler catalogues as well as keeping their eyes and ears open for unique opportunities.
- Selling periods – many bookshops operate on a quarterly basis, reviewing their stock, returning some unsold titles to make way for new launches; assessing what sold in order to inform what to buy next; planning certain promotions in tune with social calendars, local or national events etc. Many have a quarterly budget allocated and endeavour to work within it.
- Need early information: authors wishing to maximise their chance of presence within bookshops should plan early. Send an AI sheet to target bookshops; follow up with phone calls wherever possible and/or mailshot. If the booksellers are impressed or simply interested, they will order books and any associated promotional material or paraphernalia ie. shelf-talkers, dump-bins, posters etc.
- Catalogues – many publishers have long ceased issuing catalogues, having a sales force to talk to the chain stores and relying more heavily on wholesaler/ distributor catalogues to reach the independent bookshops. One independent bookseller at the IPG Conference last year advised, however, that the inde-booksellers like to receive simple announcements

about new books; they do get looked at, considered, sometimes filed for future reference and sometimes they prompt an immediate book order.

- Events – book retailers will happily host an event if there are going to be sales as a direct result of the event. If the author strikes them as a person who will organise the whole event, ensure there is adequate promotion of the event, will bring in at least a modest crowd of buyers etc then they are happy to provide their 'space'. Bookshops, however, will shy away from hosting an event that looks likely to be a flop. They hate to see an author sitting shyly in a corner of their shop, waiting sadly for people to approach them so be pro-active and dynamic.

- Instore promotions – Booksellers won't give shelf space to that which has no marketing behind it, as these are obviously invaluable spaces to attract spontaneous purchase, but booksellers do not give this space away for nothing. They have either bought into the book at a senior level, believing it to have great potential or they sell the space. Publishers can buy window space and front of shop promotional space but this can be very expensive. A report by Danuta Kean (freelance writer on the book business) advised recently that the Asda promo chart includes charges of around £25,000 for display and promotion, which is obviously out of reach for most authors. The only other way to achieve good presence is for independent authors to demonstrate marketing and associated sales potential. Organising an event is one great way to get some books into a local shop window and/or prominent front of store tables and ends of aisles.

- Sale or return is the standard practice for bookshops. They will take the book for an open-ended period of time and will return the book at some point if it doesn't sell. They are under no obligation to return it within any specific time frame, unless you agree otherwise, nor return it in any specific condition. It may come back damaged or spoiled, although personally I have received very few back in a poor condition. The general feeling is poor - *"Publishers don't sell books; they merely lend them to booksellers"*

- Discounting is a standard practice across the board, although in the high street it is generally reserved for top sellers or a price promotion across a range and/or against a specific campaign ie. Mother's Day 3 for 2; Holiday Read 3 for 2.

## How to approach the retailers

Most self-publishing authors are working within an incredibly restricted budget, trying to balance the cost of learning curve with the need to just get out and sell. Mainstream publishers have the benefit of established processes, economies of scale and established accounts whilst self-publishing authors must plan the places to target very carefully whilst investing the minimum amount of time and money. For instance, you should submit books to relevant buyers at the head offices of major chain bookshops, but it is not realistic or sensible to make this an integral part of a campaign. The chance of them buying 5,000 copies on the first print run is slim; they will first be looking for demonstrable demand.

Always remember - **retailers seek to retail.** No retailer will turn down a product that has a ready market and will make an easy sale. Prove to them that you have a ready market and can make the sales, and they will stock you.

## *Let them know the book exists*

Issue a book announcement – a simple advanced information sheet either sent by email or post with the critical information. This may be in the form of an advanced information sheet (see

Best Practice: AI Sheets on pp 79) or an announcement card (see Promotional Material on pp 213).

### Email versus royal post

Some prefer to receive emails; some prefer to receive information by post. Short of phoning them all up and asking them, creating two different databases and operating two different systems you are best making your decision on:

(i) what suits you the self-publisher best
(ii) how many can you reach by email

### Give them more than just work to do

Every time you send literature to a bookseller, you are asking him to do some work. You are adding to his 'things to do and things to look at' list. Also, sometimes to get the message across quickly and easily (and put a smile on the face of the recipient) it's good to send a gimmick; maybe something that you will be using when selling to the public. This is dependent on how much budget you have for promotional activity and whether the gimmick can be used in a multitude of ways, as discussed under the Promotional Material chapter. Independent authors must always make their investment stretch much further than the cost of the item.

Other good gimmicks can be ideas-based rather than a tangible gizmo. Some authors do 'mock reviews' ie. "if Jeremy Paxman/Jonathan Ross interviewed me it would go something like this...". Put a smile on someone's face and cheer up their day by making them laugh – it's a great route to starting a business relationship.

### Help them to create the opportunity...

When approaching a retailer, therefore, demonstrate quickly and succinctly that your product will sell. Have your 'pitch' ready prepared.

### ... and help them to close the deal

Convince them that you have a sound marketing plan in place, with evidence of how you are drumming up awareness and driving traffic, and tell them how it could work.

### Setting up a retailer account

Assuming you have published your book professionally (see *"What do I have to do to get a book published!"*) you will have an ISBN number and a barcode. If you don't, then stop reading and go and get these two pre-requisite items. Nobody is selling anything without these – not through the retail trade.

Most chains have to buy through their Central Buying facility and/or any local level ordering that takes place has to go through a recognised wholesaler/distributor.

Most independent booksellers will have a single buyer who prefers to buy through the wholesaler/distributor channels, but they will consider buying direct off the publishers. For direct purchases, they will negotiate with you their terms – percentage discount, sale/return, re-ordering or returning contact details.

### Ongoing approaches

Announcing a book to a bookshop should not be simply a 'one-off' activity even when you have published only one book. Book marketing is an ongoing activity for as long as you hope to make sales.

*The day you stop marketing your book is the day the sales drop off – and they come to a grinding halt very quickly.*

Once you have made the initial announcement, follow up with postcard announcement and ensure that they can contact you easily to confirm any interest they may have. Also ensure any ordering instructions are clearly visible.

113

Look to the year ahead and create a calendar of dates when your book subject may become topical, and remember to send the bookshops a news release / flyer to remind them of your book.

Be ready to be reactive should the newspapers suddenly start talking about your subject. Create a news release, drawing a bookseller's attention to the article, and issue it. Suggest a small display to capitalise on the public's interest on such a topic, and suggest that you send them some posters or flyers to create an interesting display.

Always be ready to react, and to react quickly. It is worth investing in the creation of your bookshop database, and there are several ways to do this from a standing start of having no information. Firstly, contact Indepublishing.com as we maintain a good up-to-date, digitally-based list. Secondly, contact The Bookseller and buy a copy of The Directory; become a member and you can buy labels from them for one-off use or multiple uses.

## THE HIGH STREET BOOKSELLERS: The Chains

There are currently five main chain booksellers – Borders/Books etc, Blackwells, Ottakers, Waterstone's and WHSmiths. This is currently on course to reduce down to four when/if Waterstone's owners, HMV, buys Ottakars. The question will then only remain as to whether they seek to fully integrate the Ottakars shops with Waterstone's and implement all centralised buying policies. Even if they do, it can take months to implement so this book is going to talk about Ottakars and their buying policies as they currently stand.

## BORDERS AND BOOKS ETC

"Borders Group Inc has more than 1,200 Borders Books & Music stores and Waldenbooks stores around the world with 47 stores in the UK and 33 Books etc stores. Borders Books &

Music shops sell not only books, but also audio books, CDs, DVDs, magazines & newspapers, gift items and games, as well as stationery via Paperchase which it acquired in 2004; and coffee via a licensing agreement with Seattle's Best Coffee cafes, a wholly-owned subsidiary of Starbucks."

### Borders Group mission statement

*"To be the best-loved provider of books, music, movies, and other entertainment and informational products and services. To be the world leader in selection, service, innovation, ambiance, community involvement, and shareholder value. We recognize people to be the cornerstone of the Borders experience by building internal and external relationships, one person at a time."*

Two of the supporting attributes to the mission statement that I found particularly motivating for self-publishing authors is

1. *Selection: To offer the best selection, based on the evolving needs of our customers, through an expert buying staff, superior inventory management, and state-of-the-art fulfillment systems,* and
2. *Community involvement: To enrich our diverse customer communities, while respecting each community as unique.*

### How to approach Borders

Borders Group Inc considers books from small and independent publishers, and they have a process for reviewing and considering each title for placement in stores (see www.bordersgroupinc/artists/publishers.htm). This is the US process, and in the UK they operate a similar process, as follows.

Send two copies of the book with a cover letter to the following address. The cover letter must provide your address and contact information, your confirmed marketing programme, distribution channels and proposed terms. Books submitted will not be returned, but you will hear back from Borders within 90 days of receipt. Use of distributors and wholesalers greatly increases the opportunity for your book to be considered. Send books to:

Lada Kritz
New Acquisitions Dept
Borders Stores Head Office
120–122 Charing Cross Road
London WC2H 0JR

Jay Cochrane
New Acquisitions Dept
Books Etc
122 Charing Cross Road
London WC2H 0JR

### *Interview with Lewis Hill, Borders Book's Buying Team*

"The most efficient way is to send a finished copy, AI and any previous sales information to our New Press Department who will evaluate it. Decisions are based on a balance of the usual judging criteria (which are, of course, how the buying customer judges the book) ie. cover design, what the jacket is communicating, how it is written and the price of the book. Other criteria including locality, subject matter, and market position. By the latter I mean whether there are established titles that cover this subject with a proven sales history.

"We look at most correspondence sent to the New Press Department but, again, we do not have the resources to respond to every mailshot etc. However, where possible we let an author know our decision, even if it is negative. We don't invite people in to present due to the sheer volume of requests, and arriving at our offices without an appointment is not recommended - it is inconvenient and will not speed up or positively influence our decision. The best method is to mail in the book and any information to our New Press Department.

"We wouldn't like to discourage anyone from publishing their own titles, however we strongly advise them to methodically research the market from a customer's point of view. For instance, they should consider 'Is there a gap in the market for this book?' 'How have other publishers packaged similar titles?' 'How does the binding/jacket / font and general appearance compare to similar titles?'

"Borders has a positive reputation in the industry as being a company that allows local buying and promotional activities. We are in the business of selling books, and any successes at a local level would certainly be communicated to Head Office and across the business."

## BLACKWELL – The Knowledge Retailer

Blackwell has its history in 'informational' texts and this remains the calling card of the business although its 70 stores around the UK also sell fiction and literature, leisure and lifestyle titles. It opened its doors in 1879 in Broad Street, Oxford, in order to promote self-education; it encouraged reading as well as religion, with separate rooms for non-alcoholic refreshment and silent reading.

By the 1960s, Blackwell had built an international reputation for bookselling excellence with links to academic institutions and libraries around the globe. It has continued to expand its UK base and is now seen on high streets and in university campuses up and down the country. In 1995, www.blackwell.co.uk became the first transactional online bookstore in the UK, giving people across the world access to over 150,000 titles.

Today Blackwell UK is the leading academic bookseller and has over 70 outlets across England, Scotland and Wales. Their staff is still renowned for their expertise, depth of knowledge and love of books 125 years after Mr. Blackwell's 'little shop' first opened its door. They are still searching out rare books and catering for every taste, Blackwell has a number of specialist stores including several medical outlets, a store specialising in the oil industry in Aberdeen and a science fiction and fantasy store in Reading.

### How to approach Blackwell Bookshops

Individual buyers in each shop decide if a title is suitable for their market. Publishers should post an AI Sheet to the relevant buyer via their title ie. The Fiction Buyer, The Health

Buyer. Most of the buyers do not have access to email so post is preferred. Do not send general book information to campus or specialist shops as these only carry books recommended by lecturers.

Copies of AIs can also be sent to Bob Johnston at Head Office for consideration for central promotions or listing in the weekly book information bulletin. Blackwell do very few central purchases and will normally advise shops to order direct where possible. Shops can set up an account for a new supplier if they believe they will do more than £250 (net cost) business with that supplier during the year. If not, or if they are unsure, they should source books via a wholesaler until sales indicate otherwise.

Blackwell's preferred wholesaler is Gardners and for ease of payment/terms etc. we would encourage small publishers to approach Gardners with their books. This information should be included on any AIs sent to shops.

*Things we like:*
- An AI including cover shot (B+W is okay), ISBN, Release date, Supplier Info (incl. Wholesalers if applicable) and a good write-up on book content.
- Local press coverage that creates real demand.
- Contacting the shop 3 months after supply to see if the book has sold – half the time you get a reorder, half the time you get returns!
- Clear invoices with ISBNs, discount, cost and retail prices marked.
- Letting local bookshops know about books of local interest.

*Things we don't like:*
- 'But students like baseball… if you put this book in your student shops it will sell' – publishers need to be realistic about their market and who shops where.

- 'Here is a sample of our new book... please post it back if you don't require it' – don't send books unless you can afford it.
- Supplying a book and then not contacting the shop again.
- Trying to get a central promotion on a book with limited or local appeal.

***Head office address:***
Blackwell UK Limited
Beaver House
Hythe Bridge St
Oxford
OX1 2ET
tel: +44 (0)1865 792792

***Brief flurry of emails with Bob Johnston***
Bob is the Product Manager for Trade Promotions. Despite being an incredibly busy time of year (September is the start of the academic term which rolls straight into Christmas, enough said), he endeavoured to assist by providing the above information in a word document, and giving the following advice:

*"Blackwell likes to remain open-minded to opportunities in the future. Like publishers, our focus and methods of doing business will change to meet the needs of the business - nothing is set in stone! In terms of types of books – we specialise in academic and professional titles. We also cover all main book genres in our flagship store, however we do not generally take much stock in the more 'leisure' oriented areas such as sport, general health, mind-body-spirit etc. Advice to authors... focus on the 'what we like' as it will generally have positive results for both of us. We can help you if you can help us."*

## OTTAKAR'S – A love for books

Ottakar's has a reputation for strongly individual high street shops staffed by book enthusiasts able to offer superlative levels of customer service. Ottakar's began in 1987 when its current Managing Director, James Heneage, realised that there might be an opportunity to establish a chain of bookshops offering high levels of range and service across the market towns of England; Philip Dunne joined him to open three bookshops. At that time the idea of a national chain of bookshops was a relatively new one. Waterstone's and Dillons were busy opening bookshops within the major cities but otherwise the book trade comprised a series of regional chains (such as Blackwells), WH Smith and a large number of independent booksellers which existed in every town, large or small.

Ottakar's grew slowly to begin and rapidly in recent years, acquiring Thin's Booksellers in 2002 and Hammicks Bookshops in 2003, with its 35-year history of bookselling, and boasting an outstanding staff base of knowledgeable and enthusiastic booksellers. Ottakar's now comprises over 130 branches from Elgin to Truro and from Aberystwyth to the Isle of Wight

Ottakar's today is a paradox – a national book chain striving to offer uniform excellence in range and service across over 130 branches, at the same time as offering intensely individual bookshops, run with great autonomy by staff whose commitment to books is matched only by their commitment to provide a bookselling service tailor-made for their communities. Some shops serve smaller communities, while others are much larger branches and offer coffee shops, seating areas and space given over to events, such as book-signings or children's activity sessions.

Ottakar's believes that the secret of great bookselling lies in the recruitment of people who enjoy a real passion for books and who are able to articulate that passion to their customers, and the success of Ottakar's has been founded on allowing these individuals the freedom to create very original and individual shops.

## How to approach Ottakar's

Send AI sheets by post to the Head Office in Salisbury, addressed to the Fiction Buyer, Non-Fiction Buyer etc. These will always be passed to the right person, however it is rare that immediate action is taken, and the advice is to approach your most local branch of Ottakar's and build up the momentum locally. Most decisions are made by local buyers, with central buyers for core stock/backlist and new titles. Self-publishers are advised to approach local buyers in the first instance and focus their energies on getting good media coverage and strive to achieve good sales over a couple of months in order to demonstrate there is a potential bigger market out there. Any book selling more than 50 copies per month over a 3 month period tends to get noticed – which is not unfeasible quantity if you put the effort in.

Ottakar's operate a very good internal communications system; if a book is selling well it will go onto the intranet and shared around the business in order to ensure Ottakar's constantly buy better and wider ranges. Some branches specialise in certain genres, and their intranet ensures specialist shops access certain titles.

Ottakar's buy mainly through Gardners and other wholesalers & distributors. They rarely peruse publisher catalogues as prefer to have separate AI's and split them up into piles and they overhaul all the categories twice yearly.

## Interview with Peter Quartley

"We review some 1,500 titles per month out of the 3,000 or so titles that come in every month. Each one reviewed is rated against various different but pre-agreed criteria which isn't just based on quality alone. We listen out for titles or authors that we have heard are very good, we watch growing subject areas and seek to fill in the gaps.

"Ottakar's have recognised the increasing number of self-published titles and, not only that, but the gradual improvement of self-published books in overall quality terms – standard of writing, plot and overall production values. But it is a buyer's market, unfortunately for authors. Fictional titles, such as crime thriller, are extremely competitive areas and authors need to be presenting something really unique and superb to be able to cut in and gain visibility. Non-fiction is probably easier to market as you have a definite hook; for us, a really good index can give us an excellent steer on a book's point of uniqueness and difference.

"The market is very difficult at the moment for everyone. There is a homogenisation in the high street due to the extreme discounting by the supermarkets. WH Smith's is competing head on, but for booksellers like Ottakar's we focus on competing on other fronts – like hosting events and immersing ourselves in the business of books. The degree of discounting taking place in the book market at the moment is a real problem; Amazon Marketplace can sometimes undercut booksellers on the same title in as-good-as-new condition by half the price. How can we possibly compete? And yes, a moratorium period on discounting would certainly help. Books need to have a value."

## WATERSTONE'S

The first Waterstone's bookshop opened on Old Brompton Road in London in 1982, founded by Tim Waterstone after he was sacked by WH Smith. It brought modern marketing techniques to the sale of highbrow, academic and literary books, providing a "browser friendly" atmosphere, with knowledgeable booksellers, a wide range of titles, and smartly-designed shops.

In 1989, WH Smith took a share in the chain, and Waterstone sold out to them in 1993. Five years later, WHSmith sold the chain to HMV and in 1999, all Dillons stores were rebranded as Waterstone's. Waterstone's had started selling books online, but in 2001 franchised its Internet operations to Amazon. Waterstone's trades as Waterstone's, Hatchards (in London) and Hodges Figgis (in Dublin).

Waterstone's runs regular national promotions including Waterstone's Book of the Month and children's book of the Month, as well as The Paperbacks of the Year promotion in the run-up to Christmas. They also publish Waterstone's Books Quarterly which aims to recommend across all genres and encourage readers to consider books and writers previously unknown to them.

In recent years, Waterstone's has been under more pressure from other chains, and have responded with a *"more aggressive and commercial focus... without compromising on the unrivalled range authority for which the chain is renowned."* Nevertheless the current management has been criticised for concentrating on fewer, best-selling titles at the expense of range.

In September 2005, Waterstone's parent company HMV tried to buy Ottakar's, a move which would give HMV nearly 25% market share of the book trade. The independents and publishers were fearful of the power this would give Waterstone's, and the bid has now been passed to the Competition Commission. HMV have indicated that they still intend to buy Ottakar's should the Commission find in their favour.

Waterstone's have a wholly centralised buying and promotions policy, despite various protestations from Head Office that local managers have local buying and promotional powers. The reality is that they rarely choose to exercise these. Occasionally a friendly face pops up and says they'll host an event or stock your book, but on the whole Waterstone's tend to focus only on named authors for events, and independent authors will only occasionally see their book stocked at Waterstone's.

The curious thing is that many authors report seeing their books in stock at ad hoc branches of Waterstone's round the country, at no particular request from themselves nor in response to any local marketing activity. This is a shame, as the author would happily implement some form of activity if they realised a local buyer was happily stocking their book. Sadly, Waterstone's appears to suffer from the usual ailments of large corporations where left hand does not know what right hand is doing, communication is poor and great opportunities are missed. If they ever got themselves truly organised, they could probably put all other book-selling chains and non-specialist independents out of business.

Waterstone's have also nominated Gardners as a preferred wholesaler, although will order from and run accounts with other recognised wholesalers and distributors. They have allegedly ceased to order direct from local shops to the publisher, although many of the branch managers seem oblivious to this fact and still endeavour to place orders locally. This has caused major fulfilment issues for the self-publishing author as books take several weeks to have their orders processed by Gardners, delivered and checked into the store and the end-customer to actually receive their book.

This leads us to another strange conclusion that the customer would have been better buying the book online and getting it within 48 hours. This gives more power and profit to the online booksellers such as Amazon, which is precisely the activity that HMV's buy-out of Waterstone's is trying to curtail.

Waterstone's advise that they closely watch the press to see what is being talked about, and they monitor what is being demanded via instore ordering and customer request; they are responsive to this form of demand.

### Interview with Peter Saxton
"We request authors send us their advanced information sheet well ahead of the launch of their title, but only after they have registered it with Nielsen BookData. Even if we decline to stock it at the outset, we will ensure the book is available to

order on our Phoenix system – and no, we do not charge postage to the customer when we order a book in.

"Good approaches to Waterstone's encompass a demonstration of your planned marketing activity, proving that it WILL happen and is not just a vague hope. Obviously good cover design and professional book production will play a part in drawing our attention and making our assessment, but it isn't the only measure. One piece of advice for self-publishing authors is that digitally printed books tend to have a brighter, thicker page which can be a negative. Many people buy books to read in bed or on the train; if it's too heavy it can be a drawback."

**Interview with Scott Pack**
"We believe that self-publishing provides a viable and credible route to market. Big publishers don't have a monopoly on good books, but what they do have is good marketing knowledge and good design. Many self-published books let themselves down by looking self-published; the authors simply haven't researched the market or don't invest in paying for good design. The books that draw my attention are the ones that I can see as selling - which shouldn't come as any surprise to anyone – but the important thing is the content, and lots of self-published books are wonderfully written. It is just a shame when they let themselves down by not appealing to a reader.

"For self-publishing authors to be successful, they must recognise that they have to work hard. One new self-published author on the scene at the moment is Ian Hocking, who has set up his own website, a PODcast and a Blog. He is making his presence felt, and this means a constant tapping at the opportunities.

"We are more than happy to look at the material sent in, although we buy very few books centrally. We have created the role of Independent Book Buyer to ensure that we get the best of the small press and self-publishing authors. So I say yes, go for it but do your research and be prepared for hard work."

## WH SMITHS PLC

W H Smith originated as a news vendor business established in London in 1792 by Henry Walton Smith and his wife Anna. After their deaths, the business — valued in 1812 at £1,280 — was taken over by their son William Henry Smith, and in 1846 the firm became **W H Smith & Son** when his son, also William Henry, became a partner. The firm took advantage of the railway boom by opening news stands on railway stations, starting with Euston in 1848. They also made use of the railways to become the leading national distributor of newspapers.

WH Smith now manages 542 high street stores across the UK with 200 Travel Retail stores at railways stations and airports, which function mainly as newsagents together with selling books.

In 1948, WH Smith was made a public holding company and shares sold to staff and the public, due to onerous death duties of the then-owner. The Smith family's control gradually slipped away and the last family member left the board in 1996. the only real rival to WHSmith's has been John Menzies, however a swift purchase of all Menzies stores in 1998 eradicated the competition.

WHSmith is the proud claimant of two historic events – they were the first ever chain store and they originated the ISBN numbering scheme for books. After a few tough trading years, they are now two years into a turn-around programme which has seen market share and share price increase significantly, although high street trading conditions remain highly competitive for all booksellers.

WH Smiths has a wholly centralised buying policy which is controlled by monthly sales meetings to decide stock, and stock range and levels are continually evaluated on sales performance and returns levels. They stock a range numbering some 28,000 titles across bestseller and range. The main route to getting books into WH Smith is:

1.  via established distributors if you are a big publisher, – Collins, Central, LBS TBS etc – with emails, presentations and meetings
2.  via Independent Publisher Scheme* if you are a small publisher
3.  via local instore buyers, who have a small local budget. However, this has proved to not be the case in 2005 as local budgets were frozen, the more books were returned than were bought from small publishers.

### *Interview with WH Smith Buying Team*

"We recommend that self-publishing authors contact WH Smith through the Independent Publisher Scheme which is co-ordinated by Gardners. Their books will then be discussed at a meeting with the WH Smith buyers and will be considered for inclusion in our range, and this is a better route than trying to contact the buyers directly. Our local stores have regular area meetings at which they share useful information and advice on bestselling products, events and sales advice. They use this opportunity to identify strong sellers for the area and will then raise this with the central buying team if appropriate."

### The Independent Publisher Scheme*

This is a scheme managed by Gardners (currently Aiden Lunn at Gardners). Author/publishers need to contact Aiden Lunn in order to establish terms. An interview wasn't forthcoming, but Gardner's sales reps meet with the WHSmith buyers every 2 months to present their selected titles, and this way you get your lines in front of Smiths without buyer bombardment.

## THE INDEPENDENT BOOKSELLERS

The independents are currently suffering from the discounting madness that is abounding. They cannot compete either on volume or price and are therefore losing out on the 'easy-wins' of popular titles. This undermines their ability to support the riskier new & midlist authors, and authors need to be understanding of their risk-averse attitude. The more you can do to help sell books, the more they will be able to do to help you.

In recent weeks, big-name authors such as JK Rowling have led the way in coming out in favour of the independents, urging shoppers to support them – or lose them.

The independent booksellers are fighting back in their own unique way, increasingly becoming information portals, focusing on hand-selling, book knowledge, cosy environments and sheer friendliness. Overall, they are adding experience to a world where selling is commodity based and is predominantly pile it high, sell it cheap and add no value. Shoppers want to feel rewarded for their custom, they want to know they are buying the right item not simply the easiest or cheapest.

*"Philip Blackwell, chairman of Blackwell Ltd, has predicted the resurgence of independent bookshops as consumers react against the limited range and staff knowledge offered by some retail chains."* The Bookseller, 16/9/05

### How to find the independent booksellers

Listings can be found in your local yellow pages, on the internet (www.upmystreet.com), the Bookseller directory and via Indepublishing.com.

### How to mutually help

The more the independent author can do to help the independent bookseller, the better the mutual benefit. The well-prepared author will reap greater rewards, simply by making it easy for bookshops to order, display and sell your book. A few tips include:

- offer promotions ie. order 5 and get one free
- provide promotional material
- contact the local media to promote and/or cover your event, or in response to something newsworthy on your subject-matter
- make yourself visible; ensure you can be found
- make ordering and re-ordering easy
  - Have an order pad
  - Discount schedule

## Order pad
You can either buy a duplicate pad in a stationers; consider getting a stamp made with your name and contact details or printing these out on stickers and adding them to the top copy that you give to the book retailer.

Or make your own template (see over).

## Chart of discounts
1-10 book at 25% firm sale
11-20 books at 30% firm sale or 25% sale or return
21-50 books at 35% firm sale or 30% sale or return
51+ books at 45% firm sale or 40% sale or return

## Cost of carriage
Most independent booksellers do not wish to, or simply refuse to, accept the cost of carriage. Therefore, when working out your chart of discounts, remember to DO THE MATHS. What discount can you afford to offer whilst absorbing the cost of freight? Knowing that you must never sell at a loss, it is important that you set the price having done your calculations.

**Robert Smith: "I wish I was there"**
**P: 01564 000000 E: Robert@wanabee.com**

# BOOKSHOP ORDER FORMS

*Copy for the bookseller*

*This is a receipt to confirm that the following bookshop has taken books for sale:*

**BOOK TITLE:**  *"I wish I was there"*
**ISBN-10:** 1-456-xxx-322   **ISBN-13:** 555-1-456-xxx-323
**AUTHOR:**  *Robert Smith*
**RRP:**  *£7.99*

**NUMBER OF BOOKS:** ......................................

**DISCOUNT OFFERED:** .......................... ..........

**TERMS:** ..................................................

**ORDER REF:** ...........................................

**ORDER DATE:** .........................................

**PAID:  YES / NO**

---

**Robert Smith: "I wish I was there"**
**P: 01564 000000 E: Robert@wanabee.com**

# BOOKSHOP ORDER FORMS

*Copy for the author*

*This is a receipt to confirm that the following bookshop has taken books for sale:*

**NAME:** ...............................................

**ADDRESS:** ...........................................
.......................................................

**PHONE:** .............................................

**EMAIL:** .............................................

**NUMBER OF BOOKS:** ...................................

**DISCOUNT OFFERED:** .......................... ..........

**TERMS:** .............................................

**PAID:  YES / NO**

## THE SUPERMARKETS

Supermarkets generally only sell the blockbuster titles and stellar authors. They have a very centralised buying policy, and any self-publishing authors going into their local branch of Tesco's, Asda's or Sainsbury's to enquire about stocking their book locally, will be directed to Head Office. The details are below, and it is always worth trying as every now and again a local author will enjoy success with getting his book into the local store.

### Tesco plc

The Headquarters for the Tesco book buyers is in Chesham, however they stipulate that they only take big sellers and very specific local author titles. It is still worth approaching the local managers and discussing your titles with them ("never say die" as they say) and maybe your book will get through.

### Sainsbury's plc

Sainsbury's do not stock local ranges of books, but have a very centralised buying policy. Book submissions should only be made against a very established track record of sales and evidence of further market potential; additionally, Sainsbury's tend to stock very specific genres with women's fiction and cookery doing particularly well.

Their advice for self-publishing authors is to develop your market and find a publisher. This won't guarantee a place in a Sainsbury's store, as they don't take every book even from a mainstream publisher.

If you can prove a solid track record and feel your book is in the right genre for Sainsbury's, then send your book for consideration to The Book Buyer, J Sainsbury plc, 33 Holborn, London EC1N 2HT. You may wish to call to obtain the correct name to address the correspondence to: 020 7695 6000.

### Asda plc
They have a Central Book Buyer and a Local Book Buyer. Central Book buying is block buster authors only, but call them and ask to speak to the Local Book buyer, as below.

### *Local Book Buying Process:*
Set up a meeting with 3 or 4 of your nearest stores, asking to see the Store Manager or H&L Manager (Home and Leisure). Show them your book, saying why you think it will sell at a local level. If they are interested, they will fill out a Store Request form on The Wire, the Asda intranet system, which logs all your details. This is submitted to Head Office, who then contact you to complete the purchasing agreement.

Their address is: Asda House, South Bank, Great Wilson Street, Leeds LS11 5AD. Phone: 0113 243 5435

### CO-RETAILERS

Look at other co-retailer opportunities and book clubs. Make notes on who else may be interested, and why/how they are promoting similar titles. A range of retail outlets you might consider are below.

- o Newsagents: The NFRN (National Federation of Retail Newsagents) have recently signed an agreement with Bertram's to supply books and maps into newsagencies around the country.
- o Gift shops ie. Past Times has recently signed an agreement with Gardners to supply gift books on humour, sports, gardening and historical; and Past Times have an online bookstore with 12,000 books on history, antiques, collectibles, architecture and literature.
- o Petrol stations or via the motoring organisations such as the AA or RAC

- o Garden centres ie. www.notcutts.co.uk: garden centres around the UK with shops offering a comprehensive range of products. Head Office: 01394 383344
- o Department stores ie. Selfridges
- o Gourmet food shops
- o Airports/trains/bus stations
- o Sports & outdoor shops
- o Pet shops

**How to approach co-retailers**

Generally, approach them much as you would an independent bookseller, suggesting your chart of discounts inclusive of cost of freight. You will quickly discover what a time-consuming activity it is for what is invariably a handful of books. But if you are following the principle of **"make a big noise in a small area"** then this form of direct selling activity may build up a groundswell of noise and attract attention to yourself and/or your book.

They tend not to replenish stock if it sells out because it was only a side-line business, not their core business. You would be advised to call them after several months and see how it is going.

This concludes the review of the different channels through the market to your end-customer. On the next few pages, we look at the some best practice ways of approaching and managing these channels.

## BEST PRACTICE : APPROACHING BOOKSELLERS

- o Before approaching a bookshop, verify what books they stock. If it is local to you, then go and have a look around, browse the shop and/or ask the sales assistant if they stock books on your subject matter, making notes on how, where, category and what shelf its merchandised in etc. Check how many they have, how they compete with yours and find out how many they sell. Have they ever done any events or promoted it in any particular way? Staff in bookstores are always ready to help out.

o  This is a critical activity to undertake at least once during the writing, publishing and marketing process, and hopefully only once, as it can become very time-consuming.

o  If approaching books in other regions, you can contact:

- The Bookseller and buy a copy of The Booksellers Association Directory (ISBN 0907972691, price £34, contact 020 7802 0802).

- For free you can go to www.upmystreet.com. Type in the name of the town into the Location search bar and the words BOOK SHOP into the Find a... search bar and up they all pop.

- Indepublishing.com also offers this service

o  Establish whether they are general trade or specialist subject, or whether they sell new or remainder/second hand books, or maybe they are a co-retailer and you could merchandise or give away a gift item with your book.

o  Call them and give them a very brief outline of the purpose of your call. Be ready to be able to send them an Information Sheet about your book. If you cannot get them on the phone immediately, send a flyer or postcard to them with information about your book, and follow up with a phone call.

o  If your book is selling well in the area or in a similar outlet, tell them – *"This book is selling well in outlets similar to yours"*. This might prompt them to give it a go with a small quantity.

o  Always keep a log of who you contacted, when and the outcome.

**The art of negotiation**
It is simple really although many people become very tense or nervous when the subject of money comes up, and most

authors claim to be bad sales reps. Unfortunately, as a self-publishing author, you will need to learn this craft and hone it to perfection.

o Keep one objective clearly in your head: your book and your time has a value; you are seeking to sell books up-front rather than you having to chase for money further down the line.

o You have done the maths (see Marketing Budget) and know what your upper and lower limits of sale are ie. not cheaper than £3.50 per unit and upper price is the RRP of £6.99.

o Your opening gambit will be a 'standard' ie. £6.99 less standard 25% = £5.24.

o For any negotiations, try to retain a Firm Sale and negotiate on other areas.

o The areas of negotiation are:
  • Firm sales versus sale/return
  • Cost of carriage
  • Added value extras ie. promotional material or give-away gizmos

o Know the unit cost on each of your areas of negotiation:
  • Have the Chart of Discounts already calculated on an easily referable sheet
  • know the cost of postage-per-book, or per box of ten books, to UK mainland including the cost of packing.
  • know how much your promotional material or give-aways cost per unit and add this onto the price of each book (see Marketing Budget section)

o Always know how much you can give. Everyone knows you are not self-publishing for entirely altruistic reasons.

o Start haggling. If they don't want to buy firm, then offer a fairly unattractive S/R percentage or suggest they take the cost of carriage.

o When you have got your way on something, then swiftly follow up with the generous offer of some freebie postcards, posters or give-aways; or one book free etc. Always leave the bookseller with a feel-good-factor.

o   When negotiating, try to keep the tone light. I often think of the 'haggling' scene in Monty Python's Life of Brian. It takes the heat out and reminds you that it is simply two people trying to agree on the most equitable deal.

o   Have a duplicate order pad or print outs of an Order form that you can leave immediately to confirm what is agreed. If you are including free promotional material, add this onto the Order Form.

o   Leave a business card and ensure it is clear how they can order more copies.

**How to get into the bookstores:**

o   make them an offer they can't refuse (but that they can buy) ie. free freight, a freebie or gizmo

o   offer a good, fast, efficient, no-fuss service

o   provide updates; send them newsletters by their preferred method

o   offer them point of purchase or promotional material

o   offer "special date" discounts ie. order by or pay by a certain date; deduct another 5% if they pay immediately so you don't have to chase payment

o   have a supply of books in your car so you can optionally drop them off immediately

o   leave behind a card so they can contact you easily without hunting around; contact them

o   draw the media and relevant audience's attention to the shop in return for a display; get on the radio and tell people to buy the book from that particular shop.

**BEST PRACTICE:  Managing bookseller accounts**

There are 4,500 bookshop outlets, which are a mix of book chain-stores, independent booksellers, specialist bookshops, co-retailers and bargain bookshops. Publishers hold accounts with distributors as well as direct to booksellers, all of which need to have book stocks.

You will need to set up an account with a distributor to ensure both the chains and independent booksellers to facilitate ordering. Distributors will take 40–55% which includes the bookseller percentage. But remember, any discounts applied by the store or online shop at the moment of sale are invariably passed back to you.

Most booksellers will prefer to order direct from the distributor, and some are happy to buy from you as the publisher, although this is becomingly increasingly uncommon as the number of publishers and book titles increases. Most chains will now only buy via a distributor/wholesaler, and increasingly many independents prefer to.

The benefit derived from direct sales is obviously the lower discount taken by the bookseller, usually around 25-35%. It is reasonable to request 25% firm sale for orders under 5 copies. For larger orders, they might ask for sale/return, which means they can return the books to you after 3–6 months (sometimes even longer). Having books out there increases the chance of the browsing customer buying it, but you cannot count it as a firm sale until you have been paid!

## Guidelines

1. Have a chart of discounts with variables based on whether firm sale or sale/return, volumes, terms of carriage etc
2. Chase up payment only when you (i) need the money or (ii) are ready to have the unsold book returned to you.
3. Don't send unsolicited books; they get sold and you never see the money.
4. Send them announcements of new book titles – if you can afford the mailshot; but many independents say that they do look at them. Many of the chains have a central buying

policy, so you may as well save your money or just go local.

5. Have a calendar of notable dates and suggest a few dates to tie in with a nationally recognised date.

6. Be prepared to organise an exciting event, supply all promotional material, participate in setting up the display, arrange all the announcements and media coverage etc.


## SUMMARY

Achieving instore distribution is the Holy Grail in the UK market. Whilst people might hear about a certain book via the media, by the time they are shopping for books, they have forgotten that they wanted to read your book. Unless the nudge is there ie. spotting it in Waterstone's or Borders, the chances are that the media coverage won't result in a sale.

Now to contradict this statement that having books in bookshops is the Holy Grail - having all your books in stores around the world won't actually make people notice and/or buy your book. In fact, selling your book in a bookshop amidst thousands of other books is a difficult feat in itself.

Raising awareness of the title is critical; all marketing and publicity efforts must be backed up with a clear message to the interested reader as to how they can obtain your book ie. where & how it is distributed. This may well to point people to certain high street bookstores, but increasingly it points people to your own website and online purchasing methods.

## *The issue of book-selling*

Selling books is not just an issue and problem area for self-publishing authors. It presents as many problems to independent bookshops and major chains – although obviously on a completely different level. Intensive discounting on blockbuster books and celebrity authors are just one part of the market, albeit a big part, which will prevail for as long as it is allowed to, and the supermarkets and internet will loss-lead these titles as much as they like.

Bookselling is entering a whole new phase and discounting blockbusters to mere pounds is undoubtedly a practice that is here to stay. The wise bookseller will give discounted books shelf-space but little energy, and focus the real effort on servicing the customer, finding information, running events and regular promotional activities – and charge full cover price for the book in order to pay for this.

The fact is, the majority of people are happy to pay for a little bit of service. Nobody wants to be ripped off, but when prices are so rock-bottom the service being offering obviously suffers and at the moment, service in the high street chains has gone AWOL. Pile it high, sell it cheap. If you complain about something, the staff attitude is invariably to shrug it off... "take it or leave, it doesn't really matter to me. I get my rock-bottom wage whatever."

You can fly to Malaga for £49 return nowadays so why would you pay British Airways' £150 return? Why? Because of service.

My experience of booksellers has been generally poor although there are obviously exceptions. You just need to read the list of comments made about some independent booksellers in the UK today (see Guardian Unlimited bookshops database) to see that some booksellers are really going for it, and are benefiting as a result. But the bookselling trade is dominated with unimaginative marketing focussed solely around a price promotion and restricted by central purchasing rules.

I have worked with authors around the UK, arranging events, promotions, activities and displays in shops. Too often, the bookseller has done precious little to promote the book and raise awareness of the event. Despite the fact that posters, leaflets and cards are provided for free, the resulting display has been fairly invisible. Nothing in the window, nothing at the tills and not a book display with a card announcing the event. When questioned on whether we can do something, they are happy for us to do then put up posters and set up book displays, but it was as though it simply never occurred to them. Some have explained that they are too busy restocking shelves and selling, but surely when an author is giving up a day or an evening to drum up sales, it would be sensible to do what you can to promote it.

The other curious observation is the lack of liaison with the local community. Many bookshops are seemingly not liaising with the local schools, local book groups, writers' circles, local universities and colleges and old people's homes. Events that are relevant to the community are organised but not maximised. Ottakar's run a great programme where staff can write up their book recommendations and place on cards around the store. This could be extended to reading groups about What's Hot and maybe attribute a display to them each month. Get local schools to vote on the Best Children's Book of the Week/Month. Get the local old people's homes and hospitals to vote on best Biography of the Week/Month. Ensure that all book-sales within the community come your way.

I also understand that they cannot alert the local media every time they host an event, but they could build up an image library of events they have hosted. A shop assistant takes a handful of photos and they create a "press cuttings book", which builds up an impression of a busy, happening place. People start to look out more regularly for "this week's event" or promotional activity.

Book-selling energies should be more community-based and closer to readers. Bookshops need to exploit their specialist skills – knowledge of range, helping people to find books and buy books, running events and creating excitement. Most publishers willingly supply promotional material when asked.

I recall doing some research many years ago about the most exciting part of a supermarket. Respondents' answers ranged from the Oils & Vinegars aisle, the Coffee aisle, the Food of the World aisle and the Organic aisle. The common thread with all of these was the display. Colour, information and give-aways were all evident and people visibly slowed down as they entered these aisles, pausing to browse and participate in the experience and atmosphere. Books really have the perfect platform on which to do this.

Booksellers should be looking to build campaigns around the content of a book and trends that make people want to buy a particular book, or genre, ie. creating a display on Asian fiction one week, collating the relevant books, punctuating a display with some flyers, fabrics, ornaments and posters. As I write this, it was both Australia Day and Chinese New Year yesterday yet in the bookshop I was in, neither was evident. Why not, when the Australian Tourist Board is running extortionately expensive 5 minute docu-style ads on the television? Why not when Wild Swann-style books are a hot topic? A great display, front of shop, around an enticing image of red-hot Aussie outback; or an image of a beautiful Chinese woman in a chung-sam as a backdrop to a range of Chinese novels, travel guides, cookery etc. I appreciate it takes time, but it may excite the buying public into buying something that wasn't top of mind. It may even encourage readers to venture outside of their comfort zone genres and try something new. I know how much I have enjoyed my reading since having to read across genres for a living.

When discussing this with some booksellers, particularly the chains, they say that the stop window, front-of-store display and end-of-aisle display is all paid for and they can't meddle. Given that the abolition of the NBA was intended to empower booksellers to run their own promotions to keep book selling lively, this is a complete turn around. The removal of a price control that was intended to help them is now cutting them off at the knees. Book selling needs to be democratised. Success should be merit-based, not budget-based. Paid-for displays and shop window presence may provide valuable income, but the local reading community may equally have a point of view. Centralised book buying and promotional activities should be reserved for blockbuster titles across a percentage of floor space for a percentage of the year. Other than that, shouldn't bookshops respond to local community demand?

At the moment, the bookshops provide little more than the internet offers. Both are shop fronts piled high with books with price discount tags attached. Online bookshops are increasingly finding ways of replicating the benefits of high street bookshops – flicking through the book, associated promotional material, staff advice and the immediacy of purchase. Amazon offers the 'search inside' facility, reviews and comments, paired titles and, of course, 24 hour delivery on most titles.

The medium of the internet forces the pace of democratisation – both in the music industry as much as the book industry. There are some great sites out there (as seen in Chapter VII Direct Selling, which invite online reviews and allowing the reading public to decide. They also provide extras such as 'best' chapter, first chapter, email the author, signed copies etc. Bookshops need to find a way to compete. Chairman of HMV, Alan Giles, has just resigned for a multitude of reasons, amongst which he sighed that the internet has proved to be HMV's bete-noir.

There is the belief that future value will be in Online Communities in terms of democratising what people want and what they won't tolerate. The internet has become a voice for individuals, and a meeting ground for common voices to come together and create noise. This provides fantastic opportunity for self-publishers to find their audiences and interact with them, building ideas and gaining attention. Self-publishing authors will definitely have an online presence, and the serious self-publishing author will exploit every opportunity available.

In the meantime, the great thing about bookshops not focussing all their efforts to delivering the above list of exciting book-selling activities is that it enables the independent author to do it all for themselves. The author who is prepared to do all the event organisation, promotional activity and media coverage will usually find a welcoming independent bookshop that is prepared to let you use their space.

# PART IV

# PROMOTING THROUGH THE MEDIA

**Analysis of the five routes to the customer**
1. via retail display
2. via unpaid-for media
3. via paid-for media
4. via direct mail (see direct marketing)
5. via events, tours and talks (see direct selling)

**Mix & Match for effectiveness**
*Local versus National*
*How to tip the balance*

**The importance of endorsement**

**Best Practice guidelines:**
1. Obtaining endorsements
2. Getting reviews
3. Writing a release (with example)
   *Top tips for attracting media attention*
4. Doing interviews
   *What did you mean to say?*
5. Organising a book launch

**Media lists**

**How to create a database**

*Pitch perfect*

# PROMOTING THROUGH THE MEDIA

## Raising awareness of the book

The purpose of this chapter is to examine the many ways to raise awareness of a book and drive the demand through the many forms of media, both paid-for and unpaid-for. We conclude by looking at how you could consider mixing & matching freebies with paid-for to maximum value.

One of the major complexities in the book industry is the sheer volume of new books hitting the market. When you compare it to other industries, the launch rate is phenomenal. It is no wonder that the buying public feels overwhelmed and has difficulty in choosing what to read. The grocery trade is 50x bigger than the book trade but launches 1/5th new products. Furthermore, in the grocery and personal products businesses, they invest in order to secure ongoing purchasing – their products are repeat purchase. As long as the product delivers upon sampling, the customer will buy it again... and again... and again. With books, the investment to get the first purchase is sadly often the only purchase. This obviously depends on the nature of the book, but in the general trade (fiction, non-fiction, children's, self-help, biographies) this is the case. Whilst the self-publisher needs to chase volume sales, it is a riskier strategy as time invested into it may not pay off. Therefore, self-publishers are advised to focus primarily on incremental sales whilst chasing a few volume sale opportunities.

But in such a saturated market, how can self-publishers drive awareness of their book to their customer?

We are a media-dominated society with national and local daily papers, weekly and monthly magazines and a specialist magazine or newsletter for nearly every interest-area, however obscure. Books are a very popular topic to write on and most media seem to have a books section – whether review section, New Releases or This Month's Choice; occasionally some run features or extracts of books and interviews with authors that may be particularly topical to reader's interest areas.

Not only are there are vast amounts of space dedicated to selling books and plenty of media channels to talk about books and endless 'book reading' communities to speak to. With the internet, even more book-reading communities are springing up which focus on a wide-range of needs; we can find any book published, review books, read author interviews, run book-groups and writing circles and debate via blogs. This has clearly been an industry in growth and many argue that it still is – certainly in terms of volume.

Yet despite the wide range of media coverage possibilities, it is notoriously hard to 'get into the media'. You have to do something truly amazing or truly stupid to achieve it, and then you are swamped with attention. Anything inbetween is simply not interesting, and you will have to pay for any media presence.

> *"80% of bestseller books never get formal coverage*
> *in literary reviews."*

One word of warning given, not only by authors who have had book reviews, but also by book reviewers, is "be careful what you ask for as you might get more than you bargained for". Book reviews do not have to be flattering or complimentary. They are not your PR agent and will say what they think. I know one author who pushed too hard for a review, then regretted it. Remember, only send them work of which you are truly proud and confident, and then don't badger them! One phone call is often enough to establish whether they received it, but we'll get into the best practice of reviews further down.

## FIVE ROUTES TO THE CUSTOMER

Now you have devised the blueprint of your communication in previous sections, we can look at the best way to combine your methods of talking to and reach the buying public, through the booksellers and the media.

There are many routes to the customer, despite that many authors think solely of major chain bookshops and newspaper reviewers. In fact, you are better advised to invest only a little time chasing the national bookshops and media – although don't misread this for "don't do it". The best advice is to target your approaches accurately, identify who is going to be MOST interested in your title and simply send them a press release announcing your book; follow up a week later to see if they got it and are interested and other than this, leave it for the time being and focus on building your value until you have news of success via other channels. (see Best Practice: Getting Reviews on page 172).

As we have already established, most shoppers will buy on word of mouth recommendation; nobody can buy this although viral marketing methods endeavour to simulate and stimulate this. This is great for the independent author as it is accessible to you. You have to focus on achieving this.

The following list demonstrates a combination of avenues and it is important that you don't see one as replacing the other. The list comprises direct and indirect methods of promoting and selling, which in layman's terms means the ones you are in control of because you are paying for it or doing it yourself (direct) and the one's that you are relying on others wanting to do on your behalf, for free (indirect).

The self-publishing author should seek to exploit the best opportunities for the least investment by mixing and matching Direct and Indirect. It is best to view this range of alternatives routes in the context of the budget required to implement each one - but balance it by keeping your efforts relevant to the audience you are trying to reach:

1.   Display (via channels) ie. free until purchased
     This means high street bookshop display, online bookshop display, co-retailer book display or book-club catalogue display

2.   Through unpaid-for media ie. free
     This includes all media coverage, email promotion, online links, chat rooms, blogs; posters, and word of mouth recommendation.

3.   Through paid-for media ie. cost
     This is any form of paid advertising from advertorials, display ads, classified ads, online banner advertising, pop-up advertising, paying someone to put your book jacket on their site.

4.   Direct marketing (from 'home') ie. cost
     This includes posted promo cards to bookshops, targeted communities or households, direct email and telesales.

5.   Events / tours / talks ie. cost and time
     This is obviously any form of direct marketing and promotional activity that you undertake by going out ie. presentations at bookshops, fairs, festivals, workshops, seminars and training sessions.

Before we analyse the method, advantage and disadvantage of each of the above options, let's firstly focus on what <u>process</u> you should follow to create your plan for raising customers' awareness of your book.

## ANALYSIS OF THE DIFFERENT ROUTES TO AUDIENCE

### Display
This means high street bookshop display, online bookshop display, co-retailer book display or book-club catalogue display. Most of these will take their information directly from Nielsen BookData, so your information should be consistent but do take the time to check it.

### *The high street*
The high street is increasingly the domain of best-seller and mass-market titles who reap the benefits of having front of shop displays, with back of shop shelves filled with books that sell slowly but steadily. In the main, bookshops will only stock you against a demonstrable marketing campaign or if you have a proven sales record.

Bookshops pay a high price for their high street, town-centre location and this is evidenced by the percentage they take and the difficulty unknown authors have to secure instore displays. But authors should not believe that presence in a bookstore guarantees sales; you will still need to motivate people to find it, pick it up and buy it.

### *Online bookshops*
There are increasingly more and more online booksellers, and as long as you are listed for free on them then there is no harm in maximising every possible avenue. You will just need to make sure that they are taking their feed directly from Nielsen and therefore using a description that you are completely happy with.

The drawback is that many of these bookshops compete for volume sales by offering discounts that you ultimately end up paying for. It may even mean that you will never actually sell your book for the RRP which you carefully calculated to be the highest price you thought the market could tolerate and the lowest price you could afford to sell it.

Arbitrary and non-agreed discounting can leave you paying for the honour of writing, publishing and making your book available for sale. Online Selling is comprehensively covered in Part VII.

### Co-retailers

There are many shops that will take certain titles ie. like garden centres will stock gardening & horticultural interest titles as well as gift books, concept books, illustrated books etc. Some wholesalers will have a direct link into them via sales force; otherwise the only way to get into them is to contact them direct.

It can be as easy as it is difficult. Sometimes you ring and they cheerily agree to stock your book on sale/return; other times you are stone-walled by an implacable receptionist. This happened to me with one international brand. It was a bizarre experience because after many letters, emails and phone calls were ignored, I finally snapped at customer service for having the rudeness to not even acknowledge receipt of my polite enquiries when email makes it easy to respond. It was obviously a one-off, exclusive pitch aimed directly at them, and not some general mail-shot. It was bizarre because the next thing I knew I had a deal. I wasn't expecting that and had to make a very embarrassed and meek climb-down.

In order to approach co-retailers, I recommend the following course of action. Firstly, approach the local retailers in your town that you think may be interested. If they are, then spread the net a bit wider until you have covered the county. Once this has proved successful, then contact the head office of any chains and try to leverage the local success to gain national distribution.

Once you can claim "As sold through all branches of Mothercare/Nottcuts/Past-times..." you have a powerful story to encourage the big chain booksellers to reconsider your pitch for national distribution.

*Book club catalogues*
Book clubs are fantastic for small publishers and independent authors as they buy firm (so no sale/returns), usually in quantity and have a direct line into certain consumer groups. They do all the mail-shotting for you and can be responsible for making the unknown author well-known. Jamie Oliver says that it was a book-club that catapulted him into the mainstream awareness when he first published.

However, the bigger book-clubs that deal with general fiction and non-fiction titles tend to focus on the mainstream, best-seller and mass-market titles; they take a very high percentage and discount your book heavily. This has a knock-on effect to the rest of the market as the bookstores and online booksellers have to compete with the book club prices.

Because they prefer to take on the bigger selling trade titles, your efforts may be wasted here. By all means send them information about your titles, and when they want you, they will hopefully know where to look for you.

There are plenty of specialist interest bookclubs, and these ones you should definitely target. They are usually run by a central company with different catalogue brands, and can be difficult to penetrate. A list of bookclubs and how to approach them can be found on page 295.

**Free publicity: traditional media channels**
This means any form of media coverage across newspapers, magazine, TV and radio, which encompasses book reviews, editorial or letters page; email promotion; online links, chat rooms, blogs; posters displayed in prominent and relevant places, or word of mouth recommendation.

*Media coverage - general*
The first thing to understand about journalists is that they are not your PR agent. They have no obligation to (i) write about you or your book and (ii) write something nice. After all, they might not like your book.

Some people believe there's no such thing as bad publicity... maybe not if you are quick-witted, inventive and the eternal optimist. Even then, I never see anybody promoting their bad press. How often have you seen an author emblazon "This was the biggest load of drivel I have ever read, says Jeremy Paxman" across their book? The only time this happens is 10 years later when the book has proved to be a literary and best-selling success and the author is feeling both vindicated and vengeful.

*Media coverage – newspapers\**
Newspapers offer a variety of opportunities from literary reviews to feature articles and social comment / human interest pages; if all else fails, there is still the Letters page. They tend to need information 6 weeks prior to any critical deadline dates, so if you are trying to get coverage before launch then send it in good time. Further information on how to approach newspapers is on page 172 "Best Practice: Securing media reviews and editorial".

*Media coverage – magazines\**
Magazines are published weekly, monthly or quarterly. They tend to work a long time in advance – weekly magazines need information 6–8 weeks in advance of publication date; monthly magazines need around 4–5 months and quarterlies tend to work 6–7 months in advance of publication date. And don't forget, they are generally available in advance of the issue period ie. January magazines are in the shops from mid to end December, so publication date is earlier than you might calculate.

Find out exactly what their deadlines are, and if you want coverage then deliver your material well in advance. Last minute submissions easily get omitted due to the complexity of changing everything round.

*Media coverage – television\**
This is obviously a fantastic medium to bring your message to the masses. There are hundreds of television channels available – local channels, specialist interest channels as well as national channels. The big hairy goal will obviously be Richard & Judy – but bear in mind that this is a big hairy goal to millions of different artistes (writers, actors, artists, spokespeople whatever) so your chances are slim. By all means send in information, but put your efforts into more likely programmes.

Again, forward planning will always optimise your chances, so gather your information early and approach them according to their required needs. Involve as many of your friends and family as possible in your research – what channels, what programmes, what tv shows and chat show hosts etc might be interested. You're your database ready so you are ready to strike during that hectic time of pre-marketing.

Who you contact varies considerably – for local television it will probably be the News team; for specific shows you will probably need to speak to the Planning, Forward Planning or Research teams.

*Media coverage – radio\**
Radio is, like television, a great route to talking to your audience en masse. With the emergence of Digital Audio Broadcast (DAB), there is a renaissance of interest in radio and a wealth of channels available. But again it is indepth, time-consuming work to research all the different channels, shows

and hosts to find out exactly what show or show-host will be most interested in your subject and your book.

Forward-planning, indepth research, roping in friends and family to keep an ear out – all of this helps.

*Bear in mind that The Indepublishing Consultancy can help you with this as we have a good database of information which we constantly update, expand and utilise.*

*Media coverage – online*
The online possibilities are endless, and you are going to saturate your boredom threshold long before you run out of websites. This is covered in Online Selling (see pp 262) and covers such suggestions as doing a search to see who might be interested in your book and email them to see if they are.

Suffice it to say here that most newspapers, magazines, television and radio stations have an online edition or at least offer headlines of articles they are featuring. So once you have identified the best newspapers, magazines, television and radio channels then don't forget to approach their online editors and see if they want to run a support feature.

**Free Publicity: Online promotion**
The internet presents such a huge opportunity for unknown authors to self-promote and become part of relevant communities, see section VII for indepth information.

**Advertising**
This is any form of paid advertising across traditional media channels and the internet. It includes advertorials, display ads, classified ads, online banner advertising, pop-up advertising and paying someone to put your book jacket on their site.

According to Book Marketing Ltd's research, advertising scores very low in terms of prompting people to buy a certain title. If you are very well-known, it will alert people that the book is available and next time they are in the bookshop, they may well make a bee-line for it. Therefore, often their advertising requires little more than to say "John Grisham's next title is released".

However, for the rest of us we need to approach paid-for advertising more judiciously. Advertising for an unknown author will rarely prompt an immediate purchase, but it will put the book into the person's subconscious. If you advertise locally and the consumer then sees the book in the bookshop, they might be prompted to try it because they had heard of it before.

Unknown authors are best advised to headline their advertising by focussing heavily on an issue within the book ie. "*A story of office politics and corporate bullying*". This should encourage potentially-interested people to tear the ad out and set aside for next time they are shopping (high street or online). Particularly if you then convey its tone by including an adjective such as: "*A funny story of...*" or "*A true story of...*" or "*A tragic story of...*". The adjective may be the clincher that tells people that this book is one they want to read. This might be the difference between people thinking that they might look out for it or people going out of their way to search for it. The latter is more likely to convert to a sale.

## Advertorials

Advertorials are usually full page, if not a double page spread, across the pages of a magazine. They look, to all intents and purposes, as a piece of editorial but in fact have been paid for. By law they have to clearly say "Advertising" or "Advertorial" at the top of the page. They are great if you are struggling to get editorial but you need to 'talk' to you audience about what you are selling. Equally, they can be expensive and yield little more than a handful of enquiries or book sales.

---

### Display ads

Display ads are the larger advertisements that you see in magazines and newspapers. They often include an image of the product – or book – and provide plenty enough space to communicate some key selling points and where to buy it. Most people would use these as a one-off or short-term form of advertising or promotion.

### Classified ads

Classified ads are the little box ads at the back of newspapers and magazines. They are sold per word and people only see them when they are hunting for certain services or products. Most people would use this on an ongoing basis to ensure that potential customers can find them in the future (in case they need them) or once they have identified a need for that service or product and are hunting for a supplier.

### Sponsored advertising

Maybe a local company or related business is happy to share the cost of advertising as long as the link between you/your book and them is made clear.

### Online banner ads, pop-ups and advertising

See Online Selling.

## Direct Marketing

Any form of direct marketing is going to be time-intensive, but this where the real opportunities exist for the serious author. It is time consuming, and we look at many forms of direct marketing and how to best implement them in Section VI.


## HOW TO MIX AND MATCH

Invariably the self-publishing author is working on a shoe-string budget, therefore any expenditure must be carefully evaluated in terms of its likely return. We look at Marketing Budgets more fully in a chapter of its own, but there is one golden rule to follow when paying for promotion...

> *Only spend money when*
> *it is paired with some freebie activity*

This means that you should always be seeking to get two promotional hits for the price of one, or buy one get one free. For example, once editorial is confirmed, book a piece of advertising for the following edition in case someone read the article, was interested but needed reminding or prompting to go and buy the book; buy online advertising like banners and pop-ups if there is some form of reciprocal benefit in place ie. they are actively selling your book on one page of the site or on some offline activity whilst you are advertising on another page.

## TOP TIPS

### TIP 1: Progressive planning
A marketing plan is a structured approach to achieving a multitude of ideas. You can't do it all at once, and if you implement it out of sync you lose your opportunities. It is critically important to carry out all activities in a structured fashion in order to exploit all the outcomes. With media, the ideal is to start local and start to build; create news and exploit opportunities as they arise.

### TIP 2: Give people a reason to believe
You can't buy editorial, but if it's good editorial then it is worth its weight in gold. The author/publisher's objective is to set the wheels in motion in a motivating enough way that journalists and booksellers pick up the momentum and promote your book for free on your behalf. You are trying to

encourage people to promote it and therefore you must always provide them with a reason to believe and a benefit for them. Journalists require an interesting enough story and booksellers require a good enough reason to believe it will sell.

### TIP 3: Recycle success

◊ Keep progressing your plan; widen the net at each opportunity, looking for more audience groups that you can talk to, different ways and places to talk to them, gather more reviews & interest

◊ Use success at one level to jump into national interest ie. bookshops, national media; always gather reviews & keep in a presentation folder.

At the end of this chapter are a series of BEST PRACTICE guidelines to help you with approaching the many audiences you speak to – how to get the best out of a journalist, write a great press release, get a book display etc. Firstly, we are going to look more indepth at the range of alternative routes to the customer, their advantages and their disadvantages.

## ISSUE: Local versus National

Many people are derisory about local launches and local media coverage. It is criticised as being the 'sad' way into bookselling, yet this is completely unfounded and unfair. Many authors have achieved success by getting it right and proving their market at a local level.

The desire for national media remains high on everyone's list of priorities, particularly as most chain bookshops *insist* that you must prove interest at a local level to even get a look in at national level. However, there are as many authors who know that national media actually did not result in a huge uplift in sales as there are authors who know that the moment of success was the day they appeared in *The Times* or *The*

*Guardian*. Therefore, it is as broad as it is long. Sometimes national media tips the balance, and other times it doesn't.

My advice to anyone launching a book is to ensure that you have local covered off, even if you have some opportunities at national media and promotion. Don't ever ignore the opportunities that local communities and media can offer. Primarily, it is easier to communicate to a smaller audience and to gain visibility in a smaller crowd.

It is increasingly being said that the future of selling (anything, not just books) is in the creation of communities. Know the clusters of people you are selling to and sell them what they are looking for, and this is easier to implement on a small scale then build rather than trying to reach out to all and sundry in one hit.

## ISSUE: How to tip the balance

No doubt somewhere deep inside you is the hope that your book will suddenly 'explode' onto the market place; that shoppers up and down the country will be flocking to read it and demand will go through the roof; that a top London agent will hunt you down begging to represent you and/or a publisher will offer you hundreds of thousands of pounds to publish your next books. Maybe the moment of success to you is when you have signed a film deal. Therefore, at some point you have to approach the film industry, which means you need information.

Any author/publisher longs for that moment where the ongoing promotional activity takes on a life of its own and starts recycling itself. No longer do you have to keep flicking the message along from customer to customer.

But how do you tip the balance to achieve this? We have seen that a continual and consistent effort will keep reminding people of your message, that having endorsements can build credibility or achieving guru status will certainly ensure your message is out there. But what else can you do? How can you make these things happen?

Somewhere you need to 'tip the balance' by implementing a few Big Hairy Goals. Most successful people were not successful by accident. Very few people get 'discovered' simply by existing. Successful people are usually people who are looking for their opportunity – they talk, they listen, they self-promote and they focus on their ultimate objective, which is success.

Therefore, running alongside the implementation of the planned stages of any author's marketing plan, is the route to achieving the dream. Know what your Big Hairy Goal is and don't lose sight of this. Instead, keep your ears and eyes open for the opportunities as you go about your business of promoting and selling your book.

If you ask enough questions to enough people, the information will come. Who best to approach? How to approach them? What information are they looking for? Where are they?

From one person you might get a name of the best person to approach; from another person, you might get told who their agent is, or someone else who contacted them and may still have their address; another person may advise you on a better angle or approach. It's incredible how helpful people are once they know what information you are looking for. Most people simply don't ask the right questions.

# BEST PRACTICE GUIDELINES

## For Raising Customer Awareness and Demand

This section looks at the many routes to raising customer awareness and demand through the media channels, discussed in terms of Best Practice advice. It covers:

1. Chasing endorsements
2. Getting reviews
3. Writing a press or news release
4. Doing interviews – press, radio, tv
5. Launching your book

**The importance of endorsement**

The book publishing and selling industry is a world which relies on endorsement. Most agents or publishers advertise that they do not accept unsolicited manuscripts ie. only those privately introduced to them which means endorsed by someone whose opinion they respect. The best form of bookselling is by word of mouth recommendation. Individuals know exactly what their friends and family like.

*The real objective in book marketing is to get everyone to market the book for you – via recommendation.*

Selling by endorsement and recommendation obviously has a very low cost margin – the complexity is in achieving it.

Books of fiction generally have a poorly defined, elusive audience. Most people struggle to define what type of fiction they like to read, often defaulting to generic categeries, such as "crime thrillers" or "light-hearted fiction" or "sagas" etc. but underlying this, they are looking for a certain quality in the writing – a tone, a style, a way with words and power of description. But this is difficult for readers to express, and it is even harder for the publisher to articulate on a book jacket.

Hence the system of reviews and endorsements that is so commonplace in the bookselling world. Amazon's system of "If you like this book, you'll also like…" or "Other people who bought that book, also bought…" is a step towards online recommendation based on quantitative data. This is just statistical database information but it draws people to other titles they didn't know existed, which is positive.

### *Exploit "quantifiable" endorsements like Amazon's IF…*

Endorsement works successfully as a form of recommendation, particularly if the endorser is well-known and carries credibility. Publishing is an ART not a SCIENCE, and therefore everyone wants someone else to endorse the book before them. Nobody wants to waste their time or, worse, jeopardise their own reputation by sticking their neck out and endorsing that which subsequently becomes a real howler.

But who are these endorsers? Invariably the endorser must be someone whose judgement one can respect. Endorsement works a bit like a chain of command: publishers want the approval of a literary agent; book buyers want the endorsement of a major publishing house, although this is changing in today's book market; book reviewers want the reassurance of a reputable publishing house; the end-reader accepts endorsement on many levels – a book reviewer, a TV personality, recommendation by a friend. In today's competitive market, being stocked in a bookshop acts as a form of endorsement, as does any form of positive media coverage.

Some areas of 'endorsement' that reputedly do not add to the end-user purchase decision are the publisher logo (too disparate a range) and advertising (this is a paid-for service, not an endorsement). At best, advertising drives awareness and recognition so when they see it in a bookshop they may pick it up to consider it; it will then be book jacket information and endorsements that inspires the purchase.

As a self-publishing author, without the endorsement of a literary agent or major publishing house, it becomes all the more critical to get endorsement. This can come from many quarters – bookshops, book reviewers, general media coverage, credible spokespeople, specialist groups, prizes and awards, festival organisers, Amazon reviews. The groundswell of opinion is increasingly playing a large role – ask the audience. If the target audience like it in a big enough volume, then who's to argue?

The journey of endorsement works back up the chain… the end-reader likes the book; it sells in volume therefore the bookshops stock more copies and create book displays to encourage even greater sale; the publishing house prints and sells more books; the distributors plug it harder; the literary agents sell greater rights on a worldwide basis. The author gains an international reputation, and people flock to buy his/her next book.

The author who really craves literary success will work hard to get endorsements, and this starts from the moment you put pen to paper (or finger to keyboard).

**QUESTION:** *Do book reviewers and libraries prefer hard-back?*
This is an oft-quoted claim but not a substantiated one. Whilst hard-back books have a greater shelf-life than paper-back, libraries pack their books into sleeves and if your paperback is a standard 198x129mm size, then it is easy for them to extend the quality-life of your book. If you create a non-standard size, you may be creating unnecessary hassles for yourself – booksellers and libraries alike prefer standard sizings.

**QUESTION: Do endorsements from non-famous people have any value?**

The general reaction from the books-sellers I spoke to is "not really." Whilst Amazon has democratised the process of reviews, these words of praise and endorsement are ultimately not sufficient to get a book stocked in a chain of bookstores.

My own view on this is that any announcements, reviews and endorsements you choose to put on the cover of your book have to work very hard for you. It must close the sale once a person has picked the book to browse it. Therefore, an endorsement by Mariella Frostrup, for example, will have far greater kudos than an endorsement by Joan Smith of Brighton.

However, the reviews that you choose to print on the inside page can be far wider-ranging… have you seen the first page of *Brick Lane*? Or the last page of *Harry Potter and the Chamber of Secrets*?

Reviews from target audience readers say more than simply an endorsement of the book. They let other readers know if it is 'for them'. If I open a book and see that the selected endorsements are predominantly from men aged 30–50 I will understand clearly who the book is aimed at. Any endorsement has a value, and this value depends on how you use it. Start small and evolve. As you get more 'named' endorsements you can shift the emphasis off the unknown endorsers.

**QUESTION: What endorsements should I use, and how?**

All endorsements have a value. The bigger the name of the endorser, the more prominently you position it. For instance, if JK Rowling says "the best children's book I have read in ages" then you would emblazon this on the front cover or back cover.

The inside front page is another great place if you have had a stream of positive approvals from a wide range of people – from the book sellers, the media, specialist communities and general public.

Good sales figures are another form of positive endorsement. Announcing "20,000 copies sold to America / Waterstone's / The Automobile Club" etc will attract attention and prompt other booksellers to consider stocking your title.

## BEST PRACTICE: OBTAINING ENDORSEMENTS

The purpose of getting an endorsement is to substantiate the claims you, your publisher or marketer may be making about the book, and your ability to write the book.

But how does an author gain the "influential" endorsement? Obviously it helps if you know someone, but many people don't, or simply don't know the right someone. Therefore you are in a position where you are asking something off a total stranger – usually for no return. Sometimes they may feel honoured that they have been asked, maybe it even strengthens their position as a spokes-person on a certain subject but generally you will not know what their reaction will be.

I tend to approach the question of endorsements by first of all turning it back round on myself. How would I react if a total stranger approached me to endorse their work? Yes, I would initially feel pleased that I had been sought out but then I would feel doubtful. Who is this author? Have they written complete rubbish which would damage my own reputation if I endorsed it? How is the market going to receive it? How are they intending to use both my endorsement and their book?

To answer these questions, I actually have to read the book yet... yet I have a stack of unread books; books which do not ask anything of me such as endorsements or reviews, but books I can read and put down at will. Isn't it simply easier to say no, I cannot give a review? At least inaction will not backfire further down the line, at most I might regret not being the one person who said that *"Harry Potter and the Philosopher's stone* is bound to be a huge success."

Ergo, I decline for the simple reason that I didn't know what was wanted of me, why and how it would be used.

Therefore, when I approach a complete stranger requesting an endorsement, I work hard at ensuring they understand their role and reassure them that it won't backfire on them.

## The golden rules to making your approach

### RULE 1: Prepare

- Draw up a list of potential endorsers, ranging from the "Most Wanted" to the "Could be Useful"
- This is not an overnight process, but something you should be doing from the moment you start writing your book.
- Always be on the look-out for celebrities of any grade (A, B, C-list – don't be fussy), tv and radio presenters, journalists, spokespeople (at clubs, events) and anyone else who represents your topic or issue.
- Keep a list, and make notes about their angle, their views and their perspective so that you can approach them appropriately.
- Start doing your research as to how you are actually going to approach them – some names may have their contact details well hidden. Start asking around; sometimes surprising people have surprising contacts.
- Prioritise who you are going to approach; don't just do an "all-out" but write an individual and personal letter to each one.

### RULE 2: Set up expectation

It is easy to feel wary, even resentful, of the unknown. We all have a lot of demands on our time and are constantly bombarded by sales pitches and people wanting something off us. A good salesman will quickly establish what he is selling and judge the reaction. Authors seeking endorsements to sell books are, in effect, salesmen. Get your pitch out quickly and interestingly. If you have covered the groundwork in preparing your marketing plan properly, then you will have some ready-to-use, succinct sentences that summarise your angle quickly and beautifully.

Use adjectives to set the tone; maybe write your own review of your book. Is your book pacy, cleverly-structured, dark, breezy, intense, hysterically funny? Tell people what your book is.

### RULE 3: Manage their response

The real task is to manage what they subsequently say about your book without bribing them. How do you do that? It is partly by setting up expectation, so this is really the same point as above, but furthermore, by sending your book to the right person. If you have carefully selected the right person/people who you know will enjoy it and you point out to them why they will enjoy it, really you are home and dry with an endorsement. After that, the book simply has to deliver.

### RULE 4: Be appropriate

In your desperation to get reviews, it is easy to approach someone with a tenuous reason. If, in your heart of hearts, you know it is a tenuous reason then you are better off either forgetting it completely or fronting it out, admitting that there is no real reason other than the fact that you admire them and hope they like your work enough to endorse it.

But if you are going to do a job, then it is worth doing it properly. Do your research and approach them with an appropriate reason. Maybe your pitch ties in with something topical that they are reported in the media as being connected to or interested in *"I saw in The Newspaper that you feel as strongly about My Subject as I do..."*

### RULE 5: Say something different.

Remember that celebrities, spokespeople and reviewers are people who are plagued with books, pitches and ideas on a daily basis. They have seen and heard it all, and if your pitch is hackneyed or your approach has been done to death, then sadly your book will be rejected.

Describing your book as being *"One woman's struggle to come to terms with the break-down of her marriage"* is hackneyed. However, by picking out something from the story, you can make it unique. How did she cope? What unusual thing did she do? Why did she do it? What prompted her to take such a course of action?

### RULE 6: Be clear about WHAT you want

One of the most frustrating sales pitches is when the salesman bamboozles you with such a wordy or lengthy pitch that you are left trying to work out what they actually want from you. The moment you have to work at deciphering the pitch is the moment they lose the sale.

The salesman who knocks on my door and announces *"Are you interested in cheaper electricity?"* is likely to get a better response than the one who starts asking me what my current arrangements are, and spouting his carefully rehearsed text before actually coming to the point. Be clear, be honest, be forthright.

*"I am approaching you to see if you might consider endorsing my book?"*

### RULE 7: Be clear about WHY you want it

To put them at their ease, you should BRIEFLY outline what you intend to do with their review, and how you are intending to market the book. Once they understand that you simply want to put a short endorsing sentence onto the back of your book and on your website, they will feel more comfortable.

On the other hand, if you are intending to use their "endorsement" as a demonstration of their support in your protest of a political issue they may feel slightly differently. If you <u>are</u> trying to whip up support as a rallying cry, then tell them. Who knows? They might sign up to the cause and give you added fire-power.

## RULE 8: Summarised review

Reassure them by advising that you will re-confirm to them what 'extract' or form of endorsement you are using, and where it is going in the first instance. Sometimes they might write a lovely letter praising your work but you simply cannot fit the whole text onto the back cover of your book. You may select only 5 words or a sentence which is fine, but you must ensure that you have not altered the meaning of their words. It is polite to let them know how you have condensed their words.

## RULE 9: No pressure

Take the pressure off them by saying you will accept it etc if they feel unable to... Thank them... and send with book and press release... confirm that you don't need the book back. They will feel more disposed towards considering your request.

If you are working to a deadline, there are polite ways of indicating this, for example: *"I realise this is a demand on your time and I appreciate your response. So as not to impose, may I call/write/email in 2 weeks' time to follow up on this? Equally, if it is easier for you, I can be reached on phone/email or the above address."*

Yes it is an open-ended question in a letter... that's the point. They will endeavour to get back to you within 2 weeks or anticipate contact from you after 2 weeks. You have politely put in place a time-frame.

## RULE 10: Make it easy for them

Emailing is the simplest form of communication today. If you are not on email, I would firstly suggest that you get on email. Failing that, enclose a stamped and self-addressed envelope.

## RULE 11: Closure

Once they have sent you a review or endorsement, write back within a week thanking them, together with the summarised version of how you will use it or confirming that you will be using it in full.

For good measure, you can say where it is first being used and add a comment about any positive reactions you have received since you last contacted them ie. *"I am optimistic about the future of this book, particularly as Borders have today ordered 300 copies of it for their stores."* This will make them feel good about supporting your book.

## BEST PRACTICE: GETTING REVIEWS

Endorsements are also taken from media coverage about the book including articles, features and book reviews. I have it on good authority that the endorsement on the back of books are usually just made up – agreed on a "can I say you said this?" basis. Personally, I have difficulty believing that nationally recognised book reviewers and newspapers would allow this practice.

Having spoken to some reviewers, they confirm that summarised endorsements are taken either from a written review which is published in the newspaper or magazine, or by agreement after the reviewer has read the book.

Many of the best practice guidelines are the same as above. You will need to set up a reviewer's expectations in an attempt to manage their response; this is done by targeting them appropriately and sending them only relevant books. Say something unique and different and make it easy for them to respond to you. In addition you will need to do the following:

### RULE 1: Send in plenty of time

The media work to a timetable. Miss the deadline dates, and you have missed your opportunity. If you are hanging your book launch on the possibility of media coverage, then start early and give them plenty of time. Most authors succumb to the temptation to start selling their book within a month of receiving review copies but this doesn't allow for media planning.

If the potential success for your book relies on simply getting the book into the market, then simply send an announcement saying it is coming and plan to update them with a news release once your book has hit the market and has something newsworthy to say.

### RULE 2: Place post-its in relevant page of book.

If you send a review copy of a book and have articulated a specific reason as to why it is important or interesting to them, then mark the interesting pages. Lead them to the information you want them to see and don't allow them to dismiss it out of hand as 'not for them'.

### RULE 3: Follow-up but don't chase

◊ Send email announcements to general email address (unless specific name available); often gets passed onto the person who may find it of interest

◊ Phone to check receipt: who has got it, and ask to speak to them about their possible interest. Sometimes they express the reason or angle/basis on which they are interested. Listen closely and be ready to build on any ideas they put forward – they are happy to be sold to if the initial interest is there.

◊ Offer to post them a copy of the book.

◊　　Phone within a week to check safe receipt
　　o　They may push-back with a "I'll look at it next month" in which case suggest to call them next month
　　o　If they decline, accept it graciously and ask for a specific reason if they didn't give one; use this opportunity to ask them what they do look for and whether other people on the paper may be interested

## RULE 4: Keep the clippings

Very few newspapers and magazines will advise you when/if they have published a review about your book. Once they have expressed their interest and said that it is under consideration, make a note to phone back later to see if they did it. If they did, or they advise that it is in the next edition, ask for either (i) a copy of the paper or (ii) the publication date so you can go and buy it yourself.

When you should make this call is dependent on whether they are a daily, weekly or monthly. Allow them enough time to have planned it in and/or actually published it. Dailies, I tend to give a couple of weeks; weeklies, I give a month; monthlies, I give 1-2 months.

### QUESTION: *What if they completely slam your book?*

They say that there is "no such thing as bad publicity". However, I wouldn't blindly cling to this notion. Not all publicity is good publicity, and there is enough choice out there in the world of book, film, theatre and music reviews, that a potential customer can be put-off. The only reason he will change his mind is if he hears enough favourable reviews coming from another quarter. One bad review requires ten favourable reviews to convert a person's opinion enough for them to go and buy the book.

The first piece of advice is to follow the best practice rules in order to avoid the risk of a bad review. Manage their response as much as you can by setting up expectation and sending only what's relevant to them. Don't annoy people by simply 'throwing mud at the wall to see what sticks'.

Don't be pushy or arrogant as they might just kick back and with good reason. If they don't want to review your book, they are under no obligation to. You are not paying them and exploiting "friend of a friend" type relationships may not pay off.

Should you get a really bad review, you may wish to try to understand what their issue with your book was. Consider on what grounds they have criticised your book and maybe even do further investigative work. Call them and ask them. Send your book to an independent editor and get their feedback. Send it to another reviewer and ask for their views, even if it is simply an unpublished view.

If this provides no greater insight than the fact that the reviewer simply took exception to your book, then simply file the review and with any luck, it will come back to haunt THEM, not you.

Remember that Paulo Coelho and Dan Brown have both been criticised by many reviewers yet the reading public buy their books any way. Dan Brown has still sold £30m worth of books!

**QUESTION:** *How many review copies should you send out?*
What's your budget? How many books can you afford to send out? What is your publishing objective? For many authors who have such a burning ambition to write, they will be prepared to send out quite a high number of free copies.

To launch *"What do I have to do to get a book published!"* I issued 100 free copies. For the majority of self-publishing authors, that represents up to £500 in paperback print costs, envelopes and postage. That is not taking into account the time you have personally invested.

Working on the principle that for every on hundred books issued to local and national media you will average a 2% return, this doesn't sound like much. Local media will provide a much higher response rate in terms of doing reviews and features, but they talk to a smaller audience. National media provide a much lower response rate, but talk to a vastly bigger audience. Clinch that, and you have saved yourself thousands in advertising costs!

When issuing books, authors should bear in mind that they will rarely see the book again. If you want your review copy back, then send a stamped, self-addressed envelope (S&SAE), but don't hold your breath as you may still not receive it back.

### QUESTION: I have heard that review copies often end up on Ebay or Amazon Marketplace?

Know who you sent what to. Many review copies I issue will be sent out with a number so I can keep track of a book. On occasion the review copy is politely returned, and I can record that on my stock levels database.

There are a lot of books hitting the re-seller websites such as Amazon Market Place, Abebooks and Ebay. It is always a positive to see that your book is popular enough to hit these re-seller sites, but is questionable when you have given books out for free to be reviewed.

## BEST PRACTICE: WRITING A PRESS RELEASE

The purpose of a press release is to announce the launch of your book with the objective of securing a review of the book, or an article about the message contained within the book or maybe even a feature about the author and why they have chosen to write about this subject.

HOWEVER, in a world where 140,000 books are published in the UK alone in one year, this is neither interesting nor motivating information unless you are Kate Moss.

In today's world, the purpose of a press release is to announce new and different news – in short, tell people why they should bother to read it when there is so much choice out there. Sell the benefits or message, not the features.

Also in today's modern context, we are all bombarded with information every minute of the day whilst struggling to do the job of three people. It is critical to supply information as clearly, succinctly and simply as possible. Your press release should ensure a journalist understands your book and feel as

though they know or recognise your book. Every word and bullet point must be relevant, and a good press release always leads with the most important and prominent point first (known to journalists as the pyramid structure of information).

## What is it?

o One captivating, eye-catching headline to motivate them to enquire further about your book, therefore you should lead with a hard-hitting point, challenge or question.

o Follow up with succinct paragraph that expands on or answers the headline, taken from your original marketing plan. It may be altered slightly to suit the specific needs of your recipient.

## Why is it?

◊ To tell the story of the book and the message behind the book ie. author raison d'etre

◊ To sell it to the media ie. get a reviewer to review it, an editor to feature it, a broadcaster to invite you on air. Therefore **sell** it!

    o Provide one or two brief facts about the author credentials/expertise or reason to believe

    o publisher credentials (what difference they bring)

    o prizes and awards won

    o endorsements

## What must be included?

1. Title, author, ISBN, price
2. Picture of the book and reference to your website (if...)
3. Book category and sub-category ie. Teen Fiction,
4. The target audience, described both as a demographic and a needs-based description
5. Order information – your website, who is distributing and selling your book
6. Who to contact and how

7. The publication date.

**How can the media use it?**

The fact that you are launching a book is not newsworthy, however the media may be interested in doing an article if you can demonstrate a human interest story ie. a triumph of the will, or a connection to a very topical issue. You should therefore create a range of press releases which lead with different issues:

◊ Note down a list of different angles that you raised in the book or you have heard discussed in the media

◊ Bullet point out your 'story' or point of view and how your book demonstrates this; give them digestible information

◊ Be clear about its purpose
  o Make it specific to a news issue; suggest possible feature ideas
  o OR general enough that they can bend to their own needs
  o Put yourself in their shoes – can they use what you have sent; remember that they are writers not readers

◊ Provide them with the information well in advance:
  o the monthlies work 4-6 months in advance
  o the weeklies 2-3 months in advance
  o the dailies 1-2 months in advance

◊ If you are sending to one person exclusively, then make an issue of it – say it clearly as this can be a real positive

**TOP TIPS FOR ATTRACTING MEDIA ATTENTION**

**TIP 1. Tailor it to the individual.**

It is time consuming, but do your research to find out what they may be looking for, arrest their attention by being relevant, give them a reason to write about you and/or your book. It is a buyer's market, and if you want to be heard you have to go the extra mile.

**TIP 2. One message, one release.**
As soon as you start detouring off the 'headline' issue and drag in other issue areas, you have confused it. The journalist won't be able to see the story, or won't be bothered. The release is just the bait, so leave out extra detail – after all, you can send them another press release with a different angle at a later date.

**TIP 3. Be ready to be interrogated.**
If they are interested in your press release, they may call up to discuss any proposed feature ideas with you. In order to vet their interest in your proposal, they will interrogate the proposal. Be ready to respond with concise and prepared answers.

**TIP 4. Follow a good reading order.**
Your press release needs to follow the same 'hierarchy of communication' principle that we talk about in the next chapter (Promotion & Publicity). Make sure the information flows in a way that you 'educate' the recipient quickly as to the purpose of the press release. Firstly arrest their attention, then secondly draw them in by an easy-to–read logic.

**TIP 5. Remember to KISS** - Keep it Simple Stupid (not my own, of course, but it makes me laugh when I see it):
  o Don't overload it with too much text ie. maximum 300 words. They are writer's not readers so don't send them huge swathes of text, so sound bites are better.
  o Keep the layout simple and accessible (see Hierarchy of Information) ie. use bullet points and don't be afraid of space.
  o Ensure Publication Date and Contact Details are clearly visible.

- o Include any Embargo Dates if you are seeking to sell serial rights, or have already sold serial rights.
- o Remember to say 'paperback original' if this book has never existed as a hardback.

**TIP 6. Emphasise any local angles** ie. if you are a local author or the book includes the local area, family or community in any way. Local newspapers will invariably cover local interest books and authors.

**TIP 7. Target a name.**
Phone up and ask for the name of the relevant editor or book reviewer. It is time consuming, but if you are going to send anything, it might as well be to a named person who you can follow up later.

**TIP 8. Avoid the hard sell.**
This is a tricky one, as what's in a definition? One man's hard-sell is another man's tentative approach. Engage in relevant conversation whereby you are either converting their distinterest to interest, or you are learning more about what they want. Don't bother with small talk, and don't pursue a conversation after they have made 'thanks for calling but...' sounds.

**TIP 9. Make it cost effective:**
- o Emailing information is the cheapest form of information-sharing but bear in mind that some companies block attachments or file size.
- o Your press doesn't have to be a 4-colour glossy flier; a one-pager Word document with one picture of the book jacket suffices.

**TIP 10.** Some newspaper email systems block emails with attachments, so send information within the body of an email.

## NEWS RELEASES

A press release by any other name, but you can use this on an ongoing basis to announce new news. All the above principles apply but it can work more like a Newsletter to remind people about your book in a meaningful and interesting way. It can help to establish you as the expert spokesperson. Send out either monthly or when something specific to say:

◊    Announce new events, developments or activities
◊    Be reactive to stories in the press or on the news
◊    Tie in with other events or activities that are happening
◊    **Make news:** sponsor a poll that is relevant to your subject matter and send findings to the local newspaper.

If you are on email, you can create a Distribution List which makes it easy each time you update your audience with information. If you are relying on post, then create a Label Table so you can easily print out a new sheet of labels each time. Remember to update your databases to keep the information as current and good as possible.

## BEST PRACTICE: INTERVIEWS

Securing newspaper, television or radio interviews is a great route to raising awareness, and local media are very ready to hear about new book launches and/or new author endeavours. The size of the resulting article and the page it is published on depends on how newsworthy you make the article. If it has a heavy local interest you will secure a decent position in the paper, or length of interview on the radio. Equally, if your book addresses a social or human interest issue you will gain a sizeable and/or prominent feature.

In my experience of working with authors, it is on the subject of interviews that most people turn pale and shudder. Most authors prefer to work alone and quietly, and are not naturally flamboyant people who relish talking about themselves. Therefore, I have endeavoured to pack in as much as I possibly can in the following tips and guidelines. I truly hope this helps, as interviews are actually quite good fun – an opportunity to voice your opinions and talk to the world…

## How to approach them

◊ Firstly – don't be shy. Be clear and forthright about why you are contacting them, and what you are hoping to achieve by this contact ie. *"I am launching my first book and I wondered if you would like to receive a press release about it, with a view to doing a review, interview or article on it?"*

◊ They will invariably say *yes*; the only time anyone has said *no* to this enquiry is when they simply NEVER do reviews, interviews or articles on authors or local people.

◊ Send a press release with current headline grabbing title – ensure you give REASON for people to want to interview you
   o Topical / interesting topic
   o Plenty of scope for discussion
   o Challenging a popular belief
   o Filling airtime in an interesting and different way.

◊ Follow up and ask if they are interested to chat on air or write about you; I tend not to send out books until they are 90% interested in an interview or article as books are costly. They may put you through to a specific show producer so you can discuss the possibilities of what you can discuss on air or in an interview
   o Have a number of different angles on hand; make suggestions

o   If they decline your suggestions, ask them what they are looking for; see if there is a good fit

o   If there is not a connection or a good fit, then be honest and agree that maybe it is not for their audience – although I hasten to add that it is a rare book that cannot be reviewed at a local level.

**TIP**: *the more articulate and confident you sound, the more they will be prepared to consider an interview or feature. Make it easy for them.*

## Organising an interview

1.   When agreed, set date immediately and offer to send a book directly to a named individual ie. the person who will be conducting the interview. Send it with another press releases (they always get lost)

    a.   Maybe mark specific pages

    b.   Maybe send suggested question list about (i) you and (ii) the book

    c.   Know what you want to say (see *What did you mean to say?* On pp 189)

2.   If you haven't yet spoken to the named person, then contact them a week or two after they receive the book and ask them if there is any particular angle they want to chat about.

3.   It is easier to be interviewed than just be invited in for an open chat – send them some guidelines together with the book; post-it note any relevant pages that pertain to the questions you propose.

4.   For radio interviews, you don't have to be in the studio to be interviewed. You can be at home, although it is preferable to go to the radio station. If you are being interviewed by another part of the BBC, you can go to your nearest BBC radio centre and they will arrange a radio link-up.

## Exploit the opportunity it presents

1.  Once you have agreement for an interview, make sure you maximise the opportunities it presents by approaching the local bookstores. Target your favoured bookstore and approach them first with the suggestion that you will announce on air that the book is available at "Their Bookstore".

2.  Push the boundaries and suggest they do a lovely display for the week before your interview with a card announcing the time/date of your interview OR the week after your interview with a card saying "As on Radio Local / Local Newspaper".

3.  See if they will host an event in the days following your interview, and make sure you announce it when you are being interviewed.

## Doing a radio interview

1.  Phone the day before to reconfirm that you will be there. It demonstrates professionalism and they feel they can trust you and relax about your participation.

2.  Get there half an hour before the show starts; it helps to settle in, collect your thoughts, get a cup of tea or coffee from someone, somewhere. You may even have an opportunity to chat with show producer beforehand.

3.  Be ready to be bowled a 'googly' – this is when they forget your name or the title of your book or what you are then to talk about. The latter has occurred to me when I was introduced as being on air to talk about the importance of walking when you have breast cancer. I wasn't and I had no specific information on that particular angle. However, rather than returning the googly, I integrated it into what I *was* there to talk about. I don't think she was any the wiser – in fact, I don't think she listened to a thing I said – but it was

kinder than bringing her to a halt by saying "I'm not here to talk about walking."

4.  **TURN YOUR PHONE OFF!!** I didn't do this the first time I was on air and someone called me. Arghghgh!

5.  Take your book and paperwork with you.

6.  Remember to mention your book title, and where people can obtain it – particularly if you have promised a bookstore that you will announce their name on air. They probably won't hear it or ever be any the wiser if you do or don't, but a promise is a promise and a deal is a deal.

    a.  Announce any events, dates and times that you may have organised.

7.  Listen closely to try to get any endorsements
    a.  Have a pen and pad ready.
    b.  If they say something suitably endorsing, note down the one critical word without getting distracted from the conversation.

8.  Follow up; ask them if they can either provide an endorsement or if you can use the endorsement they said on air.

**Doing a press interview**

* Phone the day before for the same reasons as above.

* Turn up early at the arranged meeting place, together with several copies of your book and crib sheets for the journalist ie.

    o  a press release
    o  biography
    o  question/answer sheets
    o  interesting excerpts from the book

* Give the paperwork to the interviewer and hold onto the book/s for use as props in the photo (see over).

- Remain clear and focussed about what you want to say. The resulting article will expound about 3–5 points, issues or elements about the book so make sure they are the points you wish to be making.
    o Double-check that your press release, biography, question/answer sheets support the points you are making.
- Remember to mention where the book can be bought and any promotional activity you are launching.
- You may consider taking out an advertisement the following week to remind anyone who saw the article and intended to buy the book. It acts as a good reminder, and local newspaper ads are often good value for money. Maybe you want to offer a discount voucher to encourage people to buy it.
- Press interviews may be before, during or after a launch or event, and you can exploit the opportunity it presents accordingly
    (i)     before a launch or event
    (ii)    at a launch or event
    (iii)   after a launch of event

**Doing a television interview**
Many of the above principles apply but bear in mind that airtime comes at a huge premium. Therefore, find out beforehand how long the interview will be in terms of final airtime. Ask them what questions they intend to ask you and then work out what critical points you want to make in that time in response to the questions they are asking. Note them down as single words and memorise – then go with the flow.

Also, check with them where any interested viewers may access information about your book, and whether they will be running a banner across the bottom of the screen with the title of your book and your name and website address (if…) so people can note it down.

Television stations do not tend to supply you with a tape of your 5 minutes of fame, so ensure someone at home is recording it if you wish to view it and keep it for posterity.

## Having a photograph taken

- If you are going to be photographed then choose your clothes carefully. Don't wear all black, all white or heavily contrasting colours. Newspapers print in black & white with poor contrast and resolution control, and magazines often have several pictures on one page and will 'balance up for the average'.

- Therefore, to ensure your photograph is reproduced to the best possible standard, wear tonal colours like pale and dark matching colours ie. pale blue and dark-ish blue, shades of cream to brown. Something lightly patterned (not stripes!) can also reproduce well. Stripes reproduce badly on television.

- Accessorise and take a mirror with you to do one final check on the hair and make-up (ladies) before the photo.

- Stand well forward of any background and check behind you to minimise the risk of pillars, posts, lamps and flowers growing out of the top of your head. Most photographers are professional enough to check for this, but it doesn't hurt for you to be checking for it too.

- The photographer will probably shoot 10–30 images and will invariably be using a digital camera. Ask to see them and express your preference, and ask him to delete any that you really hate. Make sure you do actually leave him with a good range however, as he is shooting for landscape/portrait usage needs; maybe with enough bleed to have space for text going over the background. He needs to go back with a good range of images.

- You could ask him if he could email you one or two, but remember that he is doing this for a living and will at the very least require crediting if you use his images for self-promotion. He will be within his rights to ask for payment if you are using it on other magazines or literature, but this should not be an unreasonably high fee.

- If he does email you any, remember to credit him <u>every</u> time you use the image; for the sake of thoroughness and politeness, you would do well to email him and let him know where you are using it.

## ISSUE: "What did you <u>mean</u> to say?"

The two biggest concerns most authors report about media interviews are firstly, that you will shoot your mouth off and say something you never intended to say and secondly, that you will be misquoted. To successfully avoid both these problems, plan beforehand what you want to say. Have a crib sheet with the main points underlined, in bold and/or in red. Feel free to consult it when being interviewed on radio or by a newspaper journalist.

Also remember that the journalist doesn't know your agenda, and may well ask you questions seemingly irrelevant to your agenda. Journalists interview people day in, day out across a wide range of subjects. These can often be on subjects where they have no prior knowledge and the wise author will help a journalist to focus on your objective by giving them the crib sheet, subtly explaining the whys and wherefores without losing sight of the main points they are seeking to make.

To understand what the interviewer/journalist needs, study some articles about other authors and their books. Count up how many key points are made about the book and you will see a basic pattern emerge:

- Intro para: sets out the one key point that the article intends to make
- Main body: illustrates 3–5 key supports to the key point
- Summary para: confirms what the article demonstrated.

Think of your book in a similar way. What do you want to say? If you were a journalist, what article would you write about your book? What ONE key point would your article be making and what 3–5 supports would you raise to illustrate that point? How would you conclude it? Take this "crib-sheet" with you to the interview in order to help you stay focussed and talk about the key points you wish to make.

Let the journalist write the article and put it into their words and their observation. Writers usually cave into the temptation of saying too much, yet a good journalist will say exactly the same points in a far more succinct and efficient way. And remember, the chances of you seeing copy before publication are slim; journalists work to tight deadlines and ultimately are not your PR agency. Let them write what they hear; it is up to you to provide them with the right information. Give it to them clearly enough and they will faithfully carry the message forward.

If you get nervous beforehand then it is important to learn relaxation techniques. Relax back into your chair, take three long, slow deep breaths and feel your shoulders drop as you exhale. As you relax, just think of the 3–5 key points you wish to make. Don't feel tempted to make too many points as people will only remember the main facts. Focus on those, and talk around those. Don't bombard people.

I did a talk recently and the person before me read some poetry out. She read it so beautifully, with such measured tone and clear voice that it completely inspired me. I wish I could take her with me for every talk I do, but sadly I can't.

Learn from others. Listen to some after-dinner speakers, watch people on television chat-shows and listen to people being interviewed on the radio. Most of all, listen to politicians. Did you actually hear what they said or did you just hear a stream of words with no real point being made? Which speakers were a pleasure to listen to and which ones weren't? When you pause long enough to consider this, you will realise that the best speakers are the ones who make a point briefly, clearly and succinctly – and slowly. They pause, they speak, they may emphasise a word or two and they speak deliberately and consciously. They don't ramble or rant. They don't digress and overload the sentence. They make one deliberate point.

If you follow these guidelines, it helps you to stay on track with the process of managing what the media will say about you and your book. It is not a guarantee, but it helps.

## BEST PRACTICE: ORGANISING A BOOK LAUNCH

Being prepared is the all-encompassing tip, and it is difficult for the first-time self-publishing author to know what this means. Therefore, you need to read the below in conjunction with the best practice feature entitled Hosting an Event on pp 307, and combine it with the below:

o Arrange it around your friends and family primarily unless you are guaranteed to draw a big media crowd.
o Have helpers:
  - Someone to help set up the room with your promotional material, posters etc
  - Someone to pour drinks and stock up any niblets
  - Someone to sit at the table with you to collect money (assuming you are selling books at your launch)
o Plan whether anyone is going to make a speech; if you are, then obviously plan out some words. If a friend or shop is hosting the event, remember to thank them.

**If you want to try to get the media there...**
  o Attract media interest by intriguing the media – an unusual venue, an interesting spokesperson who they may have difficulty reaching, some surprising activity taking place etc. Think out of the box to be creative.

- o Try to secure an unusual venue that will provide a great talking point, or have some unusual activity or visual that will help get the event going.
- o If tying in with a nationally recognised calendar event or date, make the connection visually prominent – and try to invite someone connected with that 'date'.
- o Invite lots of personal friends.
- o Make it in an accessible environment location-wise, and one that can easily expand/contract to fit enough people in but not look empty if few people only turn up; venue should be relevant to launch / book.
- o Send press release and invite 3–4 weeks beforehand.
- o Invite a photographer from a newspaper (pay him to come along if necessary).
- o Provide food and drink.
- o Do speeches 30–45mins after start.
- o Remind everyone why they are there; to buy the book.
- o Have someone there taking the money/cheques, handing out press packs, noting down who turned up from what media; try to get business cards or contact details so you can follow up.
- o Have badges for media.
- o Give something back ie. a gizmo or gift for attending; or encourage them to go forth and sell ie. postcards; tempt them ie. one chapter.
- o Provide a press pack so any attending media leave with plenty of good information.
- o Follow up in the next few days to see if they are planning to do any coverage.

**What to include in a press pack**
- o A press release which is relevant to the activity or event you are preparing the pack for
- o Author biography and photo; include any past publications, successes, prizes and awards

---

- o   Q&A about beliefs on specific message
- o   Promotional activities and planned events, together with a sample of the associated material
- o   Contact details of author, publisher and publicity agent.

This concludes our analysis of the Best Practice guidelines for using the media. In the next section, we are going to look at some of the media categories. For indepth information, self-publishers are advised to have copies of the Writers' Handbook which has more comprehensive information and contact details, or using the Media websites listed in the next section.

# MEDIA LISTS

This section looks at how you can begin to create a database of the different media. To be prescriptive would quadruple the size of this book; instead it seeks to provide information about how and where you should look to make all contact relevant to your specific subject matter.

This phase of work is relentless, but also a little bit fun as it all starts coming together. I enjoy reading the different magazines and papers and trying to see where my book could live within their pages, thinking up a specific angle and approaching them.

Sometimes it can be thankless, as you send out emails, letters and press releases which never get so much as an acknowledgement, let alone prompt any interest; or you phone and leave messages on voicemails and with other staff, but rarely speak to the person you want to reach.

Then occasionally you get a response which takes you by surprise and you have to scramble your wits quickly in order to present a cohesive pitch. The media rarely let you know when something is going into their paper or magazine, and you get texts from friends, family and colleagues congratulating you on the review in the paper, that you knew nothing about.

### How to create your database

Firstly, I would like to advise that Indepublishing.com has a comprehensive, up-to-date database of all the main media avenues you should explore in order to put together a database relevant to your subject matter. However, should you wish to undertake this yourself, I am endeavouring to put as much information here as I can.

I believe the best way to approach this phase is steadily. Slowly, slowly catch the monkey. Create the database in stages, creating lists of *"low-hanging fruit"* audience and what

media they read; "*local*" media and "*top priority national*
*media*".

Go and buy copies of your targeted media and get the
names of journalists or editors that seem most likely to be
interested in your pitch. Assess they angle or stance they take,
look at the language and tone they use to appeal to their target
reader and use all of this to get a good feel for what their
target reader will be interested in. Log all of your findings.

Bear in mind that staff turnover is high. Even the annually
updated databases such as the Writers' Handbook cannot keep
pace with the rate of staff change, so the best advice is to
phone and ask for a person by title or job role ie. the Features
Editor, the Book Reviewer. Get their name and correct spelling
before being put through to them.

To create your database, a good startpoint is to go through
the below headlined categories.

**Online media lists**
The below are particularly useful for finding media in a
certain locality, or finding media groups if you wish to
approach them and see if they will syndicate a story that may
have nation-wide appeal.

www.mediauk.com - The critically-acclaimed independent
media directory for the UK. Listing websites, addresses,
telephone numbers, live links and more for all areas of the
online media, it's your one-stop media portal. Continually
updated with 163 updates over the past week, we currently
list 748 radio stations, 481 television channels, 1699 magazines
and 1493 newspapers.

www.holdthefrontpage.co.uk - This is a website for journalists
and journalism students everywhere and offers free and
unrestricted access to everyone. If you are working, or want to
work, in the regional press, this is one of the best places to find
out more about the industry.

www.journalism.co.uk - Journalism.co.uk and dotJournalism are published by Mousetrap Media Ltd; we are an online publishing company specialising in building news-oriented and community-based web sites.

## National media Groups

There are currently 56 media groups in the UK today which own the thousands of newspapers (national, regional and local) and magazines published today. Some of the corporation names you may have heard of, such as Guardian Media Group, Daily Mail Group, DC Thompson, Haymarket and Newsquest. Others you may not have heard of. To see a full list, click on www.mediauk.com , newspapers, owners.

For news stories, these newspapers are all linked and can syndicate stories across the regions. But local stories will not be syndicated until such time as they become more widely newsworthy. Usually a local story (ie. local author book launch) will go into your most local newspaper.

## National newspapers
### Books review pages

Most of the national newspapers have a Literary Editor and regular book review pages. Again, you need to read the newspapers to find out who does what in order to see what best suits your needs. Many of the literary editors look for very specific types of work which can best be summed up as indepth researched literary works. Some have a 'paperbacks' section, but these generally focus on titles from major publishing hosues and very literary, prize-winning contemporary titles.

### Serialisation and extracts

On the whole, newspapers do not tend to run serialisations as these have been proved to not actually increase sales figures by any significant amount. Extracts or features on the author are more likely and whilst these don't increase newspaper sales, they do convey strong messages about the newspaper. Therefore the self-publishing author must approach the newspaper with a good understanding of how their book fits the newspaper's profile and audience.

- o The Independent on Sunday will run 3000 word extracts every week, including new and little-known authors. Suzie Feay advises that she looks for something edgier as well as extracts that come at a reasonable fee.
- o Guardian/Observer is a good prospect for fiction and Guardian Weekend offers Summer Fiction reviews with highlights on authors. Katherine Viner, the editor, is very supportive of fiction.
- o The Times runs a little fiction extract every week, up to 4,500 words.
- o The Telegraph: Weekend Family Book Club: the aim is to encourage parents and children aged 9–12 to get together with other families to discuss a children's book.

### Features pages
Most of the nationals run lifestyle and social comment pages, and these are always good places to watch and approach with proposals. It is critically important that you approach with a very specific idea in mind which is well thought through and you can articulate it easily when interrogated on it. Newspapers generally look for the human interest angle.

### Supplements
There are opportunities with weekend supplements as these are lifestyle focussed and often have books sections within them, although they are notoriously difficult to get any result with. They are not struggling for information to fill their pages.

## Local newspapers

Local newspapers offer a wide range of opportunities. Many are part of a larger group; features and articles are often sent out to the local and relevant paper. Some of these, like the Guardian Group of Newspapers, will also have a feed of information into the national newspapers.

Equally some, like the London Evening Standard, The Argus in Brighton, the Manchester News are large and very credible papers with a large circulation.

## Magazines

There are hundreds of magazines out there, from general lifestyle to very subject-specific and the best source of reference is either the Writer's Handbook, which includes the main contact details and a brief profile of the magazine, or going into a large branch of WHSmith.

Authors are likely to find more success by approaching a specialist subject magazine with a proposal, and you may seek to take out a small advertisement in the few weeks/months after any article about you appears. This will help ensure you exploit the opportunity of any features or interviews, and help them to find you in the following editions. However, it is also well-recognised that people will tear out relevant pages from magazines and keep them for future reference, so if you cannot afford to take out an advertisement, don't worry. The chance is that interested readers kept the information anyway.

### Writing, Literary and Poetry magazines

o The Bookseller magazine has a large new titles section which is read by the book buyers in book retailers around the country every week. They work at least 4 months in advance, so get your book in nice and early as they only review new releases.

- o  Bookseller book reviews should be sent to: Tracey Davies, 020 7420 6013
- o  The Bookseller supplements ie. audiobooks, sci-fi & Fantasy, Poetry, Buyer's Guide.
- o  The Bookseller Buyer's guide: submit to: www.booksellerbuyersguide.co.uk or email richarde@hcuk.net
- o  Writing magazines such as Writers' Forum, MS Lexia and Writers' News/Magazine are always interested in hearing writer's stories, whether mainstream published (or rejected) or self-published.

## Women's magazines

- o  They spend millions every year researching every last detail of their reader's lives, profiling them in order to constantly deliver content that is relevant to their readers. They research reader's aspirations and disappointments, and will link features closely to reader's lives. Regular readers of women's magazines will read advice and recommendations avidly, and magazines work hard at ensuring they provide information to retain that trust and loyalty.
- o  Many women's magazines like stories that demonstrate triumph over adversity, long-awaited dreams being fulfilled, spilling the beans or controversial stories or simply the off-beat to the very bizarre.
- o  Some are great for fiction (Woman's Weekly, Woman's Own), others are more health and lifestyle focussed (diet, relationships, home-making). Some magazines will take freelance-written articles and others will be open to serialisation and extract deals.
- o  Do not even contemplate taking out an advertisement, as this can average around £10,000 for a full page in one edition! Some magazines will give away a copy of

a book with the magazine, which is great for authors with a good backlist. This form of give-away is called a 'cover mount' and they will ask for a delivery of around 100,000 units. Again, not for the self-publishing author.

o Many women's magazines have a book reviewer, or run book review specials at certain times of year. Some of them regularly print short stories or extracts. Read the magazine to get the name of the current reviewer; failing that, contact the editor's assistant as they will be able to advise.

o If you are hoping for some kind of feature, the best way to approach any woman's magazine is to think of 3 or 4 feature ideas that link your book to their reader and submit this with a copy of your book.

o Make sure you do your homework before phoning randomly around, and save everyone, including yourself, time and effort.

## Men's

There are a wide range of men's magazines out there now, albeit not nearly as many as there are women's magazines. Obviously many of the above principles apply in terms of tailoring your approach... buy the magazine you are targeting in the first instance and ensure your tone fits their readership.

## Children's

Most of the children's magazines provide a limited platform for book reviews and articles about authors – except the very famous children's writers. This is because the younger age range magazines are usually tied in with a children's television channel, programme or brand. The older age range most often focus on teen celeb gossip and fashion, and books don't get a look in. We have had some success with running a competition ie. answer this general knowledge question that relates to your subject matter, and win a book. Most children's books get greater opportunity with educational magazines.

## Specialist interest

There are specialist interest magazines for most topics, and these provide plenty of scope for anyone writing on a specialist interest area eg. ethnic weekly newspapers will consider biographies by relevant authors, and subject-oriented magazines cover ie. Finance, Education, Gardening, History, Leisure interests and pets, religion and philosophy, rural life & country, travel and geography.

## Letters to the Editor

If you are having difficulty in getting any media coverage, then look to the Letters page. It is possible that you are very early to a topic, and the media just have not cottoned on. Sometimes one letter to a newspaper can result in such a flood of response that the Features Editor is quickly alerted and they will write an article about your topic, invariably featuring the originator of the first letter.

## Radio

The self-publishing author would be best advised to start with local radio stations first. Listen to your local radio for a week and get the feel of the different shows, the different presenters and their topics. Go onto the website of the local station and have a look at their weekly line up; see what issues are coming up or what specific topics they might be covering.

Contact one of the show producers or the news room, let them know about you and your book, send them a press release. If you have a launch date and an event planned, then try to tie in the timing so you can announce your event. Keep watching it, checking in on their site regularly and exploiting opportunities as they arise.

There are plenty of Book programmes on national radio too. All contact phone information is contained within

Writer's Handbook, and below is a list of *current* shows – but bear in mind that this changes quickly.

For national radio, the programme of events tends to be planned a long time in advance although local radio can respond literally within days.

### BBC Network

For BBC information, do initial research on www.bbc.co.uk. There is a wealth of information on here which constantly updates. Hunt around and opportunities abound. For instance, there is a whole section about What's On, and you can click to *Be on a Show*. The BBC research team are constantly scouring the hot topics and providing interesting programmes, and this might give you a good platform on which to talk if your topic comes up. Equally, it will put you in touch with the right programme to do a separate interview.

There is a whole section on the website on Art & Books (www.bbc.co.uk/arts/books) which is worth trawling through. Here are some of the *current* radio programmes which may well change during 2006. They all tend to plan months in advance and many focus on well-known authors, prize-winners or famous spokespeople. Even if you can't get onto them, they are good to listen to, analysing how people talk about their books, the issues and messages within their text and their connection to the book. It's all good practice for when you get your opportunity!

- o Book Club, Radio 4 – James Naughtie and a group of readers talk to leading authors about their best known novels
- o Book of the Week, Radio 4 – each weekday, a reading of non-fiction covering biographies, travel, diaries, humour and history
- o Afternoon reading – a short story or an abridged book, often by writers who are new to radio, each weekday
- o Woman's Hour, Radio 4

- Front Row, Radio 4 – a live magazine programme on the world of arts, literature, film, media and music
- Saturday Review, Radio 4
- Book at Bedtime, Radio 4
- A Good Read, Radio 4 – Sue MacGregor and guests
- Open Book, Radio 4 - Kate Moss with news from the world of books.
- Night Waves, Radio 3 – an arts and ideas programme
- The Wire, Radio 3 – new writing for radio that pushes the boundaries of drama and narrative
- The Verb, Radio 3 – a showcase of new writing, literature and performance
- Off the Shelf, World Service
- Best Book guide
- World Book Club, World Service – internationally acclaimed authors only
- Cover Stories, Radio Scotland – Scotland's brightest and best book programme presented by Richard Holloway. Contact: Cover Stories, BBC Scotland, 4 Jackson's Entry, Holyrood Road, EDINBURGH, EH8 8PJ
- Also of interest might be www.bbc.co.uk/writersroom; contact them to find out all you need to know about submitting to BBC writersroom.

### BBC Regional

All regional channels are listed in the Handbook. Visit their websites to see what local shows are relevant to you, and email your press release to the email address listed in the Handbook. They will forward it on to the most relevant person. It is sensible to phone in the next day or so to find out who it was forwarded onto, and ask them if they are interested. Most radio stations will be prepared to do something at some point if you can prove you have something more to say than just "I've written a book".

## Independent national radio

Digital Radio encompasses a range of radio station 'brands' which are part of the Digital One network: Oneword, Life, Prime Time, Virgin, Core, Classic FM, Rock Planet, Talk Sport

One programme of particular interest to self-publishing authors is ONEWORD's Between the Lines, a daily author interview show to chat about their life, their work and read an extract. This includes a children's good book guide which features author interviews, reviews of children's books and audiobooks and Rough Guides. Oneword does not shy away from self-publishing. Ana Fischel of The Zartarbia Tales has been interviewed here and it gave first airing to self-published children's story "Beyond the Hedge" by Mairi Craw.

## Independent regional radio

Most regional radio stations will be interested in inviting local authors to come on air to talk about their book. Again, I recommend that you do your research before contacting them – listen to their radio station for a week, hearing the different programmes and presenters; trawl through their website as often they are inviting people to air their views on something. Contact the News Desk, advising them that you are a local author launching a book and suggest you send them a press release. They invariably say yes, unless they are only a music channel.

## Hospital and student radio

Details for local hospital and student radio channels are to be found in the online media listings mentioned above. Depending on the nature of your book, this might be another area of interest to explore.

## Television

National television daytime chat shows are definite targets for the hopeful author, with Richard & Judy usually heading every author's Top Priority List. That and Oprah Winfrey.

If you truly believe that your book has a strong reason to feature, or you have seen your topic being discussed on a daytime chat show, then contact the show producers. If they are interested they will request further information.

The best way to find show producers is to watch the programme and get the name off the credits as they come up at the end of the programme. Equally, the Radio Times and other TV listings will invariably cite the production company. Once you have the company name, do an online search via Google or any of the search engines.

Another route, if you are seeking to contact a range of production companies is to sign up with PACT who produce a directory that lists details of most Independent production companies in the UK. You can order this by calling 020 7331 6000 or going to www.pact.co.uk. It's not cheap (at around £700 per annum) so you may wish to try your local library. They might have a copy of 2005's edition; although this is the last hard copy edition they are producing. After this, it is an online database only.

### Independent national television

The same rules apply, I'm afraid. Watch the television and likely chat shows for a week or two. See who is most appropriate, what topics they talk about, the tone and stance they take on different issues. Have a good feel for the programme before contacting the show producers. You are far more likely to get a response by targeting it closely to the show's requirements than doing an all-out, generic approach.

Regional television covers Anglia Television, Border TV, Channel 4, Channel Five, GMTV, Grampian, Granada (hosts This Morning which is another popular chat show for authors), ITV (includes Carlton, Central, HTV), LWT,

Meridian Broadcasting, S4C, Scottish Television, Tyne Tees, UTV (Ulster), Yorkshire Television.

## Cable & Satellite

The world opens up for authors writing on specific subjects, as cable and satellite television enables entire channels to be devoted to specific subject matters, for example

The History Channel
Grant Way
Isleworth
Middx
TW7 5 QD
Tel: 0207 705 3000
Email: feedback@thehistorychannel.co.uk
Website: www.thehistorychannel.co.uk

The Discovery Channel
If you have an idea for a programme or series, please write to:
Commissioning Editor
Commissions Department
Discovery House
Chiswick Park Building 2
566 Chiswick Park Road
London W4 5YB

Or, alternatively you can register and submit your ideas online at:
http://producers.discovery.com

Travel Channel International Ltd
64 Newman Street
London
United Kingdom
W1T 3EF
Tel: +44 (0) 207 636 5401
Fax: +44 (0) 207 636 6424
Website: www.thetravelchannel.co.uk

God TV (Formerly The Christian Channel)
Angel House
Borough Road
Sunderland

Tyne and Wear SR1 1RW
Phone: 08706 070447
Email: info@god.tv
Website: www.god.tv

Another good way to approach is is looking at www.sky.com and seeing the different packages you can buy as they often cluster groups of channels to suit specific target audiences, for example:

**Variety:** includes Sky One, Two and Three; Living TV, Living TV2, Sci-Fi channel, Comedy TV, Bravo, Challenge TV, Channel E4, More.

**The Knowledge Mix:** Adventure One, Animal Planet, Discovery Channel / civilisation / Wings, History channel, National Geographic Channel, UK TV Documentary / History / People.

**Style & Culture TV:** Artsworld, Discovery Home & Health, Discovery Real Time, Discovery Travel & Living, Fashion TV, sky Travel, TV5, UKTV Food, UKTV Style & Gardens, Star Plus, TVEi, DW-TV.

As advised earlier, they are broadcasters and take their programmes from independent show producers. Watch the shows you wish to be on, see who the producing company is and contact them direct.

# ISSUE: *Pitch perfect*

The first time you talk to people about your book is probably the first time they will have heard about it. You are in control of their initial response to your book, and if you describe it in an inspirational and intriguing fashion, they will be interested. Added to which, the more you talk about your book and your activities, the better you articulate your pitch when it comes to the real thing.

### *Take the heat out of your pitch*
Few people were born with a sales skill that means they can sell sand to the Arabs or convert every conversation into a sale. You have to teach yourself just as you taught yourself to write a book. This means practising your pitch on a few 'unlikelies' first in order to perfect your approach. Leave your Holy Grail until you feel quite sure and steady, and don't build it up into something that it isn't. To them, you are just the next phone call along and they are just doing their job. They are not really the Holy Grail, and if it fails then just look for the next big goal.

High emotion clouds our judgement and our ability to articulate naturally and easily. Very few people achieve their objectives when they want something too badly.

### *Stay in control of your pitch*
When you approach the media and bookshops to tell them about your book, remember that YOU called THEM. This puts you in control of the conversation. In my experience, there are only three reactions:

(i)     Yes, they are interested and please send a press release.

(ii)    No, they are not interested

(iii)   They fumble for a suggestion to give you.

In which case you respond:

(i)      what's your email or postal address?
(ii)     Okay. Can I ask what you are interested in?
(iii)    Option a: have I contacted the right person?
          Option b: can I send you a press release?

Equally, they might seize control of the conversation halfway through your introductory sentence and bark "I haven't got time." If that's the case, then accept it and hang up. But don't get put off. The next person along will probably be sweet as pie.

### Focus on the NEWS not the product

We are inundated with stuff today, and the book market is glutted with books. Don't lead with 'yet another book' story but rather lead with the issue: "In response to the increasing trend to self-publishing, I am promoting a book..." Come to the point quickly.

### Be the expert

Your pitch should be slick and professional, and this often means sounding like the expert. Always sound sure, confident and expert.

### Should you pass off that you are the publisher rather than the author?

Nobody wants to be deceived but there is a way of phrasing your approach as *"I am launching a book called... and I wondered if you would be interested in getting some information on it with a view to..."* If you have practised your pitch adequately, you will sound like a marketing expert which will reassure potential buyers. They are more likely to listen to the whole of your pitch, and maybe even place an order. Obviously, when they ask if you are the author, simply say yes. Ultimately they are only interested in the news about the book, and some like the fact that they are talking to the author.

**Be professional :** *Clear, honest and succinct*

We all have experience of complete strangers phoning us up to sell us a new mobile phone payment plan and have them ask us how we are today and trying to be all buddy-buddy. I don't know if it works for you but it switches me right off. The best approach is to deliver a straight-up "I am calling you about…" pitch which saves everyone time and hassle.

# PART V

# PROMOTION AND PUBLICITY

**Creating promotional material**
        a.  Planning the content
        b.  Writing good copy
        c.  Design the material
        d.  Assessing the material

**When to create promotional material**

**What do I need?**

**Different types of promotional material**

**Different forms of promotional activity**

**Summary guidelines and rules**

# PROMOTING TO THE END CUSTOMER

The purpose of this chapter is to look at how you create a promotional campaign and what type of promotional material you may need in order to promote directly to your audience. Self-publishers cannot afford big budget campaigns, so the critical factor is how to create the minimum amount of material with the maximum amount of uses.

We stated at the outset of this book that promotion is the activity that pushes the book to a target audience, and publicity is the media noise around a book or author. The most important rule to remember when considering any form of promotion or publicity is to focus on telling the customer how your book meets their needs or will benefit them, rather than just announcing the product:

*Promotional material must revolve around the customer*
*not the product.*

The great truth about promotional material is that it can work "out of the box". Whereas the book jacket carries restrictions in terms of size, format, quantity of text, clarity of title and author name, fitting to category etc, the promotional material can be utterly creative and challenging as long as it communicates the right message. And you don't need to spend a fortune necessarily to create the most inspiring message. What you do need to do is brainstorm, using all the knowledge about your book that you have created to date.

There are basic rules, guides, tips and advice for creating promotional material but we will endeavour to keep it succinct and brief. The following rules can be applied to any printed material you might seek to produce, but it doesn't have to be restricted to print – you may choose to produce a gizmo which better communicates your message.

In this section, we are going to look at the following steps to creating the right promotional material, and conclude with a range of top rules and guidelines to adhere to:

- how to create great promotional material: the design and content rules
- when to create it
- how much to create
- different types of promotional *material*
- different types of promotional *activities*

## HOW TO CREATE GREAT PROMOTIONAL MATERIAL

### 1. Planning overall content

Can you see in a flash, in a second, what the point is of the press release or poster? If not, then it doesn't work.

Salesmen have acronyms to help guide them in planning overall content; these should be remembered when creating any communication about the book, whether it is the AI Sheet or press releases or promotional posters and leaflets.

AIDA = Attract, Interest, Desire and Action

- Atttract: Book covers must be arresting
- Interest: once they have picked the book up you want to keep them with you – give them intriguing sound-bites that actually tell them about the book;
- Desire: stimulate that desire by great endorsements that prove or substantiate the interesting sound-bites, secondary promises and brilliantly written copy, all of which give them the reason to believe.
- Action: finally, you give them a call to action, telling them how and where they can get it.

## FAB = Features, Advantages and Benefits

- This is where you would go back to your original blueprint marketing plan, but I don't recommend you slave over this one for too long as it can get confusing, and without a "voice" making the claims, it can sound a bit hollow.
- The "feature" is the WHAT & WHO ie. it is a self-help guide for exhausted career mothers; or, it is a teenage adventure fantasy for 12–16 year olds; or, a crime thriller with an unexpected twist.
- The "advantage" of a book is the "benefit" it brings to the individual ie. that a book is unique is an advantage to the seller as it means he has little competition; that it is unique is an advantage to the buyer as it means that finally you can access information you have been looking for. How would you use this information?

> **the book you have been searching for...**
> *How to juggle domestic housework*
> *and have time for your children*
> *whilst holding down a top-flight job!*

- In this case, you are implying that no other book exists on this subject and then telling the potential reader the benefit this book will bring. The advantage / benefit is easier to define for a non-fiction (particularly self-help) title, and harder for a fiction title. An "advantage" is a tangible element of the book ie. *a beautifully written, classic story of...* and the "benefit" will then tell the reader how they will feel having read it ie. *which will uplift you and make you appreciate loved ones more.*
- You will see that these are the elements from your marketing plan that you WANT people to be thinking about your book, as much as they are how you would hope someone would endorse your book. Hence the importance of endorsement as these claims are

particularly plausible when signed off by a famous and credible spokesperson. (see "*endorsements*" on page 167). As the author, you can still say all of these things either on a book jacket or on a poster, or other promotional material, but it must be carefully written so people can feel convinced by it.

## USP = Unique Selling Point and Unique Selling Proposition

- The unique selling *point* and *proposition* are actually the same principles expressed in two different ways, but I have distinguished them here because I believe it to be helpful. The unique selling point of a book is the strapline that you devised in the marketing plan, and this is consistently and generically applied when talking generally about the book ie. *A traditional adventure fantasy with a moody, modern-day teenager.*
- The unique selling *proposition* can be varied according to the different promotional activity ie.
  - Proposition 1 – *A Halloween tale for fourteen year olds*
  - Proposition 2 – *A roller-coaster fantasy adventure with one cynical teenager and several crazy, crabby witches*
  - Proposition 3 – *Alice and her dislikeable cousin get into hot water with some witches – should Alice run, or save her cousin? What would you do?*
- In other words, the proposition can be altered to talk to different specific audiences or needs, raising different intrigues, questions and reasons to purchase. The US-Proposition invariably pulls out specific elements of the books, where as the US-Point is about the overall book, and must remain consistent.

## KISS – Keep it Simple and Succinct (aka *Keep it Simple, Stupid*)

This doesn't really need explanation. As an author, you understand the principle about "economy with words".

- Express yourself succinctly and briefly without losing meaning:
  - o  Cover off the critical information
  - o  Make the Promise
  - o  Substantiate the promise; provide a reason to believe
  - o  Expand the description, flesh it out
  - o  Tell them where they can buy it – web etc
- Use design to punch out the key points:
  - o  Consider how you will use capitals, bold, boxes, font types, font size, space, headers, colours, background graphics, foreground images and pictures, endorsements, web details etc.
- Work the words:
  - o  Always use the best word that is the most appropriate and expresses *exactly* what you want to say.
  - o  The English language comprises some 900,000 words (www.languagemonitor.com), and you should be able to find a word that captures your intended message exactly; failing that, use two words (see next).

## 2. Write great copy

- Write great copy by knowing your audience and talking directly to them, addressing their very specific needs (see *Arrest the Audience* next)
- Journalists generally believe, when writing even the briefest of articles, that you must:
  - o  Tell them what you're going to say
  - o  Say it
  - o  Confirm what you have told them or what it means to them
- This same principle should be borne in mind when creating a poster, particularly a poster that is calling for

people to do a specific action such as enter a competition or attend an event. Announce the competition/event, tell them about it then confirm to them what it means to them; lastly, the informational panel tells them how they enter/attend.

- Don't overdo the adjectives – people cannot take on board too many visual images.
- Avoid meaningless extra words; every word must actively contribute. On a poster, try removing each word in a sentence; if its removal does not alter or clarify the meaning, then lose it.
- Avoid hackneyed and over-used words. These keep changing as copywriters shift from one synonym to the next. If you want to be thorough, you might consider investing in some writing guides or reference books.
- Create an image to help people see something in a new light ie. ice-hot ice-cream.
- Use active verbs "you can see" like tumbling, zany, ferocious, ethereal etc.
- Don't patronise; be honest.
- Don't repeat the word "book" too often.
- Keep asking yourself why? Will this make me buy it?
- Offer the expert and provide a guarantee - endorser – author, spokesperson, endorser

## 3. Arrest the audience

In order to talk directly to your audience and grab their attention, you need to say something loud and clear that will resonate with a thought or issue they have been pondering:

- Make it personal *"Are you tired of commuting to work?"*
- Call to an audience group: *"Are you thinking of self-publishing?"*

- target the benefits of the book to the audience group: *"Outperform yourself in the workplace: 20 easy ways to do better than your best."*
- ask a meaningful question or set a challenge, *"How will you keep your children safe?"*
- promise results *"Look and feel younger"*
- raise a topic *"why schoolchildren are failing"*
- quote somebody *"15% of our food is genetically modified"*
- Use the imperative *" See how…"*
- Use the present tense *" Research shows…"*
- Avoid negatives and excessive words; talk positively by starting with the benefit ie.

> *Free your mind by learning how to mentally throw out rubbish and burdens*

Rather than: *This book will help you to free your mind…*
- Give facts not opinions:
  - 20,000 sold means little
  - 20,000 sold at launch starts to add value
  - 20,000 art lovers are already benefiting from this book completes the image

## 4. Professional design

Some people can lay out a page purely on instinct alone because, as a shopper, we have been inundated with sales material since the first day we spent our own pocket money. But whether you believe you can do this or not, it is worth reading the below and studying several different forms of promotional material. It will improve what you ultimately create.

### Content of visual communication

- Headline: your headline needs to arrest people's attention – and not only that, but specifically the attention of your audience group who will go out of their way to buy your book (see Arrest the Audience).

- Sub-text to expand on headline
  This is in a smaller font than the headline, and follows on from the claim made; it usually provides an answer, explanation, clarification or emphasis to the headline.

- Book jacket
  The image of the book jacket has to be very prominent whilst not overshadowing the headline. The two must work easily together, but ultimately it is the book that you are selling and you want to ensure people have it in their heads.

- Descriptive text
  You need to provide some concrete information, but keep sentences short and succinct. Don't feel tempted to say everything as nobody will read a solid block of text.

- Colours, fonts and background imagery/texture
  - People subconsciously take on board the overall colours, choice of fonts and general imagery, understanding the meanings behind them.
  - This must support and work the overall theme of the poster.
  - Don't choose a font just because you like it, but choose it because of the semiotic* understanding behind it. Just type 'fonts' onto Google and you will get directed to loads of sites; I quite like Dafont.com as you can write your text in the font and see it on screen which is helpful.
  - If you have any associated graphics, make sure it fits in with the overall tone your book is trying to convey. I felt that the cartoon graphics in my two books accurately summed up the outraged frustration most authors feel, whilst the cartoon style demonstrated that this is not a life or death situation; writing, self-

publishing and self-selling should be enjoyable past-times.

- Substantiation ie. endorsement, guarantee or comment
  - o After making a host of sales-y claims and promises, you need to provide some form of substantiation or guarantee. What is the reason for the customer to believe, or is it all just sales-hype.
  - o Shoppers in Western societies are particularly suspicious of empty promises, yet are happy to be sold something of <u>value</u>. Offer a promise, substantiate the promise, and make sure your book delivers on that promise. If it does, they will also buy your next book.

\* *"semiotics" is the study of codes and shapes that take on different meanings in different cultures.*

- Flashes
  - o You often see star-shaped or banner-shaped 'flashes' on posters or packaging, and these are used to offer a promotional claim such as a price discount, new edition, limited edition, signed copy, something free with each copy etc.
  - o Use only one maximum per piece of material.
  - o Price discounts are usually flashed in red & yellow, which are classic price-fighting, value colours.
  - o "Added value" flashes are usually done in premium colours ie. golds, royal tones (purples & blues) teamed with white, or contrasting colours. If the rest of the poster is dark and moody, the flash can be pale, pastel shades; and vice verse.
  - o Free gizmos are usually pictured with the word FREE; be sure to include parameters such as *'with each book bought'* otherwise people have the right to demand their free-with-no- purchase-necessary gizmo.

- Where to buy and contact details, including any dates and other important information.
  - o This is the must-have information that people will look for once the rest of the promotional material has done its job. Where can they get it? When is it available? Who can they contact?
  - o People generally look for a web address in this area but you can make it bigger than the rest of the information. In fact, you may even make it nearly as big as the headline in the same colour.
  - o It usually features at the bottom of a poster or other printed literature.

### Hierarchy of communication

There is a difference between the order down the page that you <u>place</u> text, and what you <u>see</u> first when you stand back. This is called the hierarchy of communication.

| Hierarchy | Order on page |
|---|---|
| Headline | headline |
| Image | sub-headline |
| Sub-headline | image |
| Endorsement | descriptive text |
| Descriptive text | endorsement |
| Informational panel | informational panel |

In terms of order, headings are generally at the top of a page, although they can work in the centre of the page. They are very rarely positioned at the bottom of a page. The book jacket image should be central and prominent, maybe ranged left or right to allow descriptive text to sit alongside it.

Go out into the street or down to the train station and have a look at some posters, and ask yourself what you see first. Compare that to the order down the page in which it is positioned, and it is different. Equally, have a look at any branded product in your house ie. a bottle of shampoo and you will see a simple order of information:

- o Brand: always large and clear
- o Sub-brand or variant: follows the brand name and is distinctive; often supported by colour of the packaging
- o Image: focuses on the need or benefit; targets the intended user
- o Descriptor: needs or benefits-based to reiterate who will use it and why
- o Volume: factual information
- o Promotional flash: sometimes some additional information appears – Now Even Bigger, New Formula etc. Always done as some form of badge or banner, usually in Red or Yellow which are standard 'promotional' colours.

5. **Assess your material**
   - Does it work?
     - o Talk about it, visualise it, mock it up and research to hear the flaws
     - o Sleep on it
     - o Stand back from it both physically and mentally. We tend to work close up, sometimes forgetting how 'new' the whole subject, idea and product may be to others. You need to attract, inspire, inform and make sure they have absolutely understood that this is for them, and they will enjoy it.
       - ▪ How does it attract them?
       - ▪ What does it say?
       - ▪ How does it call them to action?
   - Remove all the words – what do the visuals say? Put greek* into the text panels to assess how the text works (font size, emphasis, length, quantity etc).
   - Did you proof-read it?

*Designers 'greek' copy into place as they are often designing whilst the copywriter is writing. They merely know the essence of what is being said, so they know where to bold and make small, how blocks of text should work etc. In fact, their 'greek' is usually Latin, but you can just key in any letters. TIP: Remember to add spaces.*

## 6. Be flexible

The huge advantage that the independent author/publisher has over the 'big guys' is the ability to hand-sell, to talk directly to the audience, to find out their needs and adapt. The wise self-publisher will exploit these rare opportunities that are open to him.

- If you are creating a mail-out, consider printing and sending out a small sample. Ring the people you issued it to and gauge their reaction. Let's say that you have sent a flyer to bookshop buyers... were they interested, and if not, ask them why. Invariably people are honest. Aside from "I'm not buying at the moment" (which you can't control) they may say "I couldn't see what you wanted me to do" or "it's not appropriate for this time of year" etc. In which case this gives you focus to adapt your flyer and ensure that the call to action is clearer, or the reason to act / buy / believe / stock / display etc is clearer.
- Fine tune and send out some more. Again, ring to gauge reaction. When people start saying "I'm thinking about stocking it" or they order it then you know you have got it right. So then send it out more widely.
- Consider doing many smaller flyers for different audiences, creating master design and tweaking the words.

# WHEN TO CREATE PROMOTIONAL MATERIAL

Many people aim to get their promotional material ready to coincide with the book launch. However, the wise author has built in a good three months of pre-marketing activity whilst promoting their book to the trade, collating endorsements and trying to get stocks in high street bookshops. Authors are more likely to get books in bookshops if they prove viable marketing activity, and this often means demonstrating the promotional plans.

When you approach a book chain, send your promotional material along with a copy of your book, itemising how you are promoting your book in a certain locality or community. When you approach independent bookstores, you cannot afford to send your book each time, but you can send a piece of promotional material that should reflect the high production values and appeal of your book.

Remember, retailers seek to retail. If you demonstrate your involvement in pushing sales, they are more likely to want to participate in trying to sell your book.

However, if you try to produce it too early, the chances are the book cover or back text will have changed, or the page count or price of the book. There is generally only one window of time when initial promotional material can be created, and that is during the printing of your book.

## WHAT DO I NEED?

Self-publishing authors need to create the minimum amount of material with the maximum amount of uses. After all, you are ultimately trying to sell a book and do not want to be saddled with 1000 posters as well as unsold books, so don't create anything you won't use.

Below, we are going to look at a list of the different types of promotional material people generally use, and when to use the different pieces. Go through this list and mark a few that sound of interest to your needs. Then go back through the marked items and see how you can get it down to creating just two items maximum for all your promotional requirements.

You do not want to create a new piece of material for each and every occasion. When creating postcards, flyers, posters, leaflets etc, you should do the minimum that you require and the maximum to gain greater economies of scale – you need to work out the maths, and don't forget that you will have to pay for a designer for each piece of material they create.

How much you wish to invest is dependent on the sales potential of your book, (so they say), but this is unanswerable at the outset so I always work on the premise that the promotional material should not add more than 50p per book maximum. This is explored in Chapter VIII Marketing Budget.

## One Generic item

Every book requires one form of promotional material that is generic about the book and where to obtain it. This can be handed out to all and sundry, and it should be small enough that people will keep it – either pinned to a notice board at home or in their handbags or wallets. The purpose of it should be to remind people to go out and buy the book.

When talking to journalists, you want to have something that acts as a 'business card' to remind them to write that piece about your book. When talking to book-buyers, leave them with a card to remind them to follow up on your conversation, to host an event or simply to place an order for your book.

This may take the form of a business card, a postcard, a bookmark or a A5 glossy leaflet. Keep it simple and clear – include a dominant size image of the book jacket and ISBN on the front with summary text on back about your book, headlined with your succinct one liner and signed off with information about where to buy your book. Include a web address or contact details, as relevant.

Because you are intending to hand this generic item out as widely and broadly as possible, you would be wise to do a decent print run quantity. If you have 500 books to sell, it may be wise to do 1000 postcards; you then have plenty enough to place a postcard in every book you sell and hand out freely.

**One or two specific items**

You may need a couple of items that are specific to an event or activity. This may either be made as a bespoke item, or by adapting the generic item by 'over-bannering' a poster or 'over-stickering' a postcard or bookmark.

Events often require an eye-catching display poster to announce the activity and to use as a display in a bookshop, in schools and libraries and any other attended events. You may need a poster to announce a competition and one to announce an event. These clearly cannot be doubled up, therefore look for economies of scale in the design and keeping the print run very small.

If designing several posters for different needs, you would be wise to devise a consistent layout for posters – space for headline; book image, strapline and author name consistently positioned; explanation text panel and all where to buy/contact details consistently positioned. Then allow the background imagery, colours and fonts of headlines to change accordingly to suit the promotional activity.

It will not be worth your while to do less than one hundred full colour, glossy posters as most printers will have this as a minimum run.

If the event you are running is a very specific one-off event, then you may as well just run off 10-20 full colour laser copies at your local print shop.

## DIFFERENT TYPES OF PROMOTIONAL MATERIAL

There are lots of forms of promotional material, the main ones are listed below but many of these you simply won't need, such as shelf-talkers, dump-bins and display panels unless you are planning a road-show, doing events, talks, workshops etc.

The different forms of promotional material are explained below, together with a brief summary of how the different pieces get used. Then we will look at how to create it with the minimum amount of energy and fuss.

**AI sheets and press releases**
See the sample AI Sheet on pp 80 together with the guidelines for creating an AI sheet. It is unnecessary to repeat again here, but this is a form of promotional material and its content will revolve around the marketing information you create at the outset.

**Catalogue and online listings**
This is the most common form of promotional material that self-publishing authors will use. It means creating nothing other than the content itself, then emailing the text and book jacket image, but it is a critical form of promotion and important to get the content right.

**Hand-outs & announcements**
- Posters and show-cards
  - Most shops have limited space, so you are wiser to do A4 or A3. Anything bigger becomes unwieldly and space limitations can make it un-usable.
  - If you have A4 posters made, and require a "wall" of design, remember you can always get large pieces of A2, A1 or A0 size board from an art shop and create your own display by arranging the posters on the board.
  - Show-cards are usually posters on card with a self-standing mechanism at the back. Again, for big name authors they can be six foot high as space is not an issue; however for unknown authors, you may wish to get a couple of posters stuck down onto board and

fashion your own stand-mechanism at the back on the off-chance there is a space in the window display to put the show-card with a few books.

o *Your printer should be able to help you with producing these, and any of the below which are ink on paper or card.*

- Flyers
  o These are usually glossy with full-colour on both sides, printed A4 and folded either vertically or horizontally. They are obviously light-weight to send and hold a lot of information.
  o People often use these when sending out 'returnable' information ie. discount vouchers, order forms, competition entries etc, as it is easy for them to detach a section to post back, whilst retaining the rest to remind them.

- Book jackets
  o A common practice is to ask your printer to run on the cover print run in order to provide you with very cheap covers for promotional purposes. You can then use these as a 'folder' to add home-printed, tailored information such as a press release or news release.
  o They can double up in display by folding the cover and creating a nice fan of the front cover, then display the back cover separately.

- Sales presenters and press packs
  o These are the folders that hold all of the sales material should you ever get a chance to pitch your book at a Sales Conference. Publishers are slowly reducing their sales reps as the main book channels narrow and buying becomes centralised; and independents can use the book catalogues and distributor sales reps as their information channels.

- o You can use the presenter to present to bookshops if you are trudging the streets and hand-selling, but it is a rare bookshop owner who will take more than a flyer, business card or postcard as he does not want to be burdened with too much paperwork.
- o If you are hosting a launch event, you may wish to create a folder in which to insert your Press Pack, which will hold the press release, author biography, endorsements and promotional activities such as events and offers.

- Postcards
  - o Postcards are fun items that people readily pick up and pocket at events or displays.
  - o Book buyers happily store them or prop them up somewhere as a reminder if they are potentially interested.
  - o Customers can send them on to friends they think will like the book, without having to go to the expense of buying them the book.

- Bookmarks
  - o A popularly-used item which serves as both a reminder to a person to buy the book as well as being functional.
  - o Try to be creative ie. by having a serrated "business-card" size panel that people can tear off and put in their wallets to remind themselves to buy the book next time they are out.

- Business cards
  - o Every businessman has a business card, and authors really should be no different. They are ideal for leaving with shop-keepers, publishers and agents they meet in

their search for contacts, journalists as well as the reading public.

- o Many self-publishing authors swear by them as they are too often requested copies by distant family, friends and colleagues, but don't always want to give it away for free.
- o Handing a business card with the book details on it is a subtle way of saying "go and buy it".

- Cards with gizmo attached
  - o If you have a little freebie made, make sure it comes with some form of card or paper that people can pocket to remind themselves of the book and therefore encourage them to buy it.
  - o There are corporate gift companies to be found on line. One I located is www.emcadgifts.co.uk who do a wide range including badges, bags, pens and calendars. Others I found on the web include:
    - www.gb-gifts.co.uk;
    - www.image-logo.co.uk;

- Display panels
  - o If you are planning a road-show, you may wish to have a portable display system. One such company is Contour Direct Limited who can provide you with a great range of solutions from the very cost effective to the slightly-more-investment-required but very impactful and portable stands. Contact them on systems@contourdigital.com

- Book stands and dump-bins
  - o Also if you are planning a road-show, you may require a method of displaying your books. I would recommend you <u>don't</u> get a dump-bin as this looks cheap, but one good system is a cardboard book stand.

- o You can brand it with you book title, author name and background graphics/colours, having web addresses, flashes and other promotional information down the sides.
- o These usually tilt backwards to give a good visual display, yet are lightweight to carry around (when empty of books).

- Point of purchase (sale) material and shelf-talkers
  - o You may hear people talking about POP or POS material and shelf-talkers. POP and POS are the same thing – POP material is point-of-purchase material and POS is point of sale material. These include items such as sample, glossy recipe cards positioned by a recipe book, or "shelf-talkers" which are banners set into the shelves, cards stuck onto the shelves or even the projected, dangly things bouncing around on clear plastic selling something about the product or book. The chances of you being allowed to put something like this up in a shop are remote as publishers pay handsomely for this.
  - o At best, you may wish to invest in some Perspex picture frames or small table-top stands in order to put your postcard or book cover by the till on the day of an event, over-bannered with Author Instore Today.
  - o One company I found on the web are www.poscentre.co.uk; contact phone number 01279 207211. They have an online catalogue, or you can order one direct, or even drop in to see them up in Roydon.

- Something completely challenging and off-the-wall:
  - o think out of the box. If you are trying to tell people that your book is all about a "A Year in France Growing

Wine" down-sizing story, then make your poster, leaflet or launch invites look like a wine label.

o The best way to create the most eye-catching, attention-grabbing, bizarrely-appropriate kind of idea is to get a bunch of friends round, open the wine and start brain-storming. The most curious yet relevant ideas invariably emerge.

o But don't forget that whatever curious connection is made, it must be appropriate to HOW you will use it.

o Never force-fit promotional activity; people spot the discord quickly, and shrug it off as implausible and a waste of their precious time.

**Advertising**

In Chapter 6 ("Customer awareness and demand") we looked at the alternative forms of advertising which you can use for the different types of content that you are communicating. In terms of WHAT to say in an advertisement can vary widely, and you will choose the different format of advertisement depending on your objective:

- the book as it relates to specific audience or group of people (display ad or advertorial calling to them)
- the book as it relates to specific, upcoming date (headline with the need that the date signifies)
- a discount voucher between certain dates or at a certain shop (a display ad booked for a certain page in a magazine or newspaper)
- announcing an event (a display ad or a classified ad in a WHAT'S ON page).

Remember, when planning the content of your advertisement, you will need to assess it on two levels:

1. An attention-grabbing headline that arrests the target audience. Advertisements work in an environment where all panels of information have headlines, and

many people read an entire newspaper or magazine by headlines only. This truth is beneficial to self-publishing authors; make sure the headline pulls them in and they may pause long enough to read the copy.

2.  Overall impression. Stand back from it and see if it has a clear 'invitation' and 'call to action'. Does it talk to its target audience clearly and pull in the right people who are likely to rush out to buy the book?

## DIFFERENT FORMS OF PROMOTIONAL ACTIVITY

The most effective promotional activities are the ones that centre on your book. For instance, if you are promoting a regional cookery book then create a set of laminated recipe cards and hand them out at an event or function. Ensure the cards clearly point people to where they can buy your book.

Depending on your personal circumstances, I would recommend that you plan to do at least four promotional campaigns per annum, with a set number of phone calls day ie. if you have a full time job, then 1 phone call a day is at least something. If you are not working, then aim for at least 5 phone calls a day – 1 new contact and four follow-ups.

Below are a range of ideas that have been previously used by other authors I have worked with, and you can use as ideas or inspiration to start devising your own activity.

**Within the book:**
- o   If you have a website, ensure your website address is clearly visible on the cover and inside page.
- o   Create an unusual book package ie. unusual inks, textures or substrates on book jacket; package it in a box, wrap it, ribbon it
- o   Tie in with an artist; produce posters of the front cover with title/author and no other text.

- o Make limited or special editions ie. a signed & numbered hard-copy run or limited run with a different cover.
- o Combine books with other items ie. sell it as a kit. Children's books often sell with an audio tape, travel books with map of that country or area (from tourist office).
- o Bonus inserts ie. reader offers, a certificate or coupons for buyers to get a discount on the next book in the series, or to send off for a collectible toy.
- o Encourage further orders ie. insert a postcard to send to a friend
- o Include summarised reader testimonials and fan letters etc (Patti Hales)
- o Offer a limited amount of signed and 'doodled' copies
- o Include a CD of downloadable images, pdf files, games & puzzles etc.

## To lead people to the book:

- Reader offers (in printed media)
- Competitions (on radio, in printed media, sponsored with business/brand)
- Incentives and freebies (at events, online, radio, media)
- Associated events (get your book offered as the prize)
- Use online to promote offline and vice verse

## Use the media

- Seize news opportunities as they arise; watch the papers and react quickly when your subject matter arises
- Write your own features or interview; write list of questions you would want to be asked
- Advertise:
    - o Trade journals and freebie magazines
    - o consumer magazines
    - o local media

### Enlist the help of friends and connections
- Clubs, businesses, associations, opinion-leaders, spokespeople and book reviewers
- Arrange launch announcements and put into newsletters, company inhouse magazines, alumni publications, within your old college, club bulletins, company PR department
- Email all your friends to announce your book launch
- Enlist other sellers – even your family and friends around the country

### Create new connections
- Attend trade events, conventions and conferences
- Always carry a business card or leaflet with you
- Contact the writer's circles and reading clubs

### Form a consortium of authors in same genre or talking to same audience ie. education, old people's homes etc.
- Create a calendar to send out with orders, to booksellers
- Consider booklet of abridged lead titles or first chapters
- Share promotions or events with other small and relevant parties ie. other authors, small bookshops, manufacturers

### Look at associated businesses, retail or leisure outlet opportunities
- Merchandise tie-ins with an interested manufacturer – get list of manufacturers from British Library
- Get book into printed catalogues and online catalogues – search online or get listing from the British Library
- Non book retailers; remember to approach their supply chain
- National Trust, museums, theme parks
- Associations – Directory of Associations
- Get sponsorship from a business

## Other

- Enter competitions, prizes and awards: the Handbook lists many of these. Read the submission criteria and submit only where relevant.
- Sponsor an award: slightly more audacious, but if you can link with a business who is prepared to work together, this can create a bit of interest and noise.
- Donate to charity auctions: if you have a very topic specific book, then you can donate a copy of your book to a fund-raising event they are hosting. Often they give away free goodie bags and are happy to let you put a leaflet in for free because you are donating a prize.

## Use the web *(see Online Selling for further information)*

- Make sure people can find you – have meaningful web name, good search terms, update regularly
- Maximise the number of sites selling your book
- Be part of the online book and literary community (comprehensively listed and covered in the section on Online Selling).
- Consider internet auction sites if you do a limited edition
- Link as widely as you can
- Submit your book to Google Booksearch programme
- Consider Google ads
- Amazon: reviews, advertising, search inside, marketplace
- Create an E-newsletter
- Get interviewed by another site's e-zine
- Set up your own blogs
- Participate in other Chat Forums, or go to chat rooms
- Sign-off emails with your contact details
- Give away a free chapter on the internet
- Enter website awards in your category
- Run a competition and fork out for one great (and relevant) prize.

## SUMMARY GUIDELINES AND RULES

### RULE 1: Do not reinvent the wheel every time

- Go back to your marketing plan and use this to take out the essential information. It is important that the message remains consistent; you can build on it and bend it to suit alternative promotional activities, but always ensure it links back to the main message.
- Every piece of promotional material must contain the following:
  - Book title
  - Author name
  - ISBN & Price
  - Summary description (15 words max)
  - *50-word synopsis (optional, if space allows)*
  - Front book jacket image
  - Web / email address
  - Publisher/distributor name & phone number
  - Where available from

### RULE 2: Make it easily adaptable

- Adapt the piece of material depending on its
  (i) intended usage and (ii) intended audience.
  - Think hard how different audiences will want to see/hear what you are announcing. What is most relevant to them? What will catch their attention? What will motivate them to "sell" it into their friends and community?
- Set a graphic style so you can easily take the design from poster to business card, for example:
  - Have a visual style that becomes synonomous with your book.
  - Set a range of fonts that you can use in all communication, and builds recognition.
  - Own a colour palette that people will associate with your book.

## RULE 3: Make it multi-purpose

- Standardise a layout so you can easily swap the background graphic to suit a different usage or audience, and change the headline easily whilst not moving its position. Make it easy on yourself and your designer – as this will make it cheaper to buy.
- Allow space so you can over-sticker or over-banner. You will want to use posters to announce different messages:
  o Author signing event on *date*
  o Author instore today
  o As seen/heard on *local TV/radio*
  o Endorsed by *relevant body*

## RULE 4: Print as many as you will use

- You should create as many as you can comfortably dispose of to the relevant people without any of it seeing the rubbish bin. Plan to keep nothing.
- If you are doing a local launch, then get only 25 posters done.
- If you are planning many events, then print 100 posters that you can adapt.
- If you get 500 postcards made, then distribute 500 postcards.

## RULE 5: Make design work

- Use words, layout, colour and graphics to get the message across. Every element should be working hard to talk to the viewer.
- Don't have a font-fest on your poster. Pick two at maximum. Have a "character" font for the headlines, sub-headline and larger text which brings your message to life, and a simpler one for explanation text to keep it legible and clear. Don't start messing around

with crazy fonts on small, explanatory text. People get annoyed when they can't read the small print.

- Avoid excessively busy backgrounds as no-one will bother to read the words.
- Ensure text sits over one colour or shade. If you have a heavily contrasting background image, you will have difficulty ensuring the words can be seen when all typeset in one colour.
- Don't be afraid of space. Most novice designers fill up every available space whereas you should allow messages space to work. And remember, you also want space to over-banner or over-sticker different messages.
- Look professional. If you print out what looks like a home-made poster, people will sub-consciously read into it that it is home-made, lacking the support and glitz of a store.

### RULE 6: Have a call to action
- Ensure any promotional material has a call to action; tell people what you want them to do as a result of reading the promotional material. State clearly where people can find your book and don't promote anything until it is available to buy.

### RULE 7: Bring the promise to life
- It must bring the promise or benefit to life:
  - It is a piece of promotional material about the book and must clearly link to the book.
  - It is to enable people to understand what is contained within the book, and inspire them to read it.
  - It is a promise

## RULE 8: Be copy confident

- Write good motivating copy that sells to a potential buyer the reason to buy it. "Sell the sizzle, not the steak".

- Proof-read each and every word thoroughly. Nobody will buy a book if there are typos in the promotional material. Usually the biggest typo is in the headline or title of the book because authors skip over the reading of such obvious and prominent information.

# PART VI

# DIRECT MARKETING

**Direct mail**

**Direct response**

**Direct email**

**"Telesales"**

**Summary Guidelines**

# DIRECT MARKETING

The purpose of this section is to investigate the alternative methods of talking directly to your audience without going through the booktrade or media.

*"Self-publishing is what you make it."*

Direct marketing presents a massive opportunity for independent authors in a way that mainstream publishers simply cannot compete. Direct marketing enables you to get very close to your customers, finding out exactly what they want (build a knowledge base) and to create your own database over a period of time.

Self-publishing authors can choose to invest personal time to build knowledge banks, databases and communities that are relevant to their specific subject whilst mainstream publishers have to take a far more generalist approach as the individual budgets required to hand-sell simply don't exist.

Most authors report a wide range of reaction, from being totally ignored to prompting orders to be placed and selling several hundred books as a result. It is worth pointing out that generally when your approach is completely ignored, it is because you are talking to the wrong people *or* talking to the right people but with the wrong message.

Direct marketing will take the form of any of the following activities, and can be best summarised as the marketing activities with no middle-men or media:

1. Direct marketing by post ie. mail-outs
2. Direct marketing by email
3. Direct marketing by phone ie. "telesales"
4. Direct marketing by events ie. book launch, talks at festivals and fairs, workshops at courses etc.

## 1. DIRECT MARKETING BY POST (aka direct mail)

Many recommend against direct mail, claiming it to be a useless waste of money as the majority of recipients don't listen or respond to it. Others fundamentally believe in its value.

The issue is largely in the definition, however. Most people think of a direct mail campaign being a 20,000 mail-out to a vast database of names. But the independent author should see direct mail as a far smaller activity, comprising a series of small direct mail-outs to a pre-planned group or community. This can take the form of news releases and promo-cards to bookshops, targeted communities or households, and/or a direct email campaign.

The fact is, for most independent authors, you will need to engage in some form of direct mail in order to get your message to a broader audience.

### Direct promotion mail-out

The general consensus of opinion is that an all-out, blanket-blast of communication does not work. This is not to say that independent authors should never engage in any form of large-scale marketing, but always bear in mind that it is a risky strategy. It is a hit-or-miss activity. If you have bought the database, it may be outdated (people change jobs very quickly in today's world) and lists tend to be too generalist with limited ability to target by specific search criteria.

*The cons of a vast mail-out*
o It can be very expensive – designing, artworking and printing the literature, buying the database and paying for postage, given that the success rate for direct mail is around 1%. This means that for every 100 cards you send out, you may receive one sale. When you are selling a product with a large profit margin, it can be worth it but books tend to work on a very small margin.

o   If you only use the database once, you achieve no economies of scale.

o   A vast mail-out can also be very haphazard. Half the data may have been 'dirty' or heavily duplicated, and you will never know.

*The pros of a vast mail-out*

o   Large-scale direct mail-outs may provide some book sales if you are planning a series of announcements, or can use the database on several occasions to remind your target audience of your book and give them new news.

o   Direct mail can work if you team up with a number of other self-publishers who may be targeting a similar market or genre – the trick is to find them and you can waste as much time searching for them as you can searching for your audience.

o   Mail-outs can also provide some level of return if you use it as an opportunity to gather information. Most mail-outs are a one-way journey ie. a promotion. Rather than implementing a 'direct promotion' where the mail-out falls into a silent black hole, consider doing a 'direct response' (see below).

*When does a large-scale mail-out work?*

o   Large-scale mail-outs are most effective when you can amortise the cost by re-using the data time and time again, cleaning it and updating it as you go.

   ▪   For example: for books with a membership or subscription-based potential, where you might be implementing an ongoing newsletter to provide updates and developments. Book-clubs have always done very well from large scale direct mailing because they have honed their lists through memberships, closely monitor customer demand and categorise their books into subject areas.

o   Large-scale mail-outs work when you have a high profit margin item, or are approaching people that would potentially buy in volume. A mail-out for a car manufacturer is obviously very different for the self-publishing author.

o   If you are planning to publish a series of books, or an ongoing list of subject-specific books such as lifestyle, gardening, cookery etc. then buying the database at the outset could prove beneficial.

o   Large-scale direct mail-outs also work better for very subject-specific books with very specific audience needs ie. academic or medical texts, where you can buy a regularly-used list (ie. likely to be clean and up-to-date) and sell directly into establishments.

If you are interested in doing a mail-out, one good company to talk to is JEM (www.jem.co.uk):

*JEM provides a comprehensive range of distribution, mailing and digital printing services to book publishers which enable them to promote new book titles and distribute catalogues to libraries and booksellers. JEM provides shared and solus mailings of publicity leaflets, catalogues or book covers to a carefully created and regularly updated list of libraries and booksellers. JEM also provides a short run, digital print service. Phone: 01233 214022.*

Large-scale mail-outs are simply one method of implementing a direct mail programme, and these are usually a one-way communication ie. they are a direct mail *promotion*. They provide no feedback, no additional value and can be difficult to measure the success of. To gain the maximum value of a mail-out, you should use it to gather information.

Information has a value, both to yourself and other people. Targeted marketing is also known as precision marketing or customer-related marketing. One way to add value to a mail-out is to consider a direct *response* programme so you can gather data that you can use again and again in the future.

## Direct Response

This is where you create a direct mail-out that invites people to respond. The value is in building your own knowledge bank and database that is specific to your needs, therefore the question you ask them will need to inform you if this person has a commercial value to you.

However this is not the *question* you *can* ask them; the real trick is in asking them the right question. Most people are too busy today to bother with filling out a form and putting it in a post-box for somebody else's research, and no doubt to be added to a database where they then run the risk of being deluged in the future with leaflets and sales pitches.

They will, however, make the effort if the promise is to make their life easier somehow without them having to do anything. If you can create a direct response campaign that achieves this whilst meeting your own objectives, then go for it.

For example, you are planning a series of crime thriller novels which revolve around the central issue that most crime is alcohol-driven. Therefore, creating a mail-out that that addresses this social issue "Do you believe pubs should be open for 24 hours a day?" will draw a reaction. Invite opinion and demonstrate how/where response will be announced.

People are also more likely to respond when they know where and how the information will be used. If your research is intended to become part of a published article then tell them. People like to know that their opinion has influenced change.

*Make news.*
*Send your findings to the local and/or national papers.*

The real benefits in a direct response campaign will be in how efficiently you can create the optimal database and how many times you then plan to use it. Remember, that postage is expensive on a large and ongoing scale and your per unit profit margins are very low. Therefore you only want to be chasing outlets where individual orders will be a minimum of 100 books or so.

*The advantages of direct response*
o   Measure success. If you are investing £2,000 in a mail-out, you should at the very least be aiming to assess the value of this expenditure. Knowing where sales were gained will help inform your future marketing activities.
o   Personalised lists to suit your needs. Direct response can cut the rubbish data out of your list and ensure that every future mail-out using that list is well-targeted. This should increase your potential rate of return.
o   Information has a value. Firstly, you can use it for future publications by yourself, or even to set up a business on the strength of the book you have created. Maybe you can sell or rent the database to other self-publishing authors who are targeting a similar audience to you, but are not directly competitive to you.
o   Create a community. Some new communities don't have a 'centre' and maybe the creation of your database results in the creation of a community. Set up a website and act as the central pillar to that community. Other publishers will then be approaching YOU to buy access to that community.
o   Create a newsletter which people can subscribe to, thus expanding your list.

*The drawbacks of direct response*
o   If you don't ask the right question, you won't get a response. It must provide real and relevant information to

you, whilst asking them a question that they will WANT to answer.

o One truth that will be becoming increasingly evident to anyone reading this is that this form of activity is a fairly full-on job in itself. If you are running a day-time job, you will find yourself spending hours every evening developing this data and maintaining it. If you are lucky, at some point it starts to become profitable but much personal time has been invested at the outset.

o Also, to encourage a response you will have to offer FREEPOST or Business Reply, which has just increased your postage bill. One way around this is to try to use email wherever possible, and this is looked at below.

o The questions you can ask to respondents also tend to be restrictive, insofaras you cannot bombard them with as many questions as you may like to ask. Keep it to one primary question and a couple of support questions such as "what are you looking for in this subject-matter?" and "how like to be approached?" (ie. try to get email addresses wherever possible).

## 2. DIRECT MARKETING BY EMAIL (aka direct email)

With direct Email, you eradicate the postage bill immediately which means that after the original time-investment to build the database, you can implement it for free time and time again. To create an email database, the chances are you have had to implement a 'tele-sales' process first in order to get people's correct addresses, and this is time-consuming but this is important information for your knowledge bank.

*Advantages of direct email*

◊ Direct emailing is clearly considerably cheaper in terms of producing the material to mail out.

◊ If the data is correct, then your email goes directly to whom it is intended.

◊    They can respond quickly and easily if they are interested in your promotion.

◊    You can clean your database more easily – bounced back emails should be removed from your list. Once left with 10 'dead' addresses, you can more easily investigate to find the correct email address.

◊    Once you have the database, it is so quick, easy and cheap to mail-out again in the future.

*Disadvantages of direct emailing*

◊    Bear in mind that your beautifully laid out announcement may be lost on non-HTML recipients – you cannot completely control how they receive the information.

◊    Attachments are rarely opened or downloaded.

◊    Unknown senders can be hived off into a Junk or Spam mail box where you will never be read and you are unlikely to ever find out that it was wasted effort.

◊    Big files can be bounced back.

◊    It is time consuming to input the addresses into your distribution list; once you do, back it up and print out a hard-copy so you don't lose it. Keep it updated as it has a value.

◊    If you abuse it, and send out too many emails that are irrelevant to the recipient, they will simply put your name into the SPAM box and therefore never receive your emails.

**EXAMPLES:**

The most successful forms of direct mail have been when I have rapidly responded to a news item, created a tightly-targeted news release and issued it to a small and relevant audience. I sent out the below example to a small list, comprising 45 names in total, and I spent the next two weeks making five follow-up phone calls a day and sold 400 books on the strength of this activity.

**EXAMPLE** *"Austen-fever hits town"*
I issued the below press release to all book shops and gift shops in Jane Austen towns (Bath, Winchester, Dorking, Croydon) as well as to bookshops and hotels where Pride & Prejudice had just been filmed.

**EXAMPLE** *"What are you doing for Prince William's birthday?"*
This was a direct email campaign to all of the national and local radio channels, emailed out three weeks before Prince William's birthday. Because the author of Rebel Royals (Nicholas Davies) is a well-known royal spokesperson, I knew that the combination of press release and author would be appealing. He was invited onto ten local radio channels, where I promptly contacted the local stores and invited them to order stock of the title.

## 3. DIRECT MARKETING BY PHONE (aka tele-sales)
Telesales is a bad name for a very positive activity. Most people think of huge call-centres populated by people who read pre-written text off a card. For independent authors, tele-sales should be seen as direct marketing by phone.

It is one of the most time-consuming tasks and one that most self-publishing authors baulk at, yet it is one of the most effective as you are talking directly to your customer. The more you talk about your book to the middle-men and your intended audience, the better you get at making the sale; you start to convert more and more sales simply because you are pitching it better.

You can find out exactly what they are looking for and work out whether your product is suitable to their needs – even by adapting what you are saying and converting a lost cause into a sale. Once they are on the phone, you can do some subtle research and find out what his needs are, how he likes to be approached and when.

You have the opportunity to adapt your message in a way that a piece of pre-printed literature cannot, and if people are interested they will place the order immediately as it saves them the hassle of remembering to do it later.

If this sale is one copy of a book, then it is not worth the time and effort but if it ends up being several hundred books over a few months then the original time investment has paid handsomely.

**What to say**

In terms of deciding WHAT to say, authors must go back to their original marketing plan. Your opening gambit has to say a lot in the most succinct and legible fashion:

*"I am launching a book on* 'understanding the growth of crime' *and am marketing heavily in 'your area' because police reports a huge upsurge in personal crime in 'your area' today. Would you be interested in seeing some information on it?"*

Phew! There's a lot in there but you have managed to say WHAT it is and WHY you are approaching them. You closed with forcing a response either positive or negative.

Whatever their response, you have opened up a dialogue. If they say yes, you can 'chat' about the chances of doing events, how they like to order books, how they like to hear of new launches etc. If they say no, you can ask what they look for or specialise in, then discuss how they prefer to hear of new launches and order in books etc. and most of all, ask if they receive information by email. This is the cheapest form of ongoing contact and you can update them about future marketing activities.

Another important reason to keep in contact with potentially interested book-buyers is that many bookshops are poor at re-ordering low-selling titles or little-known books. Keeping them on a live database enables you to contact them a couple of months later to gently remind them to re-order the book if the initial stock has sold.

## SUMMARY GUIDELINES FOR DIRECT MAIL / EMAIL

**Rule 1: target several different campaign-based audience groups**, as per your original marketing plan. One campaign may be based on needs "Live healthily for longer" or location-based ie. "Why breast cancer is so prevalent in Surrey" or community-based ie. targeting all cancer centres. Under each campaign title, write out the list of all the people you need to contact, and this comprises one database. There will probably be only 10–20 names within each database, and this is good.

**Rule 2: take the long view.** Don't feel you have to blast the information out in one vast hit, because the chances of most people hearing it are slim. You will get your message heard if you target specific audiences with a very specific issue or need.

**Rule 3: follow-up.** You have a far greater chance of converting the sale if you follow-up and try to talk directly to the potential buyer – because everyone is a potential buyer until they have declined! Following-up is an onerous task, so plan to make just five phone calls a day to make it less daunting. However, if you get into a good stride then keep going!

**Rule 4: double up**. Any form of printed literature will incur costs. Add this to the cost of postage and you have a relatively high cost per unit. Ideally, your direct mail literature will have doubled up with some other form of promotional material. You cannot always send out a book, but sometimes the appeal is in the book jacket or print values. Ensure your promotional material reflects this ie. get a cover run-on, and send this instead to inspire interest.

**Rule 5: build knowledge.** If you buy a list, then implement some form of direct response so you have some measure of understanding of (i) the success and (ii) its value. The overriding advantage to any form of direct, customer contact is the information you derive from direct liaison with your potential buyer, which is why book clubs have done so phenomenally well. Their database is subscription, membership based and they monitor what people are buying, what they are heavily demanding and they can tailor their lists accordingly.

**Rule 6: manage your timing.** If you truly understand your market, then you will know the right time and the wrong time to talk to them. This is not just about getting romance books out in time for Valentine's Day, but also considering what buying phase booksellers are in. For example, as a small, unknown author you have a very limited chance of being seen in the weeks running up to Christmas as you can be sure that the big publishers and sales reps are forcing literature, direct mail, catalogues and books down the throats of booksellers.

**Rule 7: try to re-use the data.** The first time you create a list is the most expensive and time-consuming. Plan to implement several approaches to each database over the course of the first year of launch of your book.

**Rule 8: endeavour to chase volume sales, not incremental sales.** If you are going to do a huge mail-out with a high investment, the potential for each individual order should be in the hundreds or thousands, not in one-off book sales. Large mail-outs are better targeted at businesses, institutions and retailers who buy in bulk, rather than in customers who buy in one-off units. Remember the 1:100 rule. If the one purchase is for 2,000 books, the investment may be worth it.

**Rule 9: ongoing reminders.** Another important reason to keep in contact with potentially interested book-buyers is that many bookshops are poor at re-ordering low-selling titles or little-known books. Keeping them on a live database enables you to contact them a couple of months later to gently remind them to re-order the book if the initial stock has sold.

**Rule 10: try to measure the success.** Measuring success is invaluable for tailoring future marketing efforts. If you discovered after the first mail-out, that people in the South-East were very responsive to your mail-out but people in the Midlands didn't buy at all, this may be because your subject-matter is of little value to them. Investigate it by doing some research to a couple of bookshops. It may be they are simply not interested; equally, maybe the trend hasn't hit them yet and you are perfectly positioned to exploit it when it does.

*There's a story about two shoe salesmen... one went on a sales trip to a forgotten country in Africa where no-one wore shoes. He said to himself, this is a waste of time because nobody wears shoes here and he came back home. Then the other salesman went on the same sales trip and said, "Fantastic! Nobody wears shoes here!" He showed the inhabitants the benefits of shoes and started selling them by the hundreds.*

Sometimes, sales success is just about how you are looking at the opportunity.

# PART VII

# DIRECT SELLING

**An introduction to direct selling**

**Selling Online**

    An overview of today

    How to sell books online

    *BEST PRACTICE: Having a website*

    How to promote yourself online

    Online community sites

**Direct Selling (non-intenet)**

1. **Book clubs**
2. **General catalogue companies**
3. **Events**
   *BEST PRACTICE: Hosting an event*
4. **Specialist outlets and audiences**

**Building and managing a database**

# INTRODUCTION TO DIRECT SELLING

The biggest opportunity for the serious self-publishing author lies in direct marketing and direct selling. The purpose of this chapter is to demonstrate where and how. The opportunities are endless – limited only by imagination. This section is not prescriptive, but intended to start the creative thoughts flowing.

Direct selling falls into two very distinct camps – online and offline – but the ambitious self-publishing author will seek to utilise both to maximum effect. Offline activity will point people towards the website in order to buy books and hear about ongoing information; the website will inform people about offline activity such as events, as well as selling the book. One supports the other. And if it is your own website, then you have truly cut out any middlemen although many authors cannot afford or justify the investment into creating their own shop-site and website. We investigate all of this below.

**Five avenues for direct selling:**
1. The internet
2. Book clubs and book catalogues
3. General Catalogues
4. Events: talks, tours, workshops, conferences, festivals and trade fairs
5. Specialist outlets and audience
    a. Schools, colleges and universities
    b. Travel-related ie. travel agents and hotels
    c. Nursing homes, old people's homes, hospitals and hospices
    d. Genre-related ie. Children's, Crime, MBS, Fantasy, Paranormal, Romance etc.
    e. Other ie. collectors, talking books

# SELLING ONLINE

## AN OVERVIEW

Online retailing continues to expand at a phenomenal rate, up 68% this year (Nov 04–05) which is a growth of £8bn. This is extremely high when seen in consideration of the fact that last year we had the slowest rate of growth for total retail sales since 1947.

Amazon obviously takes the lionshare of online book site visits, at 73%, but this must be taken in the context of <u>known</u> sales ie. through the till sales. There are many, many bookshop sites and hand-sold sales that are simply not calculated into the national statistics for book sales.

High street booksellers claim that online sales do not present any concerns to them. Amazon, as the biggest online book retailer, takes only 6% of the market. Yet last Christmas, high street spending was down 44% and many attributed this to customers buying online.

High street booksellers set up their own shop-sites back in the 1990s but stepped back from this ie. Waterstone's and Borders struck deals with Amazon, which is interesting now that some of their biggest threat comes from Amazon. In the brave new world of retailing, the power of balance is slowly shifting towards online shopping, and it will be interesting to see if they pull back from selling via Amazon in the future.

Selling direct is seen as a profitable future growth area for publishers as it puts them in control of their supply chain to the market, enables brand building, cross-promotion and building a loyalty customer base. Many large publishers set up their own bookselling websites back in the 1990s, but this was costly to run and the sales were too low. They are slowly coming back to the internet as a route to talking directly to their customers, and it is proving to be an ideal route for niche publishers.

However, the internet does not completely remove the middle-men as you still need to host a website, manage it and update it as well as having a shop solution which involves having a payment provider. This is great for authors with a strong IT background, but for many it simply adds another middleman.

You could say that the emergence of the internet doubles the amount of middlemen. The optimist sees this in a positive way as it provides double the chance of your book being found by the reader who wants to buy it. The pessimist will see it as double the amount of work to get it into the market.

### *The internet is challenging business models that have worked for decades*

Whichever way you look at it, the internet has removed the *urgency* of needing high street presence. Having books in high street bookshops will always help to sell more, but not having your book in the high street no longer means that people cannot buy it at all.

This makes a phenomenal difference to the self-publishing author, and the serious self-publisher will have a website of his own. It might just be a one pager web presence that announces your book and provides some contact details, but this will be enough to ensure that anyone looking for you will find you. Having your book on Amazon.co.uk does not help people to find YOU, it only makes your book for sale. I cannot count how often I have hunted through the internet to find self-publishing authors and failed. Just think, I might have been a film producer with a large cheque in my pocket which went to someone else who had at least got a one pager site up with contact details.

Once you have a site, you must exploit every opportunity to announce it. Put it on your book, your promotional material, in any interviews that you do and just generally tell friends. Maybe you want to add reviews onto your site, or dates for any events you are doing. Make the internet work for you.

## The internet is segmenting the market

Specialist interest groups can now offer diversity, and can more easily find a value in this. Search engines help point people to the information they are looking for, so as long as you have identified your genre, key words and profiles accurately, you will be found. The future of where it is going is to be seen in the music industry ie. Firefly is one web crawler which trawls the internet to help people find music they are looking for.

Already there is a website which is developing a 'logarithm' to recommend books and refer readers to other material, and not just genre-based. I was amazed when I looked up my favourite ever book (The Secret History, by Donna Tartt) and saw that it was matched with The Godfather, a book that simply never appealed to me. I asked Steve Johnston, CEO of StoryCode about it:

*"StoryCode makes no individual editorial judgements about likely matches. The Coding process asks readers to provide a score for each of 40 questions about the story they have read. This then creates a database record with the story's 'DNA' which we then match with all the other stories in the database. StoryCode is not making conventional stylistic, subject, or genre comparisons of a story, but very sensitive, equally weighted comparisons of 40 variables.*

*Over time it is likely that the match for these stories will change, but at the very heart of StoryCode's power is the possibility that it will make legitimate, but lateral, recommendations such as the one you have discovered.*

*And your judgement that you would not read The Godfather is up for grabs in my view. I never imagined I would read A Christmas*

*Carol, which, much as The Godfather, has way too much prior knowledge from movie and TV interpretations. I did though, as a consequence of its unlikely match with Animal Farm, and was delighted. I was also very satisfied by the logic of the match having read both. I suggest you go away and code The Secret History for yourself and then read The Godfather. When you have done this come back and tell us what you thought of the match. I reckon you will be surprised."*

I think there is probably far greater benefit to StoryCode's concept than is currently being credited. I have long wondered at why booksellers SELL buy genre, yet most people hunting for books to read are actually searching for a certain quality to the writing. I would much rather see descriptions such as "Social Comment Literature", "Human observation", "Intrigue" etc. It would seem that StoryCode goes some way to addressing precisely this.

**The publishers are coming back**

Many publishers, having dabbled with the internet in the late nineties retreated, saying that they would focus on the core business rather than online marketing and selling. However, they are now reappearing online with added value offerings.

Random House are launching a "Pay-per-page" ebook project for which they are planning to charge four cents per page for fiction and narrative nonfiction, whilst informational texts such as cookery books will have a higher per-page cost.

Panmacmillan.com will host a page for every Macmillan author with a photo, profile, backlist and details of upcoming events.

The real advantage is for managed sites, such as Penguin.co.uk, which update regularly with extracts, interviews, readers' groups, competitions, digital audio downloads and instinctive microsites for imprints. Online presence also helps publishers to access niche markets as they can get into the heart of local and small markets. Penguin has partnerships with the History and Biography channels, providing content in return for links from the site. Sales add up to not an insignificant amount of money.

Reverb, a brand new publishing company, is planning to launch a book a month using the internet as its main form of marketing. Every book will have its first chapter available and there will be a huge databank of online reviews and articles covering the titles. A fortnightly newsletter will be available. The majority of books that get published and promoted will be largely on their ability to fit a marketing plan rather than originality or quality of writing. (Paul Lenz, Marketing Dir, Reverb).

Summersdale labels itself as a media company with book publishing at its backbone. It has an eye of the future of e-books and as a product to tie in with an expanding DVED range. Its e-book digital distribution facility has already produced titles for several publishers including Snow Books.

**Publishers being retailers and retailers being publishers:**

Everyone involved in book publishing and book selling is stretching their offer – publishers are becoming sellers and sellers are becoming publishers. Barnes & Noble have started self-publishing and selling a range of books, including some classics. Amazon has bought BookSurge.com, an online self-publishing POD company. Bookspan announced that it will publish its first book, James Grippando's Lying with Strangers.

*"Retailers have become publishers so why can't publishers become retailers? Everyone is trying to figure out what the right thing to do is." Pat Schroeder, President of the Association of American Publishers.*

It is evident that everybody is struggling to maintain/increase market-share by diversifying. The lines are increasingly becoming blurred, and in the resulting confusion there is plenty of opportunity for the self-publishing author.

**Radical changes include:**

### Podcast

A Podcast is an audio or video recording published freely on the internet that can be downloaded onto a portable MP3 player or iPod. It is still relatively early days, but it is very popular and I know many people who swear by them.

Websites such as www.meettheauthor.com run author interviews this way, so interested parties can hear the author talk about his/her book.

One buyer at Waterstone's was very impressed with one self-published author's website, complete with blog and podcast, that he agreed to stock the book.

*"Ian Hocking's website simply demonstrated to me how much Ian was prepared to invest in both time and money, in promoting his book. Added to which, it was a good book, so I felt Waterstone's should support it."* said Scott Pack.

### E-books

This is an electronically delivered book which can be either read on a computer screen in PDF format or on a specialised e-book reader. As the reader units improve, more people will begin to adopt this method of reading books but it will remain needs based. Neither traditional book nor e-book replaces the other entirely, and people will still like to give beautiful books as gifts or curl up with a novel in bed. Equally, doing a digital search through a training guide for a specific word or term is far more convenient than endlessly leafing through pages, and travelling light with mere microchips can provide a different set of advantages.

*"A lot has happened in the last year as far as e-publications are concerned. New reading devices have been launched, a massive*

*project is underway in Asia to provide students with e-books, the market for digital magazines is booming in both the US and Europe, and the development of new generations of e-book reader format are now well under way."*
Nick Hampshire, secretary of the E-Book Society.

*"Within 7-10 years, 50% of book sales will be downloads,"* estimates Nigel Newton, Chairman of Bloomsbury. *"When the e-reader emerges as a mass-market item, the shift will be rapid. It will soon be a dual format market."*

If you are keen to publish an e-book but want more help and support with it, have a look at:
www.successsecrets.co.uk/ebooks.
I don't know them and haven't used them, but it looks like an interesting site to explore.

### Blogs
What started off as an opportunity to air a few thoughts and grievances is turning into an industry in its own right, with bloggers landing blockbuster deals and agents/publishers increasingly watching popular bloggers in order to offer them big deals. As you weave your way through the extensive list of links on Online Selling, you will see a lot of blogs. The owner of the blog writes out his thoughts on his pet subject, just downloading and commenting. Sometimes people respond with a comment; sometimes it ends up in a heated five way debate.

Julie Powell's "Julie & Julia" was the result of a lit-blog. It gained in such popularity that the author was offered a book deal. She is not alone in this, and there are many similar stories, with, I am sure, many more to come.

### Search engines
The internet is just one big information super-highway. Instead of needing vast libraries of books in your house to find

out where the Andes mountain range is or who wrote Moby Dick, you simply 'google it' nowadays. A brand has really arrived when it becomes a verb. We still hoover our house, despite the Dyson invention. And we don't Alta-Vista-it, we google it. And now Google are enabling your entire book to be searched for key words to help people find your book. Many large publishing houses are rightly wary of this, but my advice to self-publishers is to go for it. If it gets your book found and a book sold, then it is a good thing – and it is free.

Amazon have a number of search facilities. *Amazon Search Inside* the book enables people to search inside a few pages of the book, although the text is not downloadable. Publishers are requested to submit 100% of the book but only a small amount is shown. Amazon Pages (launching '06) enables customers to buy individual chapters, pages or portions of a book for rather than entire texts, for online viewing. Amazon Upgrade (also launching '06) will offer full online access when a traditional text is purchased.

*The Internet Archive* will include content from historical works of fiction to children's books and engineering white papers, taken initially from founding members, currently two large US libraries. It is an opt-in approach and will respect copyright holder's rights. This is operated by OCA (Open Content Alliance which includes Yahoo!).

## Issues over copyright

Recent uproar has been caused by online bookseller practices of scanning in entire texts and allowing up to 20% of it to be read online for no fee at all. Owners of the copyrighted material argue that it enables the online shopper to see just the bit they want and not pay for it; Google argue that it enables buyers to see if it is right for them, much as you do in a shop by flicking through a book, consulting the index etc. If it contains the information you want, you end up buying the book. If you can't see readily whether it does, you don't buy every book on the subject in the vague hope that somebody somewhere will answer your question.

Google Booksearch and Amazon Search Inside advise that their 'preview' services actually increase the number of books sold, as people find similar but different information in a number of texts.

Publishers fear that allowing the scanning of their books will only lead to copyright abuse, claiming that lawyers can extract the chunk of text they need for a court case and students can use the information for their essays. 20% might just be enough. This is, in effect, giving the information away for free – when they should be paying for it.

The fact is that the internet opens the system up to abuse, as we saw in the music industry with Napster. People may well download the bit they need. They may well reprint it in a top-selling magazine in South America somewhere without you ever being any the wiser. And second-hand booksellers can re-sell your book on Amazon Marketplace or Ebay; they steal your customers and undercut your best online price without you seeing a penny of the profits. Personally, I have far more of an issue with resellers not giving me a cut of what is my copyrighted material than I do with Amazon or Google's 'text search' programmes.

But this is a period of change, and solutions will emerge. As regards the reselling, both of my books in the "What do I have to do..." series have a restriction which means that anyone wishing to resell the books will have to apply for a licence from Indepublishing. It's not expensive and it's not difficult to implement – a one-off payment will allow that particular reseller to sell a nominated title irrespective of quantity. This has been implemented purely to endeavour to gain some of the royalty percentage which is rightfully the author/publisher's. It is the first time a Licence to protect against reselling has been allocated to a book, and given time, I am sure some sort of standardised system will emerge from the ongoing investigations.

One interesting development is the Creative Commons Licence which is a new kind of copyright licence. It is designed to supplement the 'all rights reserved' of traditional copyright with a 'some rights reserved' alternative. Works with a Creative Commerce License can therefore be borrowed from, developed and modified which is designed to create a more fertile ground for ideas to development in the long run. This is gathering in popularity in certain circles – and obviously not in others.

## HOW TO SELL BOOKS ONLINE

The answer is clear and simple. There are two distinct ways to sell books online – by using an established bookshop site or by selling via your own website.

### The major bookshop sites

The established bookshop sites, such as Amazon, Abebooks, Play.com, Tesco.com and Bookfinder.com, generally take the title information from Nielsen Bookdata and their stock information from the distributors, such as Gardners. It should go without saying that you must ensure that your book is up on these sites.

It's very pleasing when you type in your book title in the Search bar and up it pops. You get the sense that your book is everywhere and therefore people must be able to see it and thus buy it. Amazon.co.uk recommend that to help your rating, you should endeavour to get as many reviews as you can muster up, which will help browsing shoppers to choose your book.

The best way to use Amazon.co.uk as a sales tool is to garner as many reviews as possible. Encourage anyone you can to put a review up. Watch your sales ranking and see if it improves after implementing any promotional campaigns.

I also use Amazon.co.uk prior to launching a book – to check whether there are other books with the same title. When publishing Dave Chick's book, the working title was "Access Denied". A quick check on Amazon told me that there were 25 other books listed on Amazon.co.uk of the same name. As a new author, the chances were he would end up on page 2 or more thus never be found. By changing the title around to "Denied Access", he came up as number one. Not only this, but we realised it was a better title because Dave kept referring to the fact that his daughter was *denied access* to him. All round, this bit of research led us to the best possible book title.

## Price comparison sites

Amongst the major bookshop sites there are also price comparison sites, such as Froogle and Bookbutler.co.uk which are useful to look at if you want to see who is discounting your book and by how much.

## Smaller bookseller sites

In addition to the real behemoth book-sites named above, there are a range of bookseller sites, as per the below starter list, where you should ensure your book is listed. These are not book clubs, but online bookshops; some have emerged because of a very strong regional presence or distinctive sales offer, and others are discount shops who, in the majority, take their lists from Nielsen.

o **Airlift**, www.airlift.co.uk, the leading distributor of independent publishers from the UK, U.S, Ireland, Canada and Australia. We offer a unique range of products, from classic and recently published books to audios, tarot cards and posters, all of which help to heal the body, illuminate the mind and enrich the spirit

o **Bookfellas.co.uk:** BookFellas.co.uk is part of Sprint Books, see below.

o **The Book Pl@ce:** www.thebookplace.co.uk a book shop website with interviews, features and latest extracts with an associated website, Bookends, the book place magazine www.bookends.co.uk

o **New Book Reviews** (www.newbookreviews.co.uk) is a revolutionary new scheme from The Book Pl@ce which allows the partners who link to our site to not only sell books and make money through commission but also to display up-to-date professional book reviews. Book Pl@ce partners can now manage, maintain and profit from their very own content rich bookshop. This unique offer is open to anyone with a web site and is free to join
o **Submissions:** They select all books, taking their data from Nielsen.

o **Country Bookshop:** www.countrybookshop.co.uk. A well established multi-channel retailer of entertainment, leisure and gift products offering a local alternative to customers, offering 2 million titles, discounted magazine subscriptions, music, dvds, games, software, outdoor accessories and gifts. Submissions: FAX: 01629 815659 or via email enquiry line on the site.

o **Historybookshop**.com: this site is the product of a small number of people who work in the UK book trade and who are passionate about history. We don't limit our interest to the academic discipline of History, our interests range across art, travel, literature, archaeology, world history and culture. We present our information in many different ways – events by dates, the Timeline feature cultural and social information, articles, features, quizzes, newsletters complete the picture, at least for now. info@historybookshop.com

o **Indebookshop**.com, www.indebookshop.com, the bookshop for self-published titles, to enable your book to always be in stock. No random discounts, we seek to add value to the customer by offering signed books and free promotional material, rather than remove value to the author by cutting the profit margins. **Submission**: email enquires@indebookshop.com

o **The London Bookshop**, www.londonbooks.co.uk, is the first (and only!) website bookshop totally dedicated to offering you the best books in print on our capital city. From classic fiction through to the latest travel guide, from Ackroyd through to

Zagats we aim to have all represented. Submission: use email form on the site; phone 0871 288 2429

o **Pickabook.com:** over 5m books offering great discounts, low shipping charges and fast despatch times; includes audio books. Submission: lists taken from Nielsen.

o **Samedaybooks**.co.uk: Methven's online book ordering system. If the book is in stock, you can collect it same day; otherwise www.nextdaybooks.co.uk will order it today and you can collect it tomorrow. Free delivery to store and no credit card needed. Submission: Contact your local Methven's store to get local stock if possible.

o **Sprintbooks.com:** is a new website dedicated to the low-cost supply of books with high standards of delivery and service. We are part of a company which has been supplying books by mail-order and then online for over 17 years. During this time we have built an enviable reputation for providing a fast and efficient service, rock solid security, great prices and customer service second-to-none. Email form on the site.

o **Studentbookworld.com:** StudentBookWorld where you will find 250,000 stock books at discount prices. Contact details on site, information is taken from Nielsen.

o **Swotbooks.com:** Our mission in life is dead simple: we let you buy stuff like books and DVDs via the web as cheaply as possible. No messing about, no catches - just the best discounts around... Contact details on site, information is taken from Nielsen.

o **The Book People:** www.thebookpeople.co.uk; great books at fantastic prices. One of the largest suppliers of books; not a book club – you can order what you want with no rules etc. Instead you can earn Book Points (ie. a loyalty scheme). Great for reading groups.

o **UK Book Sales:** www.ukbooksales.com; 20% off all titles with an extra 10-15% off a selected range of titles each week; part of Seek Media (www.seekbooks.co.uk) and in conjunction with

Gardners Books, the wholesalers. Submission: stock via Gardners.

But remember, these are only listings, and you will need to work hard to get people to find it by browsing. Most of the time, the unknown author will be on page 20, 30 or 40 of Amazon when pages are browsed by genre. Given that few people browse past page 2, the chances of being found are slim. None of these sites actively promote a title unless being paid to do so, or when running their own price-cutting promotion.

Obviously, the mere presence of a site amongst billions of web pages won't mean that you will be found by the browsing online surfer. Only people specifically searching for you will find you, so once you have ensured your book is available through all of these mainstream channels, **the next task is to PROMOTE your book.** To do this, you will need a website, so let's first of all look at the requirements of a website.

## BEST PRACTICE:  Having a website

The serious self-publishing author will have set budget aside to have a website. If you really want to be successful, I would say this is critical. A website, most of all, gives you presence and visibility, and you never know – a top chain bookseller may be trying to buy 20,000 copies of your book or a tv/film production scout may be out there hunting for you but is unable locate you. Don't waste all your hard promotional work because of the lack of a one-pager website (at minimum) that has your contact details on it.

In the ideal world, the serious self-publisher will have at least £5,000 to spend on a website and get a few, well-designed pages that provide good information. For £1,500, Indebookshop.com can offer you a hosted website (with nominal annual hosting charge) with top-grade specification (fast connection, back-up etc) and daily promotion to the search engines. This is well-designed site to a set formula, offering 3-pages containing Home/contact us, Book and Author with text and images, and link to your place on Indebookshop and a link to your email. If you would like further information, please email:

enquiries@indepublishing.com.

**What to have on a website**
Below is a demonstration of a £5,000 website which has updatable reviews, news and events sections. A smaller, cheaper site would not be able to offer updatable entries, but the quality (whatever your investment) should come through the content. Quality not quantity!

- **Home page:** this page should act as the summary guide that links to the other pages; always announce positive reviews received and events being done on your home page as per the following guideline:
- **About the book:** this is your opportunity to sell the fantastic qualities of your book, what it has to offer – the plot, the characters, its intrigue. You might even consider having a SEARCH text function if your book is a self-help guide and you wish to reassure people that the topic they are looking for is included within.
- **About the author:** now sell your skills and abilities as a writer; who are you and why have you written it. Keep it brief but pepper it with enough reference to richer, deeper stories that will have journalists wanting to dig for more of

## A WEBSITE: Example

# A BOY'S NAME by Stephen Queen

**The book**

**The author**

**Events**

**Reviews**

**Contact us**

**Buy the book**

A beautifully told coming-of-age story set in 1920's Scotland. The unnamed narrator of the story struggles through the mists of... read on

*"Reminiscent of Laurie Lee in visual quality without burdened description. Lovely."*
*A natural storyteller. He will go far."*

**Launching at the London Book Fair 2006**
**Limited edition posters**
**and signed books available**

Author photo

Financial and business success came early to Stephen Queen, although his school career would never have suggested so. "I was badly dyslexic and uninspired – until I read JK Rowling's books and then I knew I had to write..." read on a story. Include several different images of yourself – in colour and black & white, head shot, more casual, at an event talking to your readers etc.

- **Events:** if you are planning organised events and are coming to different festivals and fairs, then shout about it. Let people know and they might well make the effort to find you.
- **News and Reviews:** always promote any endorsements and media coverage as it firstly encourages other people to wish to read your book, and secondly this has a market value in the eyes of bookshops and potential rights buyers.
- **Buy the book:** don't just link directly to the online shop site where your book is available, but have a page that tells both customers and trade  where they can buy your book ie. via a distributor or direct from you.
- **Contact us:** include your email address at the very least and maybe even a mobile telephone number. Include a line about *"If you are interested in buying any rights or seeking permission to reprint any part of this book, please email or call me. All rights are currently available."* If you sell any, then list out which ones are no longer available.

## HOW TO PROMOTE YOURSELF ONLINE

Over the long term, you should plan to wade your way through the millions of online communities, bookseller/promoters, private websites. The next section looks at a raft of online community sites, but this is not all of them and these sites can come and go. But they are worth approaching to see if you can become a part of their community. Invariably this will mean having your own website to link to/from, as well as offering other site-owners a motivating reason to link to/from your site. Simply having a site is not enough.

This is one the critical aims of Indebookshop.com; we are seeking to create a portal link to all individual author sites so the bookshop is the central portal through which the websurfer can link. This enables the author to do his sales pitch, and convert the book-browser into a book-buyer.

Indebookshop.com also ensures that the independent author can sell his book easily, without risk of showing out of stock or long delivery lead times, as so quickly happens on the primary sites like Amazon.

## Offline promotion

In Section IV, we looked at using free and paid-for media to promote your book, and in Section V we looked at all the promotional material you can consider creating. The most important item to remember to include in all offline material is your web address.

Your offline promotional activities should push people to the website, as much as the website pushes people to your book. It is therefore important to remember to include your web address on the cover of your book or inside front page where people will easily see it, as well as remembering to include it on any and all promotional material you create from AI sheets, to posters, advertisements and media coverage.

*Offline activity pushes people to the book and website*
*Online activity pushes people to where the book can be bought.*

## The top ten ways to promote online

### Keywords and metatags

Promote a series of relevant keywords to the search engines. Keywords are the search terms that people may enter in the Google box (or Altavista, MSN etc). Metatags are the words buried in your site linked to search engines, and the person who designs and manages your website will be able to do this for you. You will just need to supply him with ie. the top 20-30 critical search terms that will lead people to your site.

### Give people a reason to return
Update your events regularly, write a blog, run a competition, put a game on there that is relevant to your book, run a newsletter or a blog... anything that encourages people to come back.

### Web links
The spirit of the internet is to unite communication, information and communities. If you participate, seek to share information and be part of the online community by linking to other sites then you will benefit by people linking to your site. The next section lists a vast range of book sites aimed at book lovers, reviewers and bookish communities. You should approach the most relevant first, and start trying to become part of their community.

### Use technology
There are a number of additional software that may help your web developer to improve your position in the search tables:
- *Cleverstat.com:* an accurate monitor for search engines which allows you to find the position of your website in major search engines like Google and Altavista for popular keyword and get more traffic to your site.
- *Adwords Clever Wizard:* An easy to use Adword suggestion and research software. Check key phrases for their efficiency and popularity. AdWords Clever Wizard will show the number of searches per month, its index and will suggest a number of synonyms which you can check then and there.
- *Site Content Analyzer* examines HTML pages on and offline to provide you a detailed report about keywords density, their weight and relevance. With it, you can get a real time report about your current standings for any keyword/search phrase.

o   *BackLinks Master* is a free software specially designed to help you monitor the status of backlinks to your site. You can check is they still pointing to you, the anchor text of links, and other info.

o   *Internet Business Promoter (IBP)* is a website promotion software tool that helps you to get the best results with your site by Getting onto the top 10 rankings on Google, Yahoo, MSN Search and others; Get more website visitors and increase your revenue and outperform your competition. IBP offers everything you need to successfully promote your website. IBP is a suite of professional web promotion tools that helps you with all aspects of website promotion and search engine optimization.

### Use online media

Don't forget that newspapers, magazines, television and radio stations have an online edition or at least offer headlines of articles they are featuring. So once you have identified the best newspapers, magazines, television and radio channels then don't forget to approach their online editors and see if they want to run a support feature. Maybe you will have more luck approaching the online editor before the offline editor.

Always be clear about the angle and basis on which you are approaching them. If you have a solid idea and good reason to be approaching one editor over another, make sure you articulate it.

### Advertise

You can pay to have banner ads and links on everything from Google to private sites. Personally, I don't favour this as it is difficult to determine how cost effective it is for the author of a book, and advertising probably has more value if you are promoting a business or offering a service.

o   *Online banner ads:* Online banner ads are the advertisements that you see on websites – either as banners across the top of the page, or boxes down the side. Google will put paying customers onto the top banner in the search results, or associated search results down the side of the web page. Again, this form of advertising tends to be longer term rather than just a one-off promotion.

o   *Online pop-ups:* Online pop-ups are those irritating little boxes that pop up when you go to a website. They block the text you are trying to read and some are programmed to go directly to the promoter's website when you click in the "X" close box which can tip me over the edge when I'm in a rush. These are best avoided in my view. I don't believe they are that cheap to programme or put onto other people's sites and I don't know anyone who buys the promotional service or product on the strength of them; but if you must use them then do so as a short-term promotion.

o   *Online advertising:* Advertising on other people's websites ie. by finding relevant websites that deal with your subject matter or talk direct to your audience and paying to display your book jacket in a good location, together with a link to your online seller.

### Email promotion

It's good to let your friends, work colleagues, ex-work colleagues, old school friends (and anyone else you have ever emailed) to know that you are launching a book. Think of a nice catchy headline that works generically to different audiences and prepare a friendly newsletter announcing the launch and availability of your book. One author of a political satire sent an email saying *"Ten Reasons to Read this Book"* and just sent the list out to everyone he knew. It was a funny list and it worked well – some people rushed to buy it (so sales revealed later) whilst others forwarded it onto friends of theirs who would like the book. A great viral marketing idea – and cheap to implement.

Another author bought an email list for subscribers to a self-help magazine / society; it actually cost more and was less effective, but still covered off a large part of the community.

### E-newsletters

If your book deals with an ongoing issue, then you can create an email newsletter (if you know what you are doing). Sometimes people read them, sometimes they don't, but they often keep them on file for that one occasion when they believe they will want the information. A friend of mine runs an 'Authentic Living Consultancy' and she sends monthly newsletters that contain a short 200 word story or observation. I love it, and I find myself reading them irrespective of how busy I am. It reminds me to slow down occasionally.

### Chat rooms

Some people are very keen visitors to chat rooms, and use this to introduce their topic and get people talking about it. Once the conversation is fired up, then they put forward the suggestion of a book that people might like to read – their book.

### Lit blogs

There are hundreds of lit-blogs nowadays. You can either start your own or join in a conversation but bear in mind that this community won't be sold to. If you start your own, make sure you give people information and perspective and are not just trying to flog your book.

## ONLINE COMMUNITY SITES

There are zillions of independent book sites when you take the whole world into account. The online community offers plenty of opportunity, from information portals to interactive sites which invite reviews and offer newsletters. Hunt around and you will find information about writing courses, festivals and fairs, writer's circles, reading groups, self-publishers and online bookshops. The internet is obviously alive with websites talking to specific communities or giving information on specialist topics. Think of angle and send them an idea.

This is a continual 'late-at-night' kind of activity for all the night-birds out there, and you will saturate your boredom level before reaching each and every site; not to mention the fact that many small sites come and go quite quickly. This is a continual activity.

Closer investigation reveals that most of them are for the American web-surfer. Whilst books travel well between the two countries, often the sites offer limited opportunity for the British self-publisher who hasn't got US distribution.

Digressing for a moment, if your book seems to be very popular in America and you are getting a lot of enquiries from the States, one cost effective way to get your book into America is to contact a company like Lightning Source. For a very reasonable and low figure (under £100) they will take your pdf of the book and cover, and make a POD demand book which they will ensure is listed on all the major US book sites and databases. We have done this a few times with them and I have found it to be a cost-effective, risk-free way to test the US market.

Returning back to the main point... listed next is a vast array of websites, starting with the UK based sites. The serious self-publishing author will immerse himself into this world, just as recommended in the last book. Whereas that immersion was aimed at building contacts and visibility offline, this is about building networks and visibility online.

I have divided it up to demonstrate how you can also start creating your network of specialist communities, and here I have started listing sites by genre. But you can also create a network by profession, target audience or need. The internet is a fantastic environment to help you find the people you want to talk to.

**UK-based sites:**

- www.achuka.co.uk: the chock-full, eyes-peeled, independent children's books site.

- www.author-network.com: Karen Scott is an author and member of The Society of Authors, The Queen's English Society and EPIC. She also runs New Writers Consultancy, a critique and editorial service for writers. E: karen@author-network.com. *Author Network, 35A Lower Park Road, Brightlingsea, Essex C07 OJX, Phone: (44) 01206 303607*

- www.author-reviews.com: The free book promotion site. We promote old and new work by any author. We do not charge any fees, and never will. We will not ask you for your credit card, the most we require is an email address to validate the review submission process.

- www.birminghamwords.co.uk: Birmingham Words is an online community for readers and writers. The site has two main aims: (i) to build community between writers, readers and all those who love words; and (ii) to publish on-site articles, reviews and criticism as well as new writing and artwork in our Birmingham Words downloadable pamphlets.

- www.book-people.net The book people: the business of publishing; editor@book-people.net Telephone: 08456 58 00 68; Book People, Queen Anne House, Lucton, Herefordshire HR6 9PN

- www.bookbods.com: undergoing development (linked to The Royalists website)

- www.bookcrossing.com: Bookcrossing, in the dictionary, is *the practice of leaving a book in a public place to be picked up and read by otherwise, who then do likewise.* Our goal, simply, is to *make the whole world a library.* BookCrossing is a *book exchange* of infinite proportion, the first and only of its kind.

- www.booktrusted.com: to help teachers, librarians and parents find out about books for young people. A fantastic site with great links for children's book-relevant sites, news, awards etc. Contact details 020 8516 2977 / info@booktrust.org.uk

- www.foxedquarterly.com: *Slightly Foxed* is the lively quarterly book review for non-conformists – people who don't want to read only what the big publishers are hyping and the newspapers are reviewing. Eclectic, elegant and entertaining, *Slightly Foxed* unearths books of lasting interest, old and new, all of them in print. Each issue contains 96 pages of personal recommendations from contributors who write with passion and wit. *Slightly Foxed* aims to strike a blow for lasting quality – for the small and individual against the corporate and the mass produced. Why not join us, and enjoy some excellent company too?

- www.thegoodbookguide.com: The Good Book Guide was established more than 20 years ago to guide readers through the maze of books published each month. We are entirely independent, accept no publisher's contributions and are therefore free to recommend books solely on merit – because we enjoyed them, they entertained and informed us or simply because we saw the world a little differently after we'd read them. Editorial enquiries: hollys@gbgdirect.com; to order a book 01626 831122

- www.thefridayproject.co.uk: The Friday Project is a new publishing house, specialising in bringing together the worlds of print publishing and web publishing. Our aim is to turn the web's best sites into the world's best books. We have two main publishing imprints – Friday Books which is responsible for our book publishing activities and Friday Online – which produces our portfolio of acclaimed websites and ezines including our flagship comment sheet, The Friday Thing.

- www.millguypublishing.co.uk: We promote new voices in writing. Each story that is published here is free to read, all we ask is that you read each one with an open mind and review it if you wish. Each story will receive at least one review from the editorial staff here, and hopefully more reviews from you. We feel the best way for writers to improve is with criticism, whether good or bad.

- www.granta.com: *Granta* magazine publishes new writing-fiction, personal history, reportage and inquiring journalism. It has a belief in the power and urgency of the story, both in fiction and non-fiction, and the story's supreme ability to describe, illuminate and make real. "*Granta* has its face pressed firmly against the window, determined to witness the world." It rarely publishes poetry, reviews or essays or other forms of writing about writing. And pieces submitted to Granta must not have been published before in English.

- Guardian Unlimited - http://books.guardian.co.uk – is the Guardian's book review and information section on the web.

- www.historicalnovelsociety.org: This is THE best place to find out about new historical fiction. (emailed)

- www.ideasfactory.com: IDEASFACTORY has been created with the aims of: helping you make the first – or next - move in your career, aiding you in your creative development, encouraging conversation with other creative people enabling you to exchange: ideas, experience, knowledge, views. E: enquiries@ideasfactory.com

- www.ideas4writers.co.uk: this is a husband and wife team based in Devon, and the site is a wealth of information about great services to help make you a better writer. Includes ideas, what ifs, competitions, newsletters, bookshops, ezine and membership. email: mail@ideas4writers.co.uk post: ideas4writers, PO Box 49, Cullompton, Devon, EX15 1WX tel: 01884 33978

- The Independent Online:
http://enjoyment.independent.co.uk/books/ cover all book, film, music and theatre online.

- www.lapidus.org.uk: Lapidus is a membership organisation, established in 1996 to promote the use of the literary arts – that is: reading, writing and performing of poetry, prose, fiction or drama; storytelling; journal writing – for personal development. Its members include writers and poets, librarians, medical and healthcare professionals, therapists and service users, academics, teachers and those having a general interest in the field. Email: info@lapidus.org.uk

- www.nowyouknow.co.uk: written by the online Scottish Writers' group and produced as printed booklet and e-book, 'Now You Know' began life as a Scottish monthly newspaper published by NYK Media. We have loads of other stuff to choose from here, including fantastic million pound free draws, writing competitions, poetry, short stories, newsboards, shopping bargains with home delivery, free stuff, earning & learning opportunities and, of course, our great magazine, 'Now You Know'.

- www.poetrysociety.org.uk: The Poetry Society is a membership-based and Arts Council England-funded registered charity, whose stated aims are to promote the study, use and enjoyment of poetry.

- www.readingmatters.co.uk: This site is about books and ideas for children and teenagers. It is written for intelligent young readers who are keen to choose their own books. It offers book and author listings, ideas and a book chooser as well as a lucky dip. Good fun.

- Tregolwyn Book Reviews, http://tregolwyn.tripod.com: *we accept independent and non-independent reviews, provided that they have not appeared elsewhere. We also need more reviewers!* Tregolwyn also publishes books; it came about because I wanted to publish my own novels and could find neither a publisher nor an agent. Mailing address for review copies and any other correspondence: P.O. Box 11, Cowbridge, Vale of Glamorgan CF71 7XT E-mail tregolwyn@btopenworld.com

- www.readysteadybook.com: *ReadySteadyBook* is an independent book review website devoted to reviewing the very best books in literary fiction, poetry, history and philosophy. Includes ReadySteadyBlog which is a top literary blog

- www.therichmondreview.co.uk: The Richmond Review was established in October 1995 as the UK's first literary magazine to be published exclusively on the World Wide Web.

- www.scottishbooktrust.com: Scottish Book Trust is Scotland's national agency for reading and writing. We are a unique organisation committed to the promotion of reading and books. We believe in the value of making every child a reading child, every adult a reading adult, and every reader a lover of good books. Books expand intellectual, emotional and imaginative horizons, enriching people's lives and experiences.

- www.spoiledink.com: Spoiled Ink is a dedicated Writing Community, providing the best networking platform for writers, poets and authors available. Post short stories and other writings here, get and give feedback, be inspired and interact with writers around the world and around the corner.

- www.spl.org.uk: The Scottish Poetry Library is *the* place for poetry in Scotland, for the regular reader, the serious student or the casual browser.

- Tls.timesonline.co.uk: Welcome to the new-look TLS website which will now give you access to all the resources of Times Online as well as reviews, debates, features and services from the TLS.

- www.unwritten.org.uk: The Library of Unwritten Books is a collection of possible books. Short interviews are recorded with people about a book they dream of writing or making. Limited edition mini-books are published from transcripts of the interviews, which are made available to readers at exhibitions and special events.

- www.whatshallireadnext.com: Search for other readers' recommendations by authors and book titles. Run by a marketing company, Thoughtplay, this is an online book reviewing community. Participate and you may find your opportunities.

- www.writersreign.co.uk: WritersReign is a stress-free zone for aspiring writers looking for practical help to improve their writing and see it published. Articles, Competitions, resources... you name it! Fortress Publishing, Brentwood, Essex U.K. Tel: +44 (0)1277 226840; editor@writersreign.co.uk

- www.writersreign.co.uk A website for the aspiring writer, it gives a host of useful information including the latest contests and competitions for short stories and poetry, writers resources, markets, useful books for the writer and much more. With just a touch of humour this site is a no-pressure, stress free watering hole.

- www.writer'scircles.com: the complete website for writers' circles courses and workshops. diana@writers-circles.com diana.s.hayden@btinternet.com

- www.wordpool.co.uk: the children's books site for parents, teachers and writers. This is a well established source of information for anyone interested in choosing or writing children's books. The UK Children's Books directory and our own web design service are both natural spin-offs from it and reflect the growing interest in author and illustrator websites.

## Specialist subject sites: Sci-Fi

- www.infinityplus.co.uk: Science fiction and fantasy still share a thriving but short fiction market; some then get picked up for reprints or translations, but a lot of excellent work becomes hard to get hold of a very short time after it first appears. **infinity plus** aims to make some of these stories available again. We've also published some excellent original fiction. We also offer stories, extracts and non-fiction chosen by the authors themselves. Over time it will grow into an archive which will republish some of the best science fiction and fantasy being written. sf@infinityplus.co.uk

- www.sfsite.com: The SF Site is dedicated to the best in science fiction and fantasy, in print and media, on the Web and off. We will continue to expand the site to include our feature reviews, news, indexed links to the best SF sites on the World Wide Web, interviews with SF writers and artists, and much more. Based in Canada.

- www.spectromonline.com:

- www.britishfantasysociety.org.uk: The British Fantasy Society exists to promote and enjoy the genres of fantasy, science fiction and horror in all its forms. We are well supported by the publishing industry and have many well known authors as members, not least our president Ramsey Campbell.

## Specialist subject sites: Romance

- www.romrevtoday.com: the best and brightest reviews on the web. See submissions guidelines (US based).

- www.theromancereadersconnection.com: a US-based review and book rating site. Contact Livia Holton at romreadcon@aol.com

- www.aromancereview.com: A US-based site, we represent several countries and many US states. We are a group of people who have been brought together by our passion for romance! Whether reading it, or writing about it, we are all dedicated to the idea that a pleasure shared is a pleasure enhanced. Submission info on site.

- www.romanceandfriends.com: your online connection for romance readers and authors.
- www.roadtoreomance.dhs.org: The Road to Romance has been online since 1998. It's a place for readers and writers of romantic and women's fiction. Our goal is to introduce new authors to readers, and new readers to authors. In a positive environment we aim to educate, entertain and support everyone who enjoys the romance and women's fiction genres. Email: webmaster@roadtoromance.ca for info.
- www.escapetoromance.com: a US-based site for authors and readers; if you would like to volunteer your time in one of EscapeToRomance.com's sections, please email me -- julie @ escapetoromance.com

## Specialist subject sites: Crime

- www.crimetime.co.uk: a whole website dedicated to crime fiction with reviews, features, interviews and profiles with a magazine that you can subscribe to. Loads of links on the Resources page, including to an online bookshop TheBigBookshop.co.uk

## Specialist subject sites: Spiritual

- www.spiritualbookstore.com: World religion, spirituality, mysticism, Buddhism, Hinduism, New Age, and more. You may send us an email to query whether we would be interested in reviewing your book, before sending a hard copy. contact us: spiritualbookstore@yahoo.com

## Specialist subject sites: Mind, body, spirit

- www.mindbodyspirit.com.au: the internet bookshop and magazine. Based in Australia.
- www.ghchealth.com: offers e-books as downloads; US-based site
- www.equinoxbooksandgifts.com: New Age Gifts, Unique Gifts, Gifts for Mind, Body & Spirit. Book section under construction at the moment
- www.veritas.ie: for books and gifts with a difference
- www.thescreamonline.com: a magazine for art, photography and literature

- www.enlightenment.com: serves the spiritual and economic needs of individuals and organizations by building a living community of transformation and interaction.

### Specialist subject sites: Travel
- www.bootsnall.com: the ultimate resource for the independent traveller. Looking for destination information? BootsnAll has travel guides, stories, book reviews, and insiders from every continent. Mailing Address: 1305 SW Claremont Terrace, Portland, OR 97225-5214 USA; Phone: +1 (503) 528-1005. Chris Heidrich is Editor/Director of N'All chris@bootsnall.com

### Specialist subject sites: Cookery
- www.cookbookswelove.com
- A guide to outstanding cookbooks, featuring original cookbook reviews; includes reviews of "Food Writing & Literary Cookbooks", a short-list of food writing, food writers, culinary writing, food articles and literature, cookery books, cooking fiction, food stories, food recipes, and outstanding cooking and culinary-related books.

On Indepublishing.com there is a section called Online Links. All of the above are listed, together with two additional sections on **International** and **US/Canada**. The lists were too copious to include here, particularly given the speed with which some arrive and disappear.

For any I have missed, and any new sites coming up, please email me on info@indepublishing.com for I am keen to keep my information live and real.

# DIRECT SELLING (NON-INTERNET)

The serious self-publisher will target all possible selling opportunities, and direct selling puts you squarely in control. It is worth bearing in mind, however, that the time you need to invest in direct selling can undermine your profit potential (if you choose to include it in your calculations!)

**Direct selling means selling directly to the end-customer:**
1) Book clubs
2) Catalogues
3) Events: talks, tours, workshops, conferences, festivals and trade fairs
4) Specialist outlets and audience
    a. Schools, colleges and universities
    b. Travel-related ie. travel agents and hotels
    c. Nursing homes, old people's homes, hospitals and hospices
    d. Genre-related ie. Children's, Crime, MBS, Fantasy, Paranormal, Romance etc.
    e. Other ie. book collectors, talking books

## 1. BOOK CLUBS

Many people would see book clubs as being part of the standard supply chain and arguably it is. I have chosen to include it here because book clubs are usually a *firm* sale, which means that you won't get the books tumbling back to you should they not sell. This makes the book club *your* end customer. They often demand very high percentages as they offer high discounts to their customer base, but you are in a position to negotiate a fixed price, which puts you in control of whether you choose to proceed or not.

Book clubs own specialist corners of the market; they hone their booklists to suit market need and demand and therefore offer an invaluable route to your specific audience. In the UK, it is dominated by BCA, as you can see below, and books are available both as online websites and offline catalogues.

- **Book Club Associates:** The gateway to a selection of UK Book Clubs tailored for both general and specialist interests - find the club that suits you! Includes:
    - Worldbooks.co.uk – which covers all female and male fictions, childrens, biography & memoir, cookery and health, home and garden, reference and entertainment
    - Mango.co.uk – the bookclub for young fashionable women; from popular culture, chicklit and crime thriller to celebrity biography, some cookery, home and gardening
    - Mysterythriller.co.uk – everything dark from adventure, crime and thriller to psychological and horror
    - Historyguild.co.uk: the ancient and medieval history book club
    - Artsguild.co.uk: for all artistic styles from fine, modern, ethnic art across all forms of sculpture, graphics, architecture and photography.
    - Fsf.co.uk: the fantasy and science fiction book club; old and young sci-fi fantasy from novel and reference to art, film and tv
    - Railway.co.uk: the railway book club for all books on all forms of train and bus transport
    - Booksforchildren.co.uk: all books from birth to 12 years
    - Militarybookclub.co.uk: a comprehensive range of books on war, military and civil aviation

- **Books Direct:** your guide to the best books. Your guide to the best UK bookclubs, all of which are part of BCA.

- **Book Giant**: www.bookgiant.co.uk - brought to you by just good books which is part of BCA (Book Club Associates) o **Bol.com**: Another BCA online discount shop with large percentage off all titles and bargain basement books.

o **Red House** Home of children's books; part of The Book People.

o **School Link:** your school receives 10% of the order value in book vouchers every time you buy books through School Link, with free delivery back to the school. Part of The Book People.

o **Scholastic**: www.scholastic.co.uk, we are committed to developing reading and literacy in children, and supporting parents and teachers. To that end, we are one of the leading providers of learning products and services in schools. Our <u>Book Clubs</u> and <u>Book Fairs</u> provide, through teachers, the chance for children to collect their favourite books and for schools to build their libraries with free books. A book fair can provide a school with up to 60% of the value of books sold in free books!

o **US bookclubs site:** www.booksonline.com: 30 different genre bookclubs across the US

*Contact and submission details:*

o BCA, Editorial Dept, Greater London House, Hampstead Road, London NW1 7TZ

o Scholastic Book clubs: send a covering letter and SAE to the Editorial Department, Euston House, 24 Eversholt Street, London NW1 1DB. It will then be forwarded onto the appropriate editor to assess, and they advise this may take around 3 months.

o The Book People: was still awaiting a response from The Book People when we went to print.

## Book club contracts

Bookclubs usually buy a good quantity of books at a huge discount (70–80% is standard) and sell these onto the final customer, passing on large discounts. It is a firm sale, therefore no books come back to you, and as they are membership-based, they can profile their audience very closely. There is scope for a slightly better percentage to publisher on second run, and this should be negotiated into the initial contract.

The Club Editor decides what goes into the catalogue, and books have to be submitted to them well ahead of publication with full information: ie. publication date, delivery date, covers, titles, descriptions, category.

Book clubs reserve the right to change covers if trade jacket is not suitable (ie. standout and impact in a catalogue), although the publisher does get a say in any changes. Some bookclubs buy the right to put their printer logo onto the spine and print it themselves.

**Checklist of contract terms**:
o   Exclusive or non-exclusive? If it is exclusive, ensure it is on a certain number of copies over fixed time period
o   term of agreement
o   cancellation of contract if book sells out and no re-order placed
o   publisher's publication date; published price
o   restriction on timing of paperback edition / cheaper editions – they often want the paperback before trade paperbacks, but this can seriously affect trade sales in that market
o   cheap offers to others restricted ie. free book on magazine
o   warranty and indemnity clauses ie. lateness
o   advance material
o   remaindering
o   published price in NZ and Aus is important for BCA
o   markets/territories – can it be published simultaneously?

**Advice to self-publishing authors**
There is huge value in subscription-based selling, and bookclubs tailor their lists based on customer knowledge. As high street discounting has reached epic proportions, book clubs are losing their point of differentiation although some people still prefer catalogues and have selections made for them.

Bookclubs, however, are buying more aggressively than ever before in order to maintain their corner of the market. We can see that the category is dominated by BCA who have recently consolidated their ranges into broader categories which homogenises the range slightly more and reduces real opportunity.

Some self-publishing authors see book clubs as being a great route to getting in front of their audience, but I would urge caution. Do the maths and see if you can afford to sell the print run at the discounts they charge. Understand what your other opportunities are, where and how you can reach your audience without selling at a huge discount. If you are making the deliberate choice to sell at a loss in the hope that it may establish your name, then see it as a gamble which may or may not pay off.

Another important consideration is that if you set a book price at £9.99 then sell it to a bookclub who retail at £6.99, don't be surprised if other sellers compete at the same price and your book is only ever available at the much cheaper price. You may undermine your ability to ever sell at full price.

## 2. GENERAL CATALOGUE COMPANIES

Hundreds of catalogues are produced every year for a range of retail, service and supplies. Some specialise in certain topics and others are more general gift catalogues.

Some of the subject-specific areas you may wish to look out for cover such topics as wine/food/chocolate, outdoor life, crafts, horse/equestrian, home/garden, historic/collectibles etc. Equally, you may have produced a book that fits perfectly into the Gift category, and there are loads of Gift catalogues. The problem is trying to find them. There is one portal information site (www.britishcatalogues.co.uk) which lists many of the catalogues available today. For the US, see www.catalogcity.com which connects you to 700 companies with catalogues and links to their sites.

My advice is to also keep your eyes peeled from August onwards when all the gift catalogues swamp you in time for Christmas; ask all your friends to save their catalogues so you can sift through them and see who you might approach. I have also listed some here:

www.boysstuff.co.uk: has a whole section on books for boys (put 'books' into the search box and they all come up. There is also a Girls Stuff section within this site. Email via the site or phone Sales on 0870 745 2000

www.past-times.com: their catalogue offers a wide range of funny, gifty books as well as historic and collectible guides.

www.elc.co.uk: have a range of books from birth to 4 years. Contact Sales on 08705 352352.

www.naturalcollections.co.uk: inspiring products for a better world; books to open the door to a new way of thinking (ecological and organic).

www.healthhome.co.uk: a range of health and home products; it has a Miscellaneous section allegedly with Books but I couldn't see any. This might draw a blank or could indeed be an opportunity.

## 3. EVENTS

This section looks at any form of direct selling to the public - talks, tours, workshops, conferences, festivals and trade fairs.

Direct selling probably rates amongst the most successful and cost-effective activity you can undertake as you are talking directly to people who have chosen to come and listen. You should sell a fair few copies on the day, and drive a certain amount of ongoing sales during the next few weeks.

The drawback to them is that they are time-intensive. A lot of time and effort is invested into preparing for the event and attending the event, not to mention the expensive of travelling to/from the event. The chances are that any sales you make on the day will not actually cover the time and cost investment, but this should not put you off.

Once you do a couple of events and it is evident that there really is a market for your book, you begin to build up market awareness and demand that money cannot buy. Use direct selling success and endorsements collated at such events as part of your Sales Success data, ensuring that any subsequent approaches to bookshops include such glowing reports.

The more events you do, the more you can tailor your presentation towards your audience, fine-tune how you pitch it to them; some people even fine-tune their book in a second edition to better suit the needs of their audience. You can use it as a form of research; you may even write a whole second book off the back of such informed data and there are economies of scale in then direct selling two books, not just one.

The critical (and I simply cannot underline this enough) aspect is to ensure you are making the effort to do your event in order to talk to the right audience. If you find you are not achieving any real sales, interest or enquiries then save yourself the hard work and hassle. Maybe you are not reaching the right audience, using the right avenue or saying what people are hoping to hear.

### Events, tours and talks

This includes any form of direct marketing and promotion activity that you undertake by signings at bookshops and libraries.

If you are just setting out on the path of talks and events, these more informally organised events provide an excellent training ground for you to build up confidence. Because they are free, people overlook it if you are a little bit disorganised or apprehensive.

A best practice sheet on hosting any form of event or talk is printed below.

## Book fairs and festivals

Many authors believe that their audience will be at the book fairs and festivals, and I am not going to disagree. Book festivals and fairs are obviously attended by people who love books and reading, but if your competition is a range of A-lister authors, you will find yourself very much on the fringes. You may not get a platform on which to speak, so arm yourself with some fascinating or intriguing promotional material and move through the crowd trying to hand out as much as possible.

Approach Fair and Festival organisers and try to get booked as a speaker, or consider taking a stand at the event if you feel you will get a good return. Before spending money, always remember to do the maths... if the stand costs £150 and your profit per book sale is £2.00, bear in mind that you will need to sell in excess of 75 books before you begin to turn a profit, and that is not including your time to attend the fair.

Find out what literature they are producing and how they are promoting their event. Do the maths and see if it is worth your while to take out an advertisement in their literature and on their website. Again, if the advertisement costs £150, you will need to sell 75 books as a result. If you are not there to inspire that purchase, the chances are you will not sell anything like it. Consider doing an ad only if you have been invited to do a talk... two for the price of one, as suggested earlier.

With certain fictional genres, there are clubs and societies (The Crime Writers Association, The Romantic Novelists Association etc) that you focus on immersing yourself in and attending all their events and activities.

Another activity authors often do is a roadshow. It is quite time intensive and you need to be a good organiser, and however good your organisational skills, you will find that things change at the eleventh hour. Always have a Plan B ie. flexible literature that can accommodate a change of date or venue, and an easy way to update people of the change.

The best events are always tailored to the audience, so how much can you use a generic talk, and how much research and individual preparation do you need to do? Try to talk to the local bookshops or libraries and discover the local interest and what angle may be particular intriguing to them.

The work involved is considerable, but well worth it if you are seeking to establish yourself as an expert spokesperson on a particular subject. In this case, you should keep at it, constantly approaching the media every time your topic emerges in the news and ensure you do one event a month on your subject.

Most self-publishing authors I talk to say that they felt compelled to "do an event" but once there, didn't really know what to actually DO. The advice is to talk to the event organisers beforehand to find out what the opportunities are. There may be a general talk about books that you can display your book; or there may be an opportunity for you to do a talk – but work out in advance what you would talk about. Sometimes the festival organisers arrange a talk around a specific genre, which you may be able to participate in. Maybe there is a one day event where you can have a stand with your book and literature displayed.

The bulk of the book fairs and festivals take place between March to September, and planning for the following year usually starts around September; some start planning a bit later ie. in the January.

For a list of Fairs & Festivals, you can either go to www.artsfestivals.co.uk or see the Writers Handbooks.

**Workshops and seminars**
This includes any form of direct marketing and promotion activity that you undertake by presentations at organised seminars, training and workshop sessions.

These more professional talks are ideal if you are writing on a very specific subject matter, or seeking to establish yourself as a spokesperson. Remember that people are invariably paying to attend and expect professionalism. Do not throw yourself into a seminar as your entry point to direct selling, unless you are experienced at seminar presentations.

The most important rules to remember are that your presentation has to be slick and you have to say something of real worth. You should talk to the organisers beforehand to find out what the audience are really after, and truly understand this. Ask to see hand-outs of previous seminars, or question them quite closely about your own intended presentation. You should also ensure you are comfortable with operating the technology ie. the audio-visual equipment; maybe turn up early and have a quick demo. Pre-load your presentation onto their computer and check you can find it when you are called up to do your presentation, or know how to plug your laptop in.

One surprising mistake that many presenters make is when they are trying to demonstrate a visual or an item, and hold up a small A4 board that the front row can barely see, and the back row can't see it at all. Any images or items should either be provided as hand-outs that people can consult, or don't bother with it at all.

Hand-outs are essential in my view. They are beneficial as people can make notes whilst you talk – not forgetting of course that the spotlight is less on you and more on the notes in front of people, so it is an excellent way of dealing with any nerves you may have! They also ensure people can remember you and contact you after the event, which is usually the point of your effort. Photocopy your slide presentation as two-to-a-page handouts, and provide with a glossy leaflet about your book or a business/promotional card.

## 4. SPECIALIST AUDIENCES AND OUTLETS

Talking directly to the communities that are interested in your subject-matter is obviously going to deliver the highest rate of sales, as well as being the most rewarding events.

The task facing you is easier if you are writing on a specialist subject ie. a self-help, training or mind/body/spirit guide. These are far more definable categories with websites, magazines and businesses you can use to research. Find out what seminars, workshops, talks and training courses they run and get on their list as a speaker.

As stated previously, fiction and certain non-fiction titles like biographies are more complex and you will need to target more generalist areas such as community centres, women's or men's groups, hospitals, old people's homes and institutions. The latter group often have lunches and like to book after-dinner speakers, but only put your name into the hat if you are up for it.

Supply the organisers with information about you, your beliefs, your book and some endorsements about your abilities as a speaker. Send them a photograph of yourself and book jacket image/s. Make sure your contact information is clearly visible. The real secret of success when hosting an event is being crystal clear on what you are providing.

### *Manage expectations*

If people think you are there to teach them how to write, and you turn up to teach them how to self-publish, then the participants will feel let down. I don't say this from experience, although I have frequently talked on radio and found that the interviewer is more focussed on WRITING a book than PUBLISHING a book, despite my fairly distinctive and descriptive book title and associated information sheet. I therefore urge you to ensure any promotional material you send clearly sets out what you are going to talk about.

Find out what magazines, newsletters, websites etc they publish or advertise on, and find out if you can write articles, get a review or feature in or consider taking out a small run of advertisements ie. 3 months for a monthly publication. This should be adequate amount of time to see if it is a worthwhile seam of interest.

Make sure all events and activities you are participating in are listed on your own website. If you don't have a website, try contacting the local media in the run-up to the event to see if they wish to cover your involvement in the event or even just publish an article about your topic – clearly announcing you and your book, of course.

Everywhere you go, every talk or event you do, every speech you make, ensure you are well-armed with copies of your book, and any promotional collateral such as business cards, flyers and leaflets. These events are very demanding on your time, and the point is to get book sales. Stay focused on this. The praise and great reception is a fantastic feel-good-factor but financially worthless.

However, don't feel bad if you don't make any sales but exploit the other opportunities presented to you. Collect all those feel-good-factor praises and comments – write them down and use them as endorsements.

***Convert praise into endorsement and use it to sell yourself.***

You may be able to identify your potential buying community either by their AGE (Children's, Teenage, Older); INSTITUTION (educational or care establishments) or by NEED (travel or other genre-related). You can achieve certain economies of scale by trying to sell your book into places where your reader congregates. Some immediate categories that spring to mind are:

o **Schools,** colleges and universities
o **Travel-related** ie. travel agents and hotels
o **Nursing homes,** old people's homes, hospitals and hospices
o **Genre-related** ie. Children's, Crime, MBS, Fantasy, Paranormal, Romance etc.

It is a huge volume of work to gather together the database. You should either choose to take the long-term view and gather it gradually or approach companies like JEM who can create a mail-out database as well as preparing the mail-out for you.

The other way to reach these communities is to 'pick them off' regionally. The UK is conveniently divided up into counties, and you would be wise to promote heavily in one county at a time. This makes the task more achievable and can prove to be an ideal way of making yourself known.

*Try to make a big name in a small area.*

Whilst major publishers see launch as being a one-shot, one-season affair, the self-publisher can take the longer term view and extend the opportunity that Right Timing can bring. There is always the possibility that, during the course of implementing a one-year, round-the-country promotional programme, some zeitgeisty event happens and suddenly your book get snapped up by local media. You have just been able to exploit the "right place, right time" ideal, which most people see as luck. In reality, it is about being prepared.

### Other ie. book collectors

There are plenty of other specialist audience groups that you might discover as a potential group to talk to, such as book collectors. Some self-published titles are produced as a "concept" title ie. the Beatrix Potter story. Scott Pack at Waterstone's says that he sees some truly beautifully produced books with unusual production values, which have huge selling potential. Equally, some are so beautiful that they can only be produced in small quantities and have too high a cost per unit to make them viable for the mainstream.

Enter the collectors... they love small print runs of special edition books. Approach the book collector magazines and send them information about your book for consideration.

As the technology for e-book readers develops, there is another possibility that books will become available as beautiful, hard-copy gift editions as well as a cheaper, downloadable e-book. You may be choosing to produce your book only as an e-book, but consider the possibility of producing a limited run of 300 "hand-made" copies, maybe with hand-painted artwork or using unusual printing or paper substrates.

Try selling limited edition books on Ebay, and don't forget to contact Book & Magazine Collector who may be interested in doing an article or review on your book.

### Other ie. talking books

We look at the possibility of selling audio rights in Section IX, but you may consider commissioning a company yourself to convert your book into a talking book and approaching different audiences. Talking books are of interest specifically to older people and young children, but also for general purpose such as drivers on long journeys or commuters. Obviously the quality has to be high and the content has to be appropriate, but with the right material you may find a rich selling vein. Some starter places to look at are:

www.rednritten.com: a great company in Sussex who publish e-book, paperbacks and audio across books and magazines.

www.rnib.org.uk: go to the Talking Books section. RNIB Talking Book Service is a library of professionally recorded audio books.

Popular fiction, classics and non-fiction titles are all available and they consider requests from all customers.

## BEST PRACTICE: HOSTING AN EVENT

The secret of success in any activity you undertake is in the preparation. The moment of delivery is merely the end-point of all the preparation you have done to reach that point. So don't skip over the important part of the process. Instead, understand what you are seeking to deliver in order to prepare accordingly.

The point of hosting an event and giving up all that free time of yours is to make book sales. You will make book sales by inspiring interest in any person in the vicinity of your stand or presentation. You will achieve that by putting together an interesting looking stand or display which encourages people to come over and have a look. Note, that a pile of books is rarely enough to draw a crowd. You may need a 'call to action' banner which arouses intrigue – or gives away a freebie!

### Preparing for the event
- Going back through your marketing plan to select the most appropriate theme you wish to focus on.
- Talk to the bookshop who is hosting the event and gather their views before making it the central theme of your event. The bookshops know their local community and how different events will be received.
- Decide what book description, excerpt, and endorsement will best support the key theme of your event.
- Get a poster designed, artworked and printed. Run off 10–50 copies. Your local print shop may well be able to create this for you, and the content of the poster is discussed in more depth in Chapter V Promotion.

- Headline your event with the "call to action" announcement, and support it with your posters.
- Have a leaflet, business card, postcard or bookmark that people can take away with them should they choose not to buy there and then for whatever reason. Ensure any website details, contact information and "where to buy" information is clearly visible.
- Supply posters ahead of the event announcing the event (either on the poster or over-stickered with the date and time). Ask them to display this in the fortnight or week before, ideally with a small window display or front of shop display.
  - o It doesn't harm to visit a number of other shops in the vicinity, including the library, asking if you can put some nicely designed postcards by their till – particularly if you can find a suitable association with their shop and the bookshop and/or your book.
- Invite everyone in the area that you know; ask them to come at different times through the two or three hours you are hosting the event. Good friends and close family members will happily hang around for a while, sliding in and out of view as required.

### Setting up the event
- Turn up 1 hour ahead of the allotted time. Expect for them to NOT have a table and chair ready which is actually a good thing as you can then be influential in its position.
- Position-wise you want it in a clear line from a main entrance-way or, if upstairs, clearly viewed from the landing.
  - o Try to position the table near an end of aisle or shelf where you can subtly remove a row or two of their display, and place yours on the shelf,

- o  another good place is near the category in which your book sells,
- o  if the event is in Borders with a Starbucks, a table near here is also a good place as people may drift over whilst stopping for a coffee.
- Try to get a sizeable table; we will always try to encourage a bookshop to order a large quantity ie. 100 books so we can create a big display. They are invariably on sale or return after all.
- Ask for one of the desk-standing mini-shelves so you can place the books flat-on with good cover presentation; fan about 10–15 books out and just stack the rest slightly messily so people feel comfortable with coming over and picking them up.
- Take more posters up on the day, with some pieces of A4 card in case you need to stick them onto something more rigid. It is good to have a little pack of blue-tak, sellotape, thick black pen and A4 white paper in case you need to stick / add notes etc
- Put posters up on doorways, pillars, staircases etc and ask for a window display for the day
  - o  Make sure that generic posters are over-stickered or bannered with the pre-printed words "Event instore today, 12–3pm upstairs".
- Ask the manager/organiser to make an announcement every now and again advising your presence and where you are located in the store.
- Ensure the shop floor staff is aware of your presence; despite posters plastered up all around shop and tills, shop staff can remain blissfully unaware. We did one event with a 7 foot crocodile-costumed man, a magic show and face-painting, posters and post-cards, tannoy announcements, the full works and still customers were told that *'there's no event happening here today'*

when they rang in to see if the Zartarbia launch was on!

- Depending on your subject matter, have a display board which is offset to your table, clearly visible as an Announcer and easily accessible ie. NOT behind you where you block people looking at it.
- Bring your own pen... ideally a nicer one than just a bic biro chewed at the end!
- Bring a bottle of water just in case you are inundated by people and talk so much you are left gasping for a drink. The staff are often very busy and will forget that you may need a drink.

## Doing the event

- Be ready to talk about:
  o the book and why you wrote it
  o its local interest / its national interest
  o the target audience or books benefits or key message/theme of the book
  o why you chose to self finance your publication
- Try to catch people's eye without accosting them... people generally will feel more comfortable engaging in chat if not being sold to; don't always sit in the seat. Get up and hover round to the side, fiddle with the books, the display board etc. whilst trying to catch people's eye, smiling etc.
- 'Hit' on people gently - choose your obvious target audience and people who are clearly browsing, not rushing.
- If trade is quiet then go for a wander, browse a few books, have a coffee; don't feel you have to just sit and wait.
- Sit and sign a few copies inbetween times as these will usually be labelled "Signed by Author" and left prominently on display.

**After the event**

Thank the store for anything and everything they have done to help you with your event. Remember, that whilst your efforts may have boosted sales for them, they may also have been involved in setting up the display – and be instrumental in the decision to leave the display up long after you have gone! They will be more inclined to help any subsequent enquiries about your book, and are more likely to re-order the book as stocks deplete.

## BUILDING AND MANAGING A DATABASE

As is becoming increasingly evident, you will need to keep a good record of the many people you will contact during the course of promoting your book.

If you are a serious self-publishing author or even a co-operative of self-publishing authors, then you will undoubtedly gather many contacts over a period of time. It is invaluable to keep a good and accurate log of each and every person you approach. It adds a bit of time to every approach you make, but once you get into the swing of updating it with each and every conversation, you will quickly see the value of this incremental time investment.

Below is an example of the database that I keep. It's quite simple and easy to update either digitally or by hand. Obviously it is not this easy to get a whole piece of editorial, but you get the point. If your contact passes the book over to someone else, then add them onto a new line and get their contact details by phoning back in. If you launch another book, then you have the previous contact details to hand. Sometimes you will get a call from another person on the same magazine many months later, and it is good to be able to lay your hands on the information immediately and sound knowledgeable about your previous dealings with them.

My example database:

| Company name & address | Contact name Phone number Email address | Who/what Information | Date of approaches & follow-up | Final action |
|---|---|---|---|---|
| Woman's Own Address Address Address | Jane Smith, Features Ed 020 7xxx 8xxx Jane.smith@x xxxx.com | Mainstream woman's mag; sometimes does author feature | Enquiry email 10/1/06 Phone chat on 19/1/06 Sent book on 20/1/06 Chased 15/2/06 | She is doing a piece in March edition |

If you are relying on post, then create a Label Table so you can easily print out a new sheet of labels each time. The reason I put the company name and address together is to make it easy to cut and paste the whole address when writing letters.

If you are on email, you can create a Distribution List which makes it easy each time you update your audience with information. Always get rid of any bounce-back addresses immediately. Ring a few days later to see if they got the email. If they didn't, then verify their address. If they forwarded it to someone else, then get this person's name, title and email address. If they have changed jobs (as they do frequently) and books are simply not relevant to them, then delete them from your address book.

If you engage them in conversation, log any information they gave you as you can use it another time.

### Listing the categories

A good database will comprise bookshops, media, specialist audiences and events places. In addition, you may wish to consider any of the below:

**Free newspapers:** There are thousands of free newspapers being issued, and the local library will undoubtedly stock these and/or be able to advise you.

**Newsletters:** there are thousands of news letters being created and issued to a vast range of different communities. A start point is to ask friends if they receive any newsletters that may be relevant to your subject matter ie. a crime book could be advertised in the Police Press, particularly if you have a friend who can introduce you, and you are prepared to offer a discount voucher. Another place to get this information from is the British Library, but you have to become a member, or a Reader as they call it.

**Writer's circles:** go to www.writers-circles.com for information. You can buy a fully updated database either as a set of labels or as a CD-rom for re-use.

### Reading Groups

Book groups tend to focus more on the literary must-reads ie. the prize-winners and the classics, although will consider suggestions from their members if someone has read or heard of something particularly niche but good. Should you propose a book to them that gets selected, you could then offer to attend the meeting where they discuss your book and you give them background information about the inspiration and chat about their assessment. People often like to know the story behind the story.

There is information about reading groups in a wide variety of places, from your local library, local bookshops and the above-mentioned online communities. Some of the online information sites include:

- www.bookgroup.info: the site that provides information for and about reading groups. They give advice about running a reading group, as well as having a newsletter and a searchable directory of book groups. If you run a bookgroup, they would like you to register it with them.

- www.fcbg.org.uk: The Federation of Children's Book Groups acts as an umbrella organisation for local autonomous children's book group around the UK. They organise activities in local areas with support from local schools and libraries.

- www.thereadinggrouponline, part of The Book People Ltd, this site is specifically for reading groups. Order 9 books and get the 10th free and collect book points. Contact queries@thereadinggrouponline.co.uk or phone 0870 191 9966

If you have any databases that you wish to share with other self-publishing authors, please email enquiries@indepublishing.com as my planned vision in the future is to create an online library of different databases for self-publishing authors. All submissions will be credited to the person who submitted it.

## SUMMARY

This concludes the section on Direct Selling; it should have given you plenty of ideas to get out there and sell. I also hope it has inspired you to want to sell which I believe is the fun part of book authoring and publishing. I will leave you with a few golden rules:

- o Make sure you can be found and contacted
- o Make sure your book can EASILY be bought
- o Manage expectations
- o Talk to the RIGHT audience
- o Build your database
- o Recycle good information
- o Have fun.

OVERALL, remember that it takes energy and commitment but can prove to be very rewarding.

# PART VIII

# MARKETING BUDGET

**How much to invest**
    **- Time?**
    **- Money?**

**Cost analysis**

**Market saturation**

**What to spend it on**

**Assessing likely return on investment**
    **- Maximising return**

*ISSUE: What price should I sell at?*

# MARKETING BUDGET

How much should an author invest into self-publishing? The rumour out there has it that you will be lucky to get away with a minimum cost input of £10,000, probably more like £15,000. In reality, this is simply not the case and nowadays you can even publish for free, albeit with major limitations, but remember that personal time investment rarely enters into the equation.

The evaluation of self-publishing companies undertaken in my partner title would indicate a completely different picture from the above statement, with prices clearly averaging around the £2,000 mark for 300 printed copies of a mid-sized paperback. For this, you get a basic edit (grammar & typos), a cover design, qualified typesetting, registrations and well-printed, well-produced books. None of the quotations include any form of marketing fees or costs for the creation of promotional material. None of the quotations include the cost of distribution and fulfilment. So how much should you spend?

Prices start from FREE from Lulu, albeit not including any editing, bespoke design, typesetting or registrations but merely being made available for sale via the company's own website; and the most expensive we saw was for the production of 10,000 hard-back copies of George Courtauld's self-published Pocket Book of Patriotism. This was a risky venture which fortunately paid off in his case, but this is not a recommended route.

### So much effort and for what return?
Only a very small percentage of authors derive any real money out of writing. Many of them have been writing for years before getting recognition. As John Banville, this year's Booker prize winner, said "Stick around long enough and it

comes to you." The sub-text of course being, "if you can afford to."

The critical question, as we saw at the outset, is 'what is your objective?' What are you hoping to achieve? This will dictate the route you should take and the amount of money you should invest.

Set a ceiling of what you can afford, and don't go beyond it because there are no guarantees. Not in mainstream publishing, and not in self-publishing. How much personal time can you afford to invest and how much in terms of cost? Many people see the cost of self-publishing purely as the cost of the publishing end of the process. But it is far more than this, both in terms of direct outgoings as well as the cost of not earning an income whilst you create the book. The cost of publication is only one part of the outgoings; it costs to sell a book, to promote yourself and creates sales aids.

**The cost of publishing must include the process of publication AND the costs of selling.**

### How much TIME to invest?

The process of selling a book is as time intensive as the process of writing and publishing that book, and can prohibit you from earning an income from a steady job. In the same way that new mothers believe they can carry on running their job from home with a new baby, so do authors believe they can squeeze the creation and promotion of a book around another job. But it is a job in itself, and a risky one at that as it doesn't come with any form of guarantee.

So how long can you really afford to take off a salaried job whilst you create, publish and sell a book? If you are intending to "go it alone" then do the maths and work out how you are going to meet your mortgage and living expenses. Factor in several thousand pounds for direct costs. Set a time limit against required expectation; don't go beyond it. if do, then extend it only once.

*"Know before you start whether you can afford to finish."*

For most people, the "go it alone" route is not tenable. Today, there are several very good self-publishing companies who can work with you through the publication process. As long as you are clear about what you want ultimately and you listen to their advice and guidance, you will end up with a viable and market-ready product whilst still comfortably running your day job. To do this properly, it is important to read *"What do I have to do to get a book published!"*

One major issue for self-publishers is the fact that many distributors do not wish to represent one-off titles, but look for volume accounts. Waterstone's have stopped their branches being able to order directly from individual publishers with their preferred supplier being established large wholesalers/distributors. Ottakar's express a similar preference. With any orders placed direct to the self-publisher, Ottakar's pass the cost of postage & packing directly onto the customer ordering the book, which means the customer may as well just buy it online – they will probably get the book a lot faster AND direct to their door.

This closed avenue results in self-publishing authors having to become distributors in their own right which is very time-consuming:

(i)    sell direct, either by door-to-door hand-selling to the bookshops

(ii)   sell online by setting up their own website and payment system

(iii)  undertake the fulfilment which means endless packing, posting and invoicing, stock warehousing and control which means your house is given over to books, brown paper, tape and stamps.

Self-publishers have to ask whether they can afford the time required to self-fulfil, or continue to find a viable solution elsewhere. Indebookshop.com, in its efforts to assist self-publishers, provides a solution which enables independent authors to get the maximum return on the sale of their book whilst obtaining all the benefits of a central distribution process.

## How much MONEY to invest?

I researched this question quite heavily, and the answers varied widely from "You should never pay to publish" to "As much as you can afford". The most advisable answer is probably somewhere inbetween.

One person suggested a total investment of around 10–20% of anticipated net sales, but I found this to be unhelpful as you don't know at the outset what this may be. If by nature you are an optimist, you would hope to sell 5,000 copies and may therefore spend far too much on production and promotional material. Equally, if you are a pessimist you would think yourself unlikely to sell more than 200 copies, and will produce a low-grade book that people reject on the grounds of poor production values rather than content.

Many authors choose to look at the cost of producing a book as simply the cost of printing it, and decide not to include the cost of editing, design and typesetting, preferring to see this as an investment rather than a cost. This is up to the individual author, of course, but my calculations that follow demonstrate the TOTAL cost based on a print run of 500. Once you have sold that 500 and are looking to reprint, your profit per book will be that much higher.

## Count your audience

### (i) the ones you know personally

The recommended start point is what you can afford to spend in relation to what you can afford to lose. Most self-publishing authors can expect to make back a proportion of what they spent, and the proportion is in direct relation to how many copies you KNOW you can sell. Add up your friends, family, colleagues and any societies / clubs etc you are a member of; add another 50% for any local bookshop and launch event sales. This might come to 300 books. That many you KNOW you can sell. It is a safe figure to work on.

| | |
|---|---|
| 250 page paperback to self-publish x 500 copies | - £2,800 |
| Promotional material | - £ 500 |
| Total cost | - £3,300 |
| | |
| Selling price £7.99 | |
| Send out 75 review copies, cost of p&p | - £ 75 |
| Total direct sales ie. 300 copies | + £2,397 |
| Less fulfilment costs for 300 copies* | - £ 150 |
| Total bookshop sales ie. 100 copies | + 799 |
| Less bookshop percentage of 35% | - £ 280 |
| Total income/loss** | - £609.00 |

*\* No fulfilment for copies sold at launch event*
*\*\*Have 25 left over unsold*

Many of the authors I have spoken to will comfortably achieve this two-thirds proportion of expenditure versus income. There are others who surpass the two-thirds relationship, but they will be the first to admit that it was hard work and time investment that got them past this point and turned them a profit. Obviously a critical factor within this calculation is the price you are selling the book for, and this is addressed in detail in this book's partner title, under the section "Setting the book price".

*"Easily accessed sales should provide a two-thirds return on initial investment"*

### *(ii) the ones you don't know*

The general public. These are the people that you may have reached out to via media coverage, a launch event or advertising but you have to work on a very low response rate:

o   At a festival or fair, 2% may buy
o   News review, 1% of readers may buy (sizable if national!)
o   TV chat show, 5% of watchers may buy (sizable if national!)

Most forms of promotional activity will drive a couple of sales, and generally the moment you stop promoting is the moment the sales start to tail off. Promotion means constantly reminding your target audience the book is there. There must be a steady drip of promotional activity which is why it must be cost effective. There is no point spending £300 per piece of promotional activity if it only nets you a handful of book sales.

Remember, that your first objective should be to sell all the books you printed. That is the first measure of a successful publication. After you have sold the first print run, remember that you cannot sell any more until you have the next print run, and this costs money. How many should you do? How many more can you sell? Should you, in fact, even do another print run or have you saturated your market – or rather, your easily accessible market?

> **"Selling the first print run is the first measure of a successful publication"**

## COST ANALYSIS

List carefully where and how you might be selling books and remember the hidden costs such as packing (labels, tape, letterhead, inks, envelopes as well as postage); attending events has the hidden costs of travel/subsistence; the phone bill quickly mounts up and the cost of sending out review copies is expensive if you include the cost of 'unsold' books. Many people edit this out either deliberately or accidentally.

o £3,300 in investment to self-publish the book
o Bracket that you might be able to 'lose' one-third if it comes to that
o Calculate the cost of review copies ie. circa 75 books to bookshops & media
o Have a ready audience of 300 people when count up friends, family etc
o Having a book event at local bookstore, and they are taking 100 copies; some will be left instore for ad hoc, ongoing sales
o Aim to retain a stock of 25 for ad hoc sales & opportunities
o Therefore need a print run of 500 books (paperback 250 pages)
o Assess the routes to publication – see options A, B or C – in order to see what your profit/loss may be in the first instance.

## OPTION A

Quoted price from self-publishing company for this is £2,800 with no 'reprinting' clause or agreement therefore authors has to fund future print runs

Cost per unit                                    £6.60 p/book
- Inc. edit, design, typeset, registrations and print at £2,800
- Inc. allowance for promo & launch event material at £500

Set book price at                                £7.99 p/book
Profit per book for direct sales,
    less 50p fulfilment allowance
    averaged out across total sales =            £0.89 p/book
Loss per book for bookshop sales
    @ bookshop 35% percentage                    -£1.41 p/book

Financial status at end of this first round of publishing and selling = -£609 down with 25 copies left in stock.

---

*Reprinting reinvestment to be seriously considered at this point as this is a further investment to be considered only if you can see a ready audience*

## OPTION B

Quoted price from self-publishing company for this is £3,000 with a fulfilment arrangement and a 'reprinting' clause

| | |
|---|---|
| Cost per unit for first 500 copies | £7.00 p/book |
| - Inc. edit, design, typeset, registrations and print at £3,00 | |
| - Inc. allowance for promo & launch event material at £500 | |
| Set book price at | £7.99 p/book |
| Profit per book for direct sales, less 50p fulfilment allowance averaged out across total sales = | £0.49 p/book |
| Loss per book for bookshop sales @ local bookshop 35% percentage | -£1.41 p/book |

Financial status at end of this first round of publishing and selling = -£810 down with 25 copies left in stock

*Reprinting is undertaken by self-publishing company, therefore profit potential changes for future books sold changes considerably; for example:*

| | |
|---|---|
| Reprint a further 500 copies | no charge |
| Profit per book sold via independent bookshop or Indebookshop £5.19 paid to publisher who keeps % for future reprints 35% paid onto author as royalties | +£1.82 p/book |
| Profit per book sold via chain bookshop/Amazon £3.20 paid to publisher who keeps % for future reprints 35% paid onto author as royalties | +£1.12 p/book |

If you manage to sell 250 copies via an independent and 250 copies via a bookchain, you stand to make around £700 for each run of 500, and ongoing reprints are paid for by the self-publishing company. It is simply up to you to keep hammering away at trying to secure those sales.

OPTION C
Print on demand, with a basic, one-off upfront charge then percentage deducted per book order.

I have based this quote on PABD who is a POD company that straddles the quality of service and production that you may get from a self-publishing 'full services' company.

| | |
|---|---|
| Upfront investment for Publishing Plus package to include all edit, design, typesetting and registrations, including Amazon.com and author getting 25 copies of their own | - £1500.00 |
| Print price per book thereafter for each book ordered | - £  4.70 p/book |
| *NB. can move to short/long print run and will be quoted separately* | |
| Assume you spend £500 on banner ads or other online advertising | - £  500.00 |
| Set book price for £7.99 for 250 page paperback | |
| Profit from direct sales via PABD website | £  3.29 p/book |
| Profit from sales via Amazon & other online at 35% discount | £  .49 p/book |
| Assume author sells 250 via direct PABD website sales | + £897.50 |
| And 250 books via Amazon | + £122.50 |

Financial status at end of this first round of publishing and selling = -£980 down with 25 copies left in stock. You don't need to consider reprinting, as this is POD. Further sales will gradually reduce your investment and over time will start to turn you into profit.

## Dividing up the total budget

Based on the above cost comparisons, you will need to divide up the total budget you have available and allocate it across the main processes you need to implement. Therefore, let's assume for arguments sake you have £3,500 in savings and you have a ready market of 300 book sales and can push this to 400 by promoting it via a local launch event. Divide it up as follows:

£1,350  edit/design/proof-reading
£1,500  print run
£  500  marketing (including review copy issuing)
£  150  fulfilment for direct sales

This is what I would call a very tight budget, with no room for manoeuvre, but is a realistic sum in terms of what the average author is prepared to invest. My recommendation is to have a total budget of £5000 which enables a realistic approach to postage, phones, travel etc as well as allowing for a couple of alternative pieces of promotional material. Equally, I know other authors who have thrown £10,000 into giving birth to their "baby."

## Market Saturation

The real task, with any of the above cost scenarios, is in knowing whether you have reached market saturation for the demand of your book – or whether you have merely exhausted specific avenues but you still have other avenues to explore.

Fully armed with the knowledge that books that do most well are the ones that touch on a nerve or are in tune with a topic in society, authors also become totally blind as to whether their subject matter is genuinely headline news. Of course it is! They wouldn't have slaved over it for the last year if it wasn't guaranteed to be a hot topic for the media to pick up and run with!

Sadly, sometimes the moment has passed, or maybe it peaked whilst your first print run was at the printers, and by the time your book is off the presses, the enthusiasm for that subject matter has dwindled. Or maybe someone more famous has already published something and owns the territory? Do your research at the outset. Try to understand what phase a trend is in. The great thing about self-publishing is that you can respond very quickly to trends. The hard work comes in trying to make a loud enough noise that people will hear you.

This is why it is critical to have a campaign plan at the outset, to have done the marketing plan before investing time and money. Endeavour to work out exactly who you can reach and how much it will cost you to reach them. Ensure you are buying the best you can for the budget allocated and determine where the greatest value lies. Understand what you can do yourself without ever affecting quality.

Stick to the plan as much as possible. Work out the likely journey; be ready to adapt as opportunities present themselves.

Most authors skip past the initial planning and research and arrive at the launch point flailing and throwing money randomly at activities that may never provide any form of return.

## WHAT TO SPEND IT ON

The cost of launching your first book is the most expensive with the least guarantee of return. Should you enjoy the whole experience and sense of achievement at publishing your first book, and maybe had some success at it, you may go onto publish another. There will be some economies of scale, particularly in terms of the learning curve and personal time investment.

But what to spend your budget on will always come down to what your objective is. You may decided to throw the bulk of your budget at high production values, creating a niche, gifty title which is, in itself, your selling tool and promotional item. Equally, you may wish to provide a standard trade book but throw money into creating some weird and wacky promotional item or activity that will be attention-grabbing. Only you can really decide, but once you are clear on your objective, then you should be able to confidently determine how much should be allocated to the main task. The rest of the budget should then be divided across the other costs.

### Investment has a direct relationship to objective

We read in Section V that a good promotional campaign will mix & match paid-for promotions with freebie promotions, with a view to doubling the impact gained. If you get something for free like media coverage or associated promotion by another company, then double your impact by taking out some advertising or giving away from freebie items. Careful investment should either push for the reviews or exploit reviews.

### Double your impact by combining investment and freebies

Your marketing plan should target as many of these free forms of promotion as possible. Focus on finding these, and your cost investments should ride on the back of them. The problem with freebies is there is no guarantee. If freebies are forthcoming, then consider what paid-for forms of promotion will best exploit them. If no freebies are forthcoming, you may need to 'buy' some promotion in order to encourage the freebies.

The caveat for this being that, if you increase advertising, you may well increase the amount of sales you make but you have also increased the amount of investment.

**It is easier to raise SALES than to raise PROFIT.**

How much you choose to invest in promotional material is dependent on the sales potential. This is difficult to assess in advance and the optimist will arrive at a different answer from the pessimist. But you can get a fairly good idea by asking yourself a series of questions... how much can you do yourself? How much time do you have available to do it? Can you do it in the time frame to meet all deadlines? Only you can answer these questions – the important rule is to ask them.

Go through your marketing plan and list out all the forms of promotional activity you WANT to do, and consider the likely return against each form of activity. How many sales can it reliably return, and focus your energies on the highest.

Other than all of this putative assessment, I work on the premise that promotional material should not add more than 50p per book maximum. If you have a print run of 300 books to sell, then divide the cost of each form of activity across the 300 books. If it cuts too deeply into your profit, then it is obviously too expensive.

Unless of course, your objective is to invest heavily in the first book or print run in order to establish a reputation... and we come back to the question of what your objective is.

## Assessing likely investment in different activities

### Talks

| | | |
|---|---|---|
| o | Build database of who to | free |
| o | Arrange series of dates | free |
| o | Do flyers, posters, business cards etc | cost |
| o | Travel to talks | cost |
| o | Contact local media for pre-announcement and/or coverage | free |
| o | Contact local bookshops | free |
| o | Develop your database | free |
| o | *Income from bookshop sales and any direct sales* | |

### Exhibitions
- o   Paid-for stand                                    cost
- o   Promotional posters and flyers       cost
- o   Time: 1+ days on the stand             time
- o   Develop database of contacts         free
- o   Follow-up and make sales               free
- o   *Income from contacts made at fair*
  *(buying books or rights)*

### Specialist magazines
- o   Chasing feature or article                free
- o   Advertise for a couple of months
  after the article comes out                 cost
- o   Contact any relevant people or businesses
  who feature or advertise in the magazine;
  sell to them or create a business synergy       free
- o   Search for information – critical dates,
  influential spokes-people, other events,
  other channels of information             free
- o   *Income from associated sales through media*
  *coverage, or direct sales by new business association*

## ASSESSING LIKELY RETURN

One's natural instinct for pessimism or optimism comes into play when trying to guestimate what the likely return of the above activities may be. I err on the side of cynicism. If the event you are chasing is clearly going to be FULL of your target audience, you can feel fairly confident that you will make a fair few sales.

Always work on the principle of dividing cost by profit and calculate the investment in terms of how many books you are likely to sell. If you have to sell 75 books to start turning a profit, then think closely:

    (i)   what are really the chances of selling 75 books?

(ii) How much time are you prepared to invest in order to get this off the ground? And how often?

Consider how many avenues you can invest time and money into, and prioritise the ones that seem to offer the best opportunity. Target those. With the remaining ones, it is still worth contacting the organisers/planners/producers and see what you can get for free, or how negotiable they are on their rates for advertising. Remember the last minute – they may have some spaces they wish to fill.

**Maximising return on investment (ROI)**
Return on investment is the cost plus time in contrast to the immediate return and longer-term benefit. The complexity lies in not knowing what the immediate or longer term benefits are going to be. Suffice it to say, don't invest too heavily into the unknown but target the more reliable income-earners primarily. It's good to have some "big hairy goals" but keep the effort in perspective, and focus on the low-hanging fruit first. Equally, many authors choose not to count their time investment at all which simplifies the maths, but should enter into the equation at least a year after launch when you may be considering whether to reprint, or launch a new title, or creating a new annual marketing plan.

The costs for the production of any new product are always heavily weighted to the front end or early selling period. Self-publishing your own book is no different.

**How to maximise the return on your investment:**

1. *Research your market first* and spend wisely: you can do a Masters course in Book Marketing for $12,000 in the States, or follow these guides in the "What do I have to do to…" series for £22.00 (if you buy both together on Indebookshop.com)!

2. ***Gain economies of scale*** by doing a print run; then work flat out to sell every single last copy; saturate your market as much as you possibly can. Pocket the money and don't do a further print run unless you have good reason to reprint ie. an order from a bookchain.

3. ***Amortise the investment*** over the longer term by planning to spend a small but regular sum on promotional activity and endeavour to establish your voice as a spokesperson on your subject matter. Maybe you are planning a series of books, and can amortise the costs of promotion because you are advertising several titles, and/or a business.

4. ***Build your presence*** by sending out newsletters, flyers, doing talks and promoting the talk, have a PR or marketing agent who taps away, reminding people you are there; immerse yourself fully, build contacts and create noise, and ensure your friends, family and work colleagues are on board with project, doing the word of mouth recommendation.

5. ***Work effectively:*** develop your database and log everything you do. Always seek to reduce duplication and repetition; use email and the web for as much as possible as it is as free as it gets; chase all freebie opportunities; double the impact by appropriate advertising with freebie opportunities; do everything logically and in the right order to maximise visibility; make a big noise in a small area.

6. ***Success breeds success:*** build on great reviews and large orders to entice the next 'target' along; obtain sales data from your distributor or a book store and shout about good sales figures to get stocks in more stores or to secure a feature in the newspaper about yourself and your book;

use reviews to encourage instore presence and vice verse - use instore presence to encourage reviews.

**Can the publishers do it better?**

Yes and no. Obviously publishers have experience, knowledge, skills and economies of scale on their side. However, they suffer from the need to globalise and focus on scale, with minimum budgets to allocate to all books. Only a handful of reliable authors will get the truly big budgets, and the rest will get a standardised promotional exercise.

Yet book marketing, in today's overloaded market, is about dedicated and constant promotion. Big publishers just cannot do that. Reliance is increasingly on authors, yet many mainstream authors suffer from a lack of knowing how they can participate. I truly believe that there has never been a better time for authors to be able to immerse themselves in the selling process and make a mark for themselves.

Having spent many months researching the industry, I was recently sent the Society of Authors' booklet on marketing books, and it advises mainstream authors to do everything that the self-publishers recommend. This was enlightening, and substantiated all my own beliefs. Ultimately, the only difference between mainstream and independent publishing is scale and who is paying for the production of the book.

Whilst mainstream offers a breadth that smaller independents and self-publishers cannot achieve, including the global selling of rights, the fact is that more books and rights have to be sold for the author to get any real return on the average 7–10% royalty. Self-publishers can afford to sell fewer in order to get a return and build a value in order to sell it to a bigger publisher.

## Issue: What price should I sell at?

Selecting a price is a bit of an arbitrary and wasted decision today, now that discounting is standard and discounts are passed back to the originator.

In fact, discounting is not really discounting but simply the practice of setting a new price. Has anyone actually seen a copy of Harry Potter and the Half-Blood Prince selling for the RRP of £16.99?

I tried very hard to not flag up Harry Potter as the example of every point I wished to make in *"What do I have to do to get a book published!"* because it is so utterly over-documented. But we must accept that the Harry Potter phenomenon is the sad example of mass-market publishing, extreme discounting and the general over-production that plagues the industry.

Some of the most extreme discounting was seen with the recent Harry Potter title, priced at £16.99 and sold, at its cheapest, at £4.00. This is clearly considerably less than the cost of the paper the 700-page book was printed on. And why did we see such extreme discounting? Was this necessary in order to sell in the volumes required to make it a success? Of course not. The chances are Harry Potter Book 6 would still have sold in the same volume as it did irrespective of the price. Market saturation is market saturation. Just because you like a book doesn't mean you'll buy two of it. Maybe the heavy discount grew the market by 25% ie. an extra 25% of buyers decided to buy it because it was cheap – it still didn't grow the VALUE of the industry. Simply the volume. More trees died with less investment to replant.

*"The Bookseller estimated that £35m was lost to the trade in the deep discounting of Harry Potter in the first two days of sale."*
Danuta Kean, The Author, Spring 2004

This illustrates a point. The majority of consumers were going to buy the book anyway – irrespective of the price. Cut-pricing did not grow the 'Harry Potter' market, it merely redistributed who gained from selling the book.

Discounted prices are not borne by the person who discounted, but by the publisher and author. Mainstream authors have to hope they sell in a high enough volume that they see some return for all their hard work being discounted to the bone, and self-publishing authors struggle to set a price which provides any profit yet is low enough to compete with the rest of the market.

It is questionable how discounting can be undertaken with no form of discussion or agreement unless the discounter is choosing to 'take the hit'. The retailer takes his self-same percentage despite the fact that his marketing effort was simply to cut the price until it sold. How does that justify his percentage? He should have to share in the reduced profit.

The small publisher and independent author should also be able to dictate the minimum selling price, or when discounts can be applied, or how long they can run for.

For small and self-publishers, discounting is a form of Barrier to Trade. Arbitrarily reducing the publisher's profit margins, at no loss to the seller, is certainly a way of squeezing out the small independent. Self-publishers invariably produce low print runs with a higher cost per unit, and cannot afford to sell a book below a certain price – yet they do not get consulted about the discounts so easily offered. Surely there is some form of control. Surely they can set a minimum price below which they cannot afford to sell?

> ***Cut-pricing is a battle between booksellers,
> not between publishers.***

So what really is the benefit of heavy discounting? Proponents of price cutting as a viable selling method claim that it has increased the <u>volume</u> in the bookselling industry;

maybe so but it hasn't increased the <u>value</u> of the industry. They argue that it encourages shoppers to buy in greater volume, but books are a one-off purchase generally.

Perpetual discounting is merely an expression of the worst aspects of consumerism where shoppers expect rock bottom prices, but sadly all they end up with is the homogenisation of range, low quality and restricted choice. There is always a minimum price below which it is not commercially viable to produce and sell an item, and in a consumerist society the first products to suffer are hand-crafted, bespoke items. Their price tags reflect the time investment and lack of economies of scale. The value of books has been permanently devalued, and service has suffered accordingly.

*I don't mind paying full price for something that I know I want;*
*I do resent paying half-price for something that I didn't want.*

Self-publishing books are price sensitive but there has to be an economic viability. Irrespective of who paid for the production of a book, people won't want to buy something purely because it is cheap. There has to be a desire for the product and a reason to believe that it will deliver a benefit or enjoyment.

Books, like products, will have a saturation point irrespective of price. If there is a high demand, then you will have a high saturation point before fulfilling all demand for your book. Most self-publishing authors never really reach the book's saturation point; instead they reach the limitations of their marketing and communication capability.

The best advice for a self-publishing author is to not engage in cut-pricing where you can avoid it. After all, what's the point of selling if you are paying for the honour of selling it? It is too easy for the self-publishing author to find himself in this position.

## Does self-publishing ever provide a return?

Yes it does. There are enough well-promoted success stories out there to substantiate the fact that self-publishing CAN provide a return, and most authors can sell around 300 copies of their book to friends, family, acquaintances, work colleagues, local community and specialist interest groups. Equally, we all know authors who have tried but not recovered their initial outlay.

The cynics will tell you that *"even if a self-publisher recoups his costs, he doesn't recoup his time investment."* To that I say, neither do many mainstream published authors. As John Banville said, *"... if you stick around long enough."* Most of us cannot actually afford to, however.

The one piece of knowledge I know for certain, having worked in the industry for two years and thoroughly researched these two books, is:

*"The common thread for all successful self-publishing authors lies in their tireless self-promotion."*

Ultimately it is up to the author. Write something good, brand it clearly, announce it widely, spend wisely, promote it tirelessly and you will find your audience. It's not easy but it is possible.

There are many who question whether self-published titles have any real worth, but reassuringly, the late Lynda Lee-Potter said of a Book Guild book entitled "The Almost Impregnable Miss Parker' by Ethel Dallin is *"One of the best autobiographies I have ever read... It confirms... this country is full of unknown creative talent, possessed by natural, powerful writers who have a dazzling ability to express what they feel with passion, purity and truth."*

# PART IX

# SELLING RIGHTS

What exactly is a right?

What rights are for sale?

How to sell rights?
    Who to sell to
    How to use book fairs
    How to pitch the idea
    How to create an initial agreement

Pricing formulas and contract parameters

Further reading

# SELLING RIGHTS

The purpose of this section is to provide new authors to the basic principles of selling rights. It is intended solely as a first introduction, as many reading this book will have no prior experience. If you seek further information, read Lynette Owen's book "Selling Rights" which is more indepth.

Selling books to the home market is only one part of the total marketplace that mainstream publishers sell to. They also seek to sell to export markets (other English-speaking countries); sell publishing or translation rights, serialisation/ extract rights and/or film/tv/radio rights. All of these areas increase the income returned to authors – and many of these areas are not easily accessible to self-publishing authors.

The value of the written word is in how many times you can re-sell the same content. Many self-publishing authors will see self-publishing as a route to selling to a mainstream publishing house in order to reap the benefits of having an experienced rights person. As a self-publisher, many have difficulty in exploiting sales rights.

**What exactly is a RIGHT?**
An author owns the copyright to his own material unless he ASSIGNS it or LICENSES it (see 1988 Copyright Act) to somebody else for an agreed fee. The standard copyright for any text is 70 years or "in perpetuity" which means 70 years. Should you assign or licence the copyright to a publisher, you are being paid a flat-fee to hand over all copyright to that material. For certain commissions, authors are perfectly happy to do this.

Other than this, you retain the overall copyright but can sell off different uses of your text ie. you are giving people permission to use your original text in different ways. Not only does selling rights earn income, but it enables your book to get to a wider and broader audience.

In a mainstream publishing house, the rights team get involved in an early decision as to whether to publish a book and the publishing programme is determined 1–2 years ahead of publication date. Income from rights sales contributes greatly to a publishing house's income.

**Some definitions**

Moral rights
This is a right which is designed to protect the artistic integrity and reputation of the author. It can only be claimed by people, not companies, institutions or employees.

They must be asserted in writing to the publisher and, once asserted, the publisher must ensure that every copy of the work published and licensed bears the author's name. There are four different rights included within the description:
- o   To be identified as the author
- o   To not have the work treated in a derogatory way
- o   To not have someone else's work attributed to you
- o   To have privacy in private photos

Volume rights
When publishers are buying rights, they will probably refer to Volume Rights which means a definition of the following parameters:
- o   the format ie. hardback / paperback
- o   the territory ie. US, UK Language & Rest of World*
- o   the reprint rights ie. hardback, trade paperback and mass-market paperback.

*Sometimes other publishers may buy world rights but cannot sub-license these rights; would have to buy subsidiary rights in order to do this.*

Publishing territories

Historically, agreements existed as to how the world was divided in terms of publishing and bookselling ownerships. UK territorial rights included the Commonwealth countries. Territorial rights have come under fire recently as the world changes, allegiances and associations change and then, of course, there's the internet which is the global shop.

**What rights are for sale?**

We will go on to explain what each of the below are, and what some standard approaches are. In reality there is no great mystery to this and the measure of success is in your negotiation skills. After all, all you are doing is trying to find the price at which someone might buy what you are trying to sell.

1. Permissions
2. Serialisation / extracts
3. Electronic rights
4. Publishing rights
   a. Translation rights
   b. Foreign distribution
5. Non-print rights
   a. Radio
   b. Audio
   c. Film and tv, inc. tv tie-ins (very popular) ideal for current event, local angle, human interest
6. Co-printing (illustrated and concept books)
7. Bookclub rights

**1. PERMISSIONS**

Anyone wishing to reproduce any part of your text to reprint into an article or book (for example) will need to get your permission. People will need to seek 'permission' for any of the following Anthology & Quotation Rights (A&Q), Radio &

TV readings / extracts, Talking books, some electronic rights (e:e, e:print, print:e, p:p), Braille, Customised ie. large print.

It is notoriously difficult to monitor this, just as it is a nightmare for authors trying to track down the correct person to ask permission from. One thing that Indebookshop seeks to do is facilitate this and make it easy for people to buy permissions and rights from the original author.

**Text:**

o  Don't spend time and effort on low-cost permissions; work out your own formula ie. minimum fee £50 x minimum transaction ie. 500 words; a picture.
o  Charge per transaction
o  Poetry is often charged by line
o  Remember: it is your right to say no if you so choose

*Formula examples:*

-  Item x territory x language x edition = £50
-  500 words x 2 territories x 1 language x 1 edition = £100
-  1000 words x 1 territory x 1 language x 1 edition = £100

**Pictures:**

o  Do you own copyright / permission in order to give permission to use, or do you have restricted use?
o  What print run quantity?
o  Sometimes it is interesting to know how they are going to use it ie. lead image in a big advertising campaign vs. small picture on a charity leaflet
o  the size being used doesn't matter (altho picture libraries charge on size to page)
o  *Formula: number of pictures x territory x edition*

**Create your own agreement\*:**

-  What you are licensing ie. book title, author, edition, extract from/to
-  Where being used ie. language, territory

- Term of licence: ie. duration or print run
- Credit / Acknowledgement line to be made
- Agreed fee
- Payment date: on publication
- No alterations may be made without signed approval
- Publisher to supply gratis copy on request
- Include a termination line: This license expires if payment is 30 days overdue, the publication goes out of print, payee's publishing house closes down, at the end of the licence term or print run

*\* The only exception to this is a BBC contract\*. Example of BBC contract is on the Publisher's Association website.*

## Electronic permissions

Electronic permissions is ultimately just another format – hardback, paperback, CDRom, e-book. Obviously this type of permission has to be multi-jurisdiction, you cannot limit to certain regions.

- o What you are licensing ie. book title, author, edition, extract from/to
- o Where being used ie. language, the internet
- o Term of licence: ie. duration (often 3-5 years)
- o Credit / Acknowledgement line to be made
- o NO SUBSIDIARY RIGHTS INCLUDED ie. they cannot sub-license it to other sites
- o Agreed fee
- o Payment date: on publication
- o No alterations may be made without signed approval
- o Publisher to supply gratis copy on request
- o Include a termination line: This license expires if payment is 30 days overdue, the publication goes out of print, payee's publishing house closes down, at the end of the licence term or print run

## 2. EXTRACT & SERIAL RIGHTS

These are sold to media who wish to use an extract or abridgement, or run a serialisation in a publication. There are two types available:

- First or pre-publication serial
- Second or post-publication serial.

**Approach**

o Send email information/advice to the editor, inviting their interest; clearly indicating why you believe it will be of interest to them.

o Upon any interest expressed, you may wish to send them a Confidentiality Agreement which binds them to not publishing the extract prior to a given date (usually 24-48 hours prior to publication date). The need for this is usually with explosive subjects and stellar authors, but do bear it in mind.

o Send a copy of the book, with clear terms set out in an accompanying letter – ie. no publication of any material without prior permission.

o If you genuinely believe you have a "crowd-puller" book, then be audacious in naming a sum, but don't be greedy. There is a difference. Consider *"what is it worth to them?"* rather than *"what can it be worth to me?"*

o Remember: if you are an unknown author, the publicity value of having an extract of your book in a national newspaper has a value in itself. Ring the major chain buyers and let them know – by phone, by email and by post, and then chase them on their response. Phone local media and see if they want second serialisation.

*Remember... build and recycle.*

**Exclusivity**

If you have several media interested, then you can stipulate the Exclusivity or not.

- o If NON-EXCLUSIVE, you can sell to as many media as you can interest
- o f EXCLUSIVE, the price should reflect this (particularly if there is a <u>lot</u> of interest)
- o Equally with EXCLUSIVITY you can stipulate the category of media ie. exclusive national daily press, exclusive weekly magazine etc or exclusive women's national magazine etc.

**Advice**
- o Buyers of serialisation and extracts usually only want the 'juicy bits' which may in turn undermine book sales. Bear this in mind when negotiating fees and either make it worth your while to sell the juiciest bit by charging higher fees, or endeavour to sell a section that builds up to the intrigue.
- o Define how much they can use.
- o Agree and stipulate the credit line, where it is being published and the date of publication.
- o Issue a letter of agreement.

## 3. ELECTRONIC RIGHTS

These are rights to allow a third party to print all or part of your book. In the modern world, these rights begin to have a greater and greater value, so be sure when selling any rights whether Electronic Rights have slipped into the small print. They have a funny habit of being overlooked.

Electronic rights can cover:
- o Electronic display rights such as E-books, as a whole or in chapters, or Verbatim use of text from part of a volume
- o Electronic multi-media rights such as the interactive adaptation of a book or the website of the book

It will begin to mean more and more as podcasting, gaming, digital book search programmes etc become more advanced over the coming years.

### Advice

- Keep platforms together (see www.ebookweb.com) ie. web, mobiles, etc; find out what platforms they can cross-produce to; internet is invariably world rights basis.
- Because it is wide-spread and constantly changing, authors are advised to keep non-exclusive wherever possible and to only sell short licences (3 months – 1 year).
- Check their security ie. DRM which tracks who has sold what rights, who owns what and that money goes to rightful owner.
- Any renewal fees should be linked to initial payment.

### 4. PUBLISHING & DISTRIBUTION RIGHTS

This means that you are selling somebody the right to reproduce and sell your title in their country. This will be defined as being:

(1) foreign publishing rights – where you are selling the rights for the book to be printed and sold in English in a foreign market; includes export publishing rights – where you are selling the rights in an English-speaking market. See also US Rights.

(2) translation rights – where you are selling the rights for the book to be translated, printed and sold in a foreign market.

(3) Distribution rights – where you negotiate a rate for a local distributor to sell your book in their market.

### Foreign publishing rights

*US Rights*

America is a massive market and as such, US rights are often negotiated independently of other rights. Agents are increasingly retaining the US rights sales to sell on behalf of their authors whilst offering up all other rights with comparative ease.

## Asian Rights

China is an emerging economy with huge growth potential in the consumer market. It offers plenty of opportunity to publishers to sell book rights. There are 100,000 retailers in China (some large, thousands of small) selling 7 billion books per annum.

*"Beijing's latest move to open up its book distribution sector has publishers and booksellers drooling, not least because IDC (International Data Corporation) has valued the China book market at some $3.33 billion. Joint-venture bookstores on a 51%–49% basis are now allowed in some 14 major cities."* Publishers Weekly 19/5/2003

There are many issues to be addressed, and the small self-publisher may suffer as a result of these. Distribution and bibliographic databases are still of a very poor standard, and piracy remains an issue albeit gradually diminishing as the Government tightens controls. E-commerce understandably lags a long way behind the West, and cash remains the main purchasing route as few people (by proportion) hold credit cards, although a report recently indicates:

*"E-commerce, including online book shopping, is quickly catching on in China. Market researcher IDC reported that Chinese consumers spent 4.8 billion US dollars in online shopping last year; the figure is expected to grow to 14.6 billion US dollars by 2005."* China Daily, 29/1/06

The main chains are:
o   Xinhua is a state-owned book organisation with 13,000 stores and other retail outlets.

- o Xooyo Chain has smart stores in the Guandong and southern provinces which targets students and businessmen.
- o Xishu is a national network of 500 bookshops and franchises.
- o 21st Century is another bookshop chain.
- o Bertelsmann is the main bookclub.
- o Online book shops include:
- o Joyo.com which is now owned by Amazon; tipped to become China's largest online book retailer
- o Dangdang.com is currently China's largest online book retailer

**Translation rights**

Publishers will seek translations rather than sale of publishing rights when they are trying to get 'brand' established in that country for wider book sale purposes despite that translation is a more expensive way of acquiring local presence. With selling translation rights, the brand name of a publisher is important and smaller companies may find it hard to compete because they are not established.

Some books cannot sell translation rights ie. they culturally don't travel, they are economically unviable to produce, are against local copyright conventions, have banned political views or have to seek translation sub-agents. The types of books that 'travel' are usually:

- o best-sellers, or books with proven sales ie. 2nd edition+
- o fiction and children's (esp on author reputation)
- o biographies of well-known people
- o books by any author who's changed status ie. won a major prize
- o academic/text books where knowledge lacks in that market

This works much as a publishing right does, with the major areas to be ironed out with translation rights is the accuracy of the translation. Are you going to demand a back-translation, and if so, who pays for it? You would be within your rights to expect them to, but they may baulk at it. For personal reputation, will you be prepared to absorb the cost?

## 5. NON-PRINT RIGHTS

Most authors dream of seeing their book on the big silver screen, and it does happen to self-publishing authors – Cold Mountain, Legally Blonde, Shadowmancer, and several others. The rights included under the descriptor "Non-Print Rights" can include any of the following:

1. Film & TV Rights
2. Merchandising
3. Dramatic rights: plays, musicals, ballets
4. Audio

A standard contract with a mainstream publisher awards authors with around 80-90% of royalty on sale of options and/or film rights. Maybe an agent was involved. They are increasingly taking 15-20% today. Additionally, within a Film Rights contract, many other rights may well be included such as merchanding and electronic rights.

The self-publishing author needs to carefully offset two opposing needs – one is to make as much money as possible (and the money is in reselling content as many times as possible for as much money) versus visibility. When an offer comes your way, you need to consider if VERY carefully. Maybe it's not as high profile as you dreamed. Maybe it's not for as much money as you'd hoped for. Maybe this is simply the beginning or maybe it's your one and only shot. Only you can decide whether you accept or decline.

### Film & TV Rights

o This includes dramatisation and animation either for cinema, television and video/streaming.
o Merchandising rights are usually included within this.

- o Sometimes it includes electronic rights although you should specify a particular use ie. electronic clips to promote their product or interactive game related to film. Don't just sign it over wholesale.
- o The other element to Film & TV Rights is the Residuals ie. after making film for cinema, might go onto TV, video and CD; you need to get percentage of these.
- o Advice: keep a tab on where it is distributed and follow up with translation sales of books.

### What books make a good film?

Not every type of work of fiction or biography will make a great film. Bestsellers are an obvious one, but for new, unknown authors the interesting factor may be that it is an originally-told story, or have a strong voice/theme or central character, or have an emotional resonance.

### Submissions

Send copies to head of drama or documentary departments at TV companies and to mainstream/small independent production companies – TV and films. Accompany your approach with as many reviews as possible. Ideally, if you have experience of scripts, write a 3–4 page screen treatment and send that.

### Contracts:

Should you be hurtling towards a Sale of Film rights, you are best advised to arm yourself with an experienced negotiator. Phone an agent. Phone a solicitor. Some top-line information is as follows:

- o "Options" are usually bought, which means the interested buyer 'reserves' the possibility of buying the film rights, and the copyright holder cannot continue to tout them round for sale. The standard options period is 12–18 months whilst the option-holder develops ideas and raises finance. The option price is usually 10% of purchase price.

o At the end of the 12–18 months, may re-option or move to Sale of Rights.

o Purchase price is usually 5% of production price inc. actors fees. Can set a floor limit ie. £100,000; they will set a ceiling but ensure it's not too low.

o Keep rights together & always try film first ie:
  - Film, TV, video
  - Electronic games / website
  - Merchandising

o Assignment / licence signed on commencement of photography
  - Includes licence to make any number of films, remakes, sequels, spin-offs in all media in perpetuity (70 years)

Reference points
  o Screen International: www.screendaily.com
  o British film Institute: www.bfi.org.uk
  o Internet Media Database: www.imdb.com: complete database of all production companies
  o The film industry's annual bible – The Knowledge: www.theknowledgeonline.com

## Merchandising rights

If there is no film in the offing, you may wish to try to sell merchandising rights anyway. The opportunity exists when you have a very strong character or design. The best place to look around for ideas is to go to Gift Fairs to spot possibilities; try to visualise your character on their product. Some products may not be worth the effort once you've done your calculations, but might have great PR value. Do your figures and bear in mind that shops take around a 50% discount off retail price.

If you are taking this route, then don't forget that the image will need trade marking; you may need to set up a company and you should also set up a website to ensure people can find you. Suddenly this becomes a job in itself.

### Dramatic rights: plays, musicals, ballets
These are rarely bought. However, if you are approached then a standard formula is 6–12% of ticket price which they can work out by formula "bums on seats x length of run of show". You will need to determine whether you are selling performance rights (you adapt) or publication rights (they adapt).

### Audio
There are 75million audio books published to date, which sounds like a vast quantity but generally only best-sellers and classics have been made into audio books. This is arguably the only range of books that are desirable to Audio Rights Buyers but this is an imbalance that RNIB are seeking to have redressed as 96% of books in the market today are not available in audio. Equally, this statistic is set to change drastically by the uptake of podcasting.

Sound quality is obviously critical and anyone investigating this avenue must ensure the company they use or sell to has an evidential and proven track record. Audio fees for tapes are often based on advance + royalty per copy sold (like books) whereas radio fees are usually paid £ per minute

Good contacts
- Talking business magazines 020 7819 1111
- Spoken word publishing 01952 680131
- The British Federation of audio 020 7930 3206

### How to sell non-print rights
In order to evaluate an offer, you may wish to consider:
- o how many people will be involved on the project?
- o who else's work will be in it ie. who enhances who?

- o how will it be marketed? Is there an opportunity to earn more income further down the line?
- o What PR value is there for you?
- o What is their budget?
- o Where is the money generated? If there is an associated product, then ask for a percentage of sales instead.
- o What would it cost them to originate the material?
- o Who are they ie. what have they done before?

## 6. CO-PRINTING

If you are producing a highly visual book with standardised templates of text which could easily be replaced by other language texts, and you believe the book has a global appeal, you may wish to try to get other foreign publishers interested in sharing a print run price.

Because full-colour books are expensive to print, and there are great cost savings to be had in a bigger print run, it may become worth your while to share the cost with other markets. But there is a lot of work in finding your co-publishers, and this time investment is only worth it against solid information that the world truly wants this book.

## 7. BOOK CLUB RIGHTS

We looked at book clubs earlier, but one point that is worth adding under this section on selling rights is this. If your book has a demonstrable 'club' value, it is worth approaching a book club to see if they want to share the cost of a print run with you. Therefore, rather than selling your book at a massive discount, you may wish to gain economies of scale in print in order to maximise your profit margin on your own stock.

## HOW TO SELL RIGHTS

Selling rights sounds more complex and inaccessible than the reality of it. The best advice is to think about what you want to sell, do a bit of research (here, Lynette Owen's book) and decide what you want to sell.

*For example*: maybe you want to get your book into America but it is cost-prohibitive to ship a UK-printed copy and you cannot interest a US-distributor because you have no viable US-based marketing plan. Consider selling the publishing rights to a US-based publisher.

To find them, subscribe to the Literary Market Place (www.literarymarketplace.com). It's not cheap, but you can subscribe on a weekly basis which may be enough for you to get a host of publisher and/or agent names.

Prepare a pitch ie. why they should consider buying your offer and why your book is so appropriate for the American market, and start contacting people on the list.

Get feedback as you wade through the rejections. Evolve and perfect your pitch. Review whether your book is indeed right for the US market? If you have UK-based success in the meantime then let them know. Add it into your pitch. Local success can only enhance your appeal.

### Using book fairs to sell rights

The best start point for the self-publishing author is to turn up to your nearest book fair and get a copy of the Directory of stand-holders. There are many international publishing companies present, as well as their Trade Council who will willingly give you information about local publishers and agents who seek to trade in rights.

There is always a Rights section but this is invariably sealed off to the public, and you can only access this area by having a meeting previously set up.

Don't fret about not being able to get into where all of the agents and publishers are, as most of them have received prior information about the meetings they are having. If you really believe you have something worth selling, then approach the publisher before the Fair and use the Fair as a place to hammer out the detail.

The below aims to give you some basis and start-point but the rules are that there are no rules. This is, in effect, a marketplace where you can barter and haggle, and expect the unexpected.

## Summary tips:

o Start planning 8–10 weeks beforehand getting meetings into the diary

o Make it clear what you want, whether you are buying or selling.

o Do most of the work the week before via phone and email; to find out who you need, go through to your counterpart and ask

o Follow up: keep a log of who you saw, when, why and get back to them within a fortnight.

o Book fair directories are the best source of information; they are like gold-dust. If you get one, hold onto it tightly.

## A checklist for selling rights

o If you are publishing completely independently, then you will obviously own all the rights and can sell them as you wish.

o If you are publishing with a company offering self-publishing services, check your contract to see (i) if they take any percentage and (ii) on what basis ie. if they are seeking to sell rights and using their contacts to do so.

o Ask yourself if there is any reason not to sell? *If you are tying up a television or film deal in America, then you won't want to sell the publishing rights – or if you do, it will have a marked effect on the price you sell it for.*

o   What alternative markets might the book be suitable for? And why? (This forms basis of your pitch or approach to them.)

o   Which publishers have published books by this author / on this subject before?

o   What Terms would you be looking for? Shipping costs, payment schedule,

## Who do I sell them to?

You can obtain information from reference directories:

o   The Writer's Handbook & Yearbook

o   The LMP: The literary marketplace

o   Contact Indepublishing.com which promotes rights for self-published titles, following a review of your book and agreement of contract.

o   Fairs, such as the Frankfurt Book Fair, have an online directory of publishers which is free.

## How to approach rights buyers

o   Face to face is always better, at trade fairs. Start setting up meetings 8–10 weeks beforehand and much of the subject matter is discussed via phone/email in the week before.

o   Send relevant mail promotion to target mailing list ie. AI sheet, author biography, cover, key highlights of the book, why it is relevant to them, promotional plans and any good sales data and endorsements gathered to date.

o   Submit exclusively with a time-limited option; be reasonable depending on form of text ie. academic needs proper reader's report etc. Submit electronically to speed up

o   If not exclusive, let them know it's a competitive situation

## Pitching the idea

You need to arrest their attention and actively sell the concept:

- o  Why book is better than competitive titles out there
- o  What it contains
- o  Expertise of author
- o  Alert them to specific points of interest
- o  Sales figures in home market
- o  Sale of rights in other languages
- o  AI sheet about book
- o  Any advance or sales material or electronic files

## Creating an initial agreement

When creating an agreement, it should cover the following parameters:

- o  Type of licence granted ie. *Publishing Rights*
- o  Territory – be careful here as much fighting going on over certain 'dependencies' ie. *Canada, India*
- o  Term of licence – 5–10 years is standard
- o  Financial terms – advance against royalties
- o  Subsidiary rights – stipulate what subsidiary rights are locked up into a Publishing Rights agreement
- o  Approval stages – especially on firm delivery dates and schedule; may request proofs or blads (book layout and design)
- o  Delivery date
- o  Number of copies
- o  Indemnities and warranties
- o  Termination
- o  Specification – may change from original concept presented
- o  Any limitations ie. distribution agreement in place in certain countries. No-one will sign a publishing agreement if an existing distribution commitment exists in that same country.

### Going to "auction"

Should you find yourself with a "hot potato" that suddenly seems to be drawing a lot of attention, you may wish to venture into auction-land.

Firstly, if you are approaching many publishers, agents or production companies, then list out who you have approached (purely for politeness, not any legal requirement). Invite offers and set a closing date with a minimum price.

Once the offers start coming in, you are bound by gentleman's agreement to ring around and see if anyone wishes to beat it. Keep doing this in order to "top out" and you have only one man left – and he's your man! Just like Ebay, and why it's not done on Ebay is anyone's guess.

### Alternative methods of selling rights

1. Sell copyright outright for a flat, one-off fee: this is risky if the book suddenly finds a huge audience. Few copyright-holders do this unless they are specifically commissioned for a task by book packager/publisher
2. Sell the publishing right: this carries less risk as you sell firm and obtain the money upfront. This is time limited, therefore if your book becomes a huge blockbuster, you can either renegotiate or not renew the publishing rights.
3. Sell a license for a specific use
4. Grant options for a specific time frame, which is renewable

### STANDARD APPROACHES FOR PUBLISHING RIGHTS

#### 1. "Flat Fee" Licence

This is an advance paid on signing for a certain amount of books in a specified time period, specified language. After that period, the licence expires or is renegotiated.

Many inexperienced people feel comfortable with this Lump Sum approach as they do not have the ability to monitor sales in foreign countries – and reputedly it is a rare publisher that will tell you honestly if they have reprinted.

This approach is good for any of the following ie. a single printing, a low print run, when book price is low, a country has a poor reputation for payment or you just don't know someone well enough to trust them.

FORMULA
*Print run x price / royalty = total payment to publisher / royalty spit with author*

## 2. "Advance against royalty" Licence
This is the other alternative to selling publishing rights. It is worth noting that English language contracts in North America do not have term of license as books are generally retained for length of copyright.
o   Advance ie. US$6,000
o   Royalty ie. 6% to 10,000 copies sold; 8% to 20,000 and 10% thereafter
o   Term of licence ie. 3–7 years
o   Language: (name)
o   Other rights included: book clubs, formats (hard/soft), sub-rights

Rumour has it that £1,500–£3,000 is standard for a work of fiction; fiction translation rights have a 7–7.5% standard royalty on foreign sales and the advance will usually be 50% of print run x price ie.
o   Per unit retail price 10 euros x 2000 books first print run = 20,000 euros
o   Head publisher percentage is 1,400 euros ie. £1,000
o   This £1,000 is split between publisher and author according to head contract ie. 50/50 is £500 each.

You should not agree to flat royalty rates but build in a rising rate as a matter of principle. Always consider their selling price, the volume they are propsosing and calculate their approximate profit; don't ask for more than they can realistically make. If you ask for more than they will make back on first print run, you won't get the contract.

**Financial terms**
- o If based on a catalogue or wholesale price, then demand a royalty rate of at least 10%.
  - ▪ Prices can be misleadingly quoted as either trade catalogue or wholesale price which is about 40–50% lower than retail so be careful you don't go for this. It should always be based on retail price.
- o Request they pay translation fees and production of all materials, including cost of couriering to you for approvals:
  - ▪ Should it be vetted? Back-translated?
  - ▪ Check all requirements have been followed ie. credits and acknowledgements
  - ▪ Consider if you need to agree any of their changes.
- o Charge for materials
  - ▪ Supply of duplicate production material
- o Collate data such as specs, shipping, documentation, insurance
- o Take references if you haven't worked with them before
- o Monitor contracts in the long term in order to extend or terminate it.

**FURTHER INFORMATION**
- o "Selling Rights" Fourth Edition, by Lynette Owen, published by Routledge, ISBN 0415235081
- o "Selling Rights" training course at Train4publishing. See their website (www.train4publishing.co.uk or contact them on 020 8874 2718 for information.)

# PART X

# CONCLUSIONS

**Ten golden rules**

*Thank you and good luck*

# CONCLUSIONS

How to summarise such a volume of advice, research, tips and guidance? The purpose of this section is to attempt to do so, but I will first draw to your attention two of my over-riding philosophies:

*Authoring is the art form, and the rest is simply business.*

To publish is to create a book with a view to selling it. Many authors get caught up in the excitement of their achievement, which is a good thing. You are right to be proud of your achievement, and long may that pride remain with you.
But do remember that a book is a product and you are a manufacturer. Nobody will come looking for your product; you need to get out there and bring it to their attention.

*Think of expenditure in terms of the number of books*
*you must sell to recoup that expense.*

Promoting and selling books often comes with a cost attached, and I have found the best way to assess whether it is worth my while to invest. For example:

o   Hosting an event (including cost of travel, postage, printing and delivery of promotional material etc = £55.00
o   My profit per book = £3.00
o   To make a return, I need to sell in excess of 28 books.
o   Do I think there will be 28 buyers attending this event?

This approach colours your view when considering a £200 advertisement. That's 66 books that must sell on the strength of that one advertisement.

Self-publishers get a very different view of their bookselling activity when you calculate expenditure in this fashion
- how good is the "call to action" of your promotional activity? Will it really convert that many buyers?
- How accurate is your view of the audience? Will their really be more than 5 people willing to part with a tenner to buy your book?

Now let's look at a summary of the golden rules of bookselling.

## Ten Golden Rules of Bookselling

### 1. Know your objective
Publishing starts by knowing your objective. Write out in 5–15 words your one single objective and focus all energy, activity and expenditure towards that. It is easy to lose sight of it as you delve deeper into the book publishing and bookselling world.

### 2. Make a plan.
Have a plan in order to be focussed and effective:
- o Take the time to 'get it right' – from cover to content and category to communication. It all needs time to work through the process.
- o Take the time to 'do it properly' – have a period of pre-marketing with a set publication date and aim to get on all the lists.

Itemise the short term activities and the long term plan in order to stay on track. Self-published books have the benefit of a longer selling period as you are in control whereas mainstream publishing is one shot, one short season. Always cover off the obvious and standard and aim to 'tip the balance' by implementing a few Big Hairy Goals.

Marketing is about making predictions and assumptions that are 75% grounded in reality and reason for believing them to be true; the remaining 25% is based on hopes and dreams – and there is no harm in this. Just make sure you get the percentages in the right balance!

### 3. Research first.
Successful marketing requires knowledge – network, read the press and exploit local. Seek to make a big noise in a small area; build and recycle success, slowly widening your net.

Know whether you have a market and understand what they need. Reach your audience by knowing who they are, where they are and what they need to know about you and your book in order to result in a sale. Target micro-groups rather than a demographic ie. don't see them as 60 year olds but as Active Retired Travellers, Hobbyists, Family-involved Grandparents etc. This will help you to "find" them.

Don't be afraid of defining your audience very specifically and narrowly. Once you have reached them, then you can widen the description. You need to know that it will sell, who to and how. Don't just write and publish to a mantra of "I'm sure this will sell, I'm sure this will sell…"

### 4. Don't publish and market in a vacuum.
During the writing and publishing of your book you should have been collecting your data – interested media and promotional channels, communities relevant to your topic, bookshops that specialise in or stock your subject-matter. Contact people, record relevant findings, build and update your database. It has a huge value.

Many people disparagingly say that most authors are only 'there' because they knew someone. If they do, it is invariably this is because they made that contact in the beginning. They lived the world they wanted to be successful within. They created their opportunity.

One author said to me recently, "Well, I'm sitting here waiting. I'm keen. I'm ready." There's one author who'll be waiting a long time, as self-promotion doesn't happen by simply being ready and waiting. Self-publishing is what you make it. Don't wait for someone else to do it for you, but build the contacts and do it for yourself.

### 5. Work effectively and recycle success.
Don't let people forget you, but don't phone up and have the same conversation as last time; take it forward or close it. Recycle the success you have in one area and take it to a new marketplace. Build and recycle.

It costs money to promote your book, but spend wisely and effectively. Combine direct & indirect forms of promotion; free and paid-for marketing and promotional activities. Always look for the Buy One Get One Free (BOGOF) opportunity.

Focus on gaining endorsements, reviews and successful sales data and recycle this to attract interest from other book sellers and book reviewers. Add endorsements onto press releases or news updates; put them on your website; sign off your emails with them; include them on the book jacket or inside front page when you do reprints. These endorsements have a value, both to potential readers as well as to bookshop buyers and the media. Remember – success breeds success.

### 6. Make a big noise in a small area.
Starting small is less overwhelming. It is easier to implement your plan progressively, to re-use success to approach the next person and to be seen.

Make a noice by doing something unusual. Publicity can be inventive, so you can think laterally. Sponsor a school sport's day or a spelling bee, or a new chair in an old people's home, run a poll or a contest. Announce the event to the newspaper and tell them how it connects to your book launch.

Build a groundswell, and play your part in taking it wider and further. Infiltrate as many small communities as possible ie. college newsletters and inhouse business publications. Phone the nationals, and send newsletters to the media.

## 7. Plan to do something every day.

The book that has no push from behind will quickly disappear from view. You need to keep at it. Aim for four major promotional campaigns a year (ie. four counties, four different target audiences).

Successful promotion is continual. You should be seeking to constantly create news, to cultivate contracts and use connections.

Depending on whether you are holding down a full-time job or not, aim to make 1-5 phone calls a day about your book.

Always remember to follow-up. The first approach is usually the most time intensive as you have to research the data. The follow-up is tedious albeit brief.

## 8. Exploit zeitgeist.

The most successful books are a result of a trend or interest capturing the public awareness because of a complex set of influences. You cannot CREATE it, but you can watch the news and endeavour to make connections with a current hot topic and your book. The chances are that you conceived the book because of some social influence that you sensed or were aware of.

Know your critical calendar dates and make as much noise as possible in line with your target media's planning dates. Have a diary of critical calendar dates, national "causes" and even be aware of new tv shows that revolve around a social issue of the time.

Create news (do a survey); know who writes about niche subjects. Maximise how you use editorial and remember, you won't get a tear sheet; you will have to chase or get clippings agency.

## 9. Help them to help you.

Publicity begets publicity. Once you have the review copy in your hand, you can then start approaching the media and other contacts. Help them to help you by making sure you send them the right material and have a distinctive and snappy one-liner or USP that they will associate with your book, or will capture their imagination. Make it easy for them to understand what you are offering and what you want them to do.

Make it easy for people to find you and your book; maximise all free listings both on/offline. Provide downloadable jacket images and author photos, a well-edited and usable synopses; target the media at appropriate times of the year; write a specimen piece on an angle. "Do's and Don'ts" or "Top Tips" pieces work well.

**10. Sell, sell, sell.**
There is no value in stock so all your efforts must be aimed at selling stock. Unsold stock merely takes up space and deteriorates over time.

Remember, bookshops will stock books that have a demand; people buy books when there is a compelling reason to. In today's competitive bookselling market, the task is to prove demand in order to secure a high street siting. You will get high street presence if you can demonstrate your marketing and how it will drum up demand. Don't let those books that were once so full of promise of returning an income turn into valueless piles of paper.

Announce success by sending information about any rights sales to the writing and book trade magazines, and create a newsletter to announce promotional activity, new edition printing, tours etc to bookshops.

*Selling means:*
o   Make sure your book is easy to buy
o   Always offer good and fast service – to the trade, the media and customers
o   Manage stock levels
o   Inspire other people to want to sell your book for you
o   Be creative in looking for other retail opportunities

- o Use your book to sell ie. via the end-pages, lead people to your website
- o Approach groups, communities and associations that may buy your book in volumes greater than just one!
- o Consider other editions ie. audio, hard-back, e-book

## THANK YOU, AND GOOD LUCK

On the basis that you create a strong communication plan and you implement it as per the guidelines here, you will maximise your chances of finding a buying audience for your book. That audience may number 100 or 1000 or more, and nobody can answer this for you.

Not all forms of communication or channels of communication will reap the intended rewards. If some seem to reap more rewards than others, then obviously focus on the ones that deliver against your objectives. If everything an author attempts seems to result in a dead-end, then consider the possibility that the book is not demanded at that time. It sounds harsh, but you still have a copy of the book you wrote and your friends & family still have it. Re-adjust your objectives and acknowledge other fringe benefits that you derived from the experience of publishing – the sheer achievement of writing a book, the exhilaration of publishing, the new people you've met and the learning curve you have been through – after all, you may well be planning another book and you will be far better versed as to how to go about publishing it and selling it.

*I hope something said in this book makes the world of difference to you and your selling skills. Please email me with your story; let me know what worked for you, and any tips or advice is missing from this book so I can include it in the next book.*

*Joanna*

# ABOUT INDEPUBLISHING

Self-publishing has definitely arrived as a credible route into publication, and many more people are taking to publish themselves – their story and their opinions.

The glass ceiling has shifted; no longer is the wall at the point of publication but at the point of selling. But with a good sound marketing plan, authors can double the amount of books that they sell, and maximise their chances of real success.

**indepublishing**
consultancy for independent authors

**The Indepublishing Consultancy** offers advice to authors seeking to self-publish and sell their books both into the trade and direct to the end-reader.

We seek to help provide information to authors that would otherwise be unavailable to them or cost prohibitive to access.

The Indepublishing Consultancy can also act as an agent, representing you in a rights sale.

**indebookshop.com**

**Indebookshop.com** specialises in selling independently published books. We don't believe in randomly discounting books but seek to add value to the customer by offering signed copies and free promotional material where it is available.

All books are assessed for suitability and the site is regularly promoted to rights buyers worldwide.

**Our published titles for authors:**

Whilst there are many routes to self-publishing, the information is scattered and contradictory and the newcomer to the industry is quickly confused. How should they go about producing a credible title that will compete effectively with mainstream-published books? My book "What do I have to do to get a book published!" will set you on the road to success, and I am available for further consultation.

ISBN: 1-905203-58-6 PRICE £12.99

Once your have created your book, how do you sell it? It is impossible to get bookshops to stock your book, very few people will review it and what is a distributor anyway? The partner title "What do I have to do to sell a book!" is packed with helpful hints, tips, information and great ideas to help you sell your book.
ISBN: 1-905203-59-4 PRICE £12.99

*BUY BOTH TOGETHER AND SAVE £4.00*
*Always in stock on Indebookshop.com*